CHANGING FRONTIERS
OF MISSION

American Society of Missiology Series, No. 28

CHANGING FRONTIERS
OF MISSION

Wilbert R. Shenk

ORBIS BOOKS

Maryknoll, New York 10545

The Catholic Foreign Mission Society of America (Maryknoll) recruits and trains people for overseas missionary service. Through Orbis Books, Maryknoll aims to foster the international dialogue that is essential to mission. The books published, however, reflect the opinions of their authors and are not meant to represent the official position of the society. To obtain more information about Maryknoll and Orbis Books, please visit our website at www.maryknoll.org.

Copyright © 1999 by Wilbert R. Shenk
Published by Orbis Books, Maryknoll, New York, U.S.A.

Manufactured in the United States of America.
Manuscript editing and typesetting by Joan Weber Laflamme.

Library of Congress Cataloguing-in-Publication Data

Shenk, Wilbert R.
    Changing frontiers of mission   /   Wilbert R. Shenk.
    p.   cm.   —   (American Society of Missiology series   ;   no. 28)
    Includes bibiographical references and index.
    ISBN 1-57075-259-1 (pbk.)
    1. Missions—Theory.   2. Missions—Theory—History.   I. Title.   II.
Series.
    BV2063   .s495   1999
    266—dc21
                                                98-51055
                                                CIP

Dedicated with gratitude to

J. D. Graber (1900–1978)
and Carl Kreider

esteemed mentors and colleagues
who graciously took on administrative duties
thus enabling me to have study leave
that laid the foundation for
much of the work collected here

Contents

Contents

PART FOUR
DISCERNING
CHANGING FRONTIERS

Preface to the ASM Series

The purpose of the ASM (American Society of Missiology) Series is to publish—without regard for disciplinary, national, or denominational boundaries—scholarly works of high quality and wide interest on missiological themes from the entire spectrum of scholarly pursuits relevant to Christian mission, which is always the focus of books in the Series.

By *mission* is meant the effort to effect passage over the boundary between faith in Jesus Christ and its absence. In this understanding of mission, the basic functions of Christian proclamation, dialogue, witness, service, worship, liberation, and nurture are of special concern. And in that context questions arise, including, How does the transition from one cultural context to another influence the shape and interaction between these dynamic functions, especially in regard to the cultural and religious plurality that comprises the global context of Christian mission?

The promotion of scholarly dialogue among missiologists, and among missiologists and scholars in other fields of inquiry, may involve the publication of views that some missiologists cannot accept, and with which members of the Editorial Committee do not agree. Manuscripts published in the Series reflect the opinions of their authors and are not understood to represent the position of the American Society of Missiology or of the Editorial Committee. Selection is guided by such criteria as intrinsic worth, readability, and accessibility to a range of interested persons and not merely to experts or specialists.

The ASM Series, in collaboration with Orbis Books, seeks to publish scholarly works of high merit and wide interest on numerous aspects of missiology—the study of mission. Able presentations on new and creative approaches to the practice and understanding of mission will receive close attention.

The ASM Series Editorial Committee
Jonathan J. Bonk
Angelyn Dries, O.S.F.
Scott W. Sunquist

Introduction

Mission is synonymous with movement. It stands for purposeful going and doing. Mission implies challenge to the status quo and invites change. Whereas mission was long regarded as a religious term that referred to attempts by a religious group to gain proselytes for its ranks, in the twentieth century mission has been secularized and appropriated freely by military, industry, and government to describe their main purpose for being. A respectable company proudly displays its mission statement, reassuring the public that it is clear as to its raison d'etre. This mission is its commitment to the public to provide certain services or products.

The essays that comprise this volume have taken shape on the road. Although all were written during the years since 1984, they have been decisively influenced by my personal experiences since 1955, when I began a formative four-year apprenticeship in Indonesia. I was associated there with two churches, Gereja Injili di Tanah Jawa and Gereja Kristen Muria di Indonesia, situated along the coast of northcentral Java.

Within weeks after the end of World War II, on August 17, 1945, the Indonesian nationalists declared their political independence of the Dutch colonials but did not win that independence until 1949. The years following independence were tumultuous. The charismatic Sukarno, father of the nation and first president, was a spell-binding orator but an inept administrator. The nation lurched from one crisis to another. Indonesia survived a civil war in 1957-58 that pitted the Javanese-dominated central government against the outer islands.

The Conference of Non-Aligned Nations meeting at Bandung, Indonesia, in 1955 signaled to the Soviets and the Americans alike that the emerging nations of Asia and Africa would not be taken for granted by the world's power brokers. But these new nations were poor and largely traditional. The post–World War II Marshall Plan—which had contributed to the rebuilding of Europe—helped inspire the development movement in the 1950s that was touted as the answer to third-world poverty.

From 1963 to 1990 I was an administrator of international Christian mission and service programs. The rapid geopolitical changes of the 1950s and 1960s, especially the ending of European colonialism and political independence of many African and Asian peoples, contributed directly to the crisis of Christian missions that spanned the 1960s. The call early in the '60s, "Missionary, Go Home!" was echoed a decade later by the demand for a moratorium on Christian missions from the West. It was not easy to keep one's bearings with regard to the course of Christian mission.

1

During these turbulent years the notion of *frontier* proved to be useful in clarifying perspective. For me the critical question was not the validity of mission. This was a settled conviction. But if mission itself is nonnegotiable, equally important is the demand that the form and patterns of mission be kept flexible and responsive to the changing historical situation. Failure to distinguish between these two elements will result in paralysis or aimlessness.

In 1800 mission leaders were ineluctably drawn to the geographical frontier, especially the continents of Africa and Asia, where there was little Christian activity. Nearly two centuries later the Christian map looks amazingly different. In the late twentieth century the simple and straightforward concept of geographical frontier can no longer be used to frame the mission task. It was a powerful symbol of mission when geographical exploration was a "frontier" activity, but in the age when the leading frontier is the exploration of outer space or personal inner space, earth-bound geography is passé. To focus the mission task in relation to the emerging situation, we need a renewed sense of frontier and symbols that accurately describe it.

Frontier entails a double meaning. On the one hand, it indicates the place where the crucial engagement is taking place. It is here the battle is joined and the future is being decided. On the other hand, to pursue the frontier requires movement, the abandonment of long-held entrenched positions in order to seize the moment. Frontier symbolizes movement outward, away from the status quo, into new opportunity, challenge, and growth. This seems highly relevant to the modern mission movement, which has reached the end of an era and is now, in its old age, floundering under the burden of institutionalism.

Missionaries and missionary agencies are patently not exempt from the laws of institutionalization. Many mission leaders have tried to address this issue. From the early years of modern missions the ever-present temptation to settle in and perpetuate program—or, in Roland Allen's scornful phrase, maintain "mission activities"—has been evident. This places missionary obedience continually at risk. Whenever the missionary prizes the comfort and security of familiar patterns and methods, the mission dynamic gets suppressed.

Two principles have guided my efforts to discern the mission frontier in our day. First, if the missionary mandate given to the church by Jesus Christ, its head, is not limited to a particular time or geography, then we must continually seek to discern where the "new thing" of the mission of God is happening. This is not to argue for novelty for its own sake. Rather, the ever-changing sociopolitical context challenges the church to remain flexible and responsive.

The second principle is to reflect carefully on the experiences of the missionary church in previous generations. There we find episodes of true creativity where the gospel has been communicated in its integrity and in the idiom of the people. The West African prophet William Wade Harris burned with a vision of the reign of God and announced this gospel of the kingdom to the peoples of Liberia, Côte d'Ivoire, and Ghana in the years 1910-15 with unusual power. On the other hand, there is plenty of documentation that the human vessels of the modern mission movement have been seriously flawed. But for reasons that elude us, God has elected to use precisely these "earthen vessels" as means of mission. And it is this highly imperfect modern mission movement that has been instrumental in the unprecedented globalization of the Christian faith in the twentieth century.

These two principles remind us that the path of Christian discipleship calls us continually to press on toward the frontier but to do so in full awareness of the path the church has taken thus far. The ultimate stage of mission will be the eschaton in which the Lord of history gathers up all things "to the praise of his glorious grace."

Several acknowledgments must be made in connection with the preparation of this volume. The Associated Mennonite Biblical Seminary gave me a faculty research grant during the spring of 1995 that enabled me to begin preparing these essays for publication. Naomi Lloyd helped with the first phase of getting the essays on computer in the summer of 1995. Karen Kuchan, Sheree Lahey, and Kristin Kvaalen, Fuller Theological Seminary, have spent many hours getting the manuscript into final shape. Without the help of Naomi, Karen, Sheree, and Kristin, this book would not have seen the light of day. To them I extend my heartfelt gratitude.

PART ONE

THE THEOLOGICAL FRONTIER

To be authentic, mission must be thoroughly theocentric. It begins in God's redemptive purpose and will be completed when that purpose is fulfilled. The God-given identity of the church thus arises from its mission. This order of priority is foundational. Yet for some sixteen centuries Christians have been taught to think of church as the prior category and mission as one among several functions of the church.

This view is based on a deformed understanding of the nature and purpose of the church. Ecclesio-centricism can be explained historically and institutionally, but it cannot be defended on biblical or theological grounds. Nevertheless, this entrenched perspective continues to shape the way most Christians think about the nature and purpose of the church. The erosion of identity and vitality widely observable in the church today can be traced to this flawed view.

The answer to ecclesio-centricism is to be found in the biblical-theological order of priorities. When we accept the significance of the mission dynamic that arises from God's redemptive initiative, we will understand how this was intended to form and inform the people of God, first in the Older Testament and then continued in the New Testament.

Mission must precede the church. Jesus the Messiah formed his disciple community for the express purpose of continuing his mission. If Jesus had had no mission, he would have had no need to gather and commission a group of disciples to continue what he had started; and they could happily have dispersed to their homes and customary occupations when he left them. But the four gospels make it clear that Jesus was imbued with a compelling sense of his mission and committed that mission to his disciples. The renewal of the church as the twentieth century ends is linked to recovery of the *priority* of mission.

A second issue on the theological frontier is the scope of the gospel. This became an issue toward the end of the nineteenth century as Christians reacted to the threat of modernity to Christian faith. The resulting polarization has been a drag on the church for much of the twentieth century. The split between "modernists" and "fundamentalists" in the first two decades of the twentieth century had long-lasting consequences. A partial recovery was made when the "word and deed" formulation was introduced in the 1960s. But we cannot be content with less than recovery of the fullness of the gospel.

1

The Mission Dynamic

The New Testament defines the raison d'etre of the church to be missionary witness to the world, thus at one stroke sharply focusing its purpose while subsuming all other functions under mission.[1] Accordingly, Christian witness and discipleship are worked out in scripture in light of that primal tension which characterizes the relationship between the people of God and a world that does not acknowledge God's sovereignty. This is the proper context for describing the implications of the church's calling to be the agent of reconciliation between the world and its Creator (2 Cor 5:16-20).

Perusal of the many works that fill theological libraries yields a different impression, however. Ecclesiology, for example, rarely engages the question of mission to the world. Theologians have conceived of their task as essentially concerned with responding to intellectual questions that the culture addresses to the Christian faith or engaging in intramural debate over points of controversy

---

This chapter was originally published in Saayman and Kritzinger (1996, 83-93). Revised and expanded for publication in this volume.

[1] The New Testament develops an understanding of the church descriptively. Paul S. Minear (1960) demonstrated the rich imagery New Testament writers use to describe the nature and mission of the church. Certain key texts do establish the purpose of the church. Matthew 10 sets the basic paradigm for the disciple community (cf. Ridderbos 1962, 37). The mandate given by the Messiah following the resurrection (Mt 28:18-20) effectively connects the purpose of the disciple community to the pattern already established and makes it normative (cf. Bosch 1991, 73-83). The Great Commission is thus a fundamental ecclesial statement. Ephesians 3:10 emphasizes the *public* and *proclamatory* role the church is to play. 1 Peter 2:9 casts the purpose of the church in terms of its responsibility to "proclaim the mighty acts of him who called you out of darkness into his marvelous light," in support of which the church should be a set-apart, holy people. Consistent with the sacramental-sacerdotal view of ministry, Christendom held to a different understanding, at once institutional and parochial. Cf. José Míguez Bonino (1975, 155), who argues that "the ecclesiological question is a critical one for all contemporary theology and traces the present dilemma to the 'classical ecclesiologies of the Reformation and Counter-Reformation' which were concerned to show historical, institutional, or demonstrable continuity with the past."

within the scholarly guild.[2] This shift from the kind of theology found in the New Testament to that produced out of the Western intellectual and ecclesiastical tradition has resulted in theology divorced from mission.

A leading theologian of mission the past three decades, David J. Bosch, was greatly concerned about theology sans mission. Bosch (1980, 21-27; 1982; 1983, 490f.; 1991) argued persuasively that the church's approach to theology, especially after the fourth century, was not shaped by the fact that "mission is the mother of theology."[3] When theology becomes disconnected from its origin, it is no longer nurtured by its true source. Such theology either will succumb to traditionalism and self-preservation or be cast adrift on cultural and historical currents. The evangelical vitality of theology will be in direct proportion to the degree to which it engages the life purpose of the church.

This chapter interprets mission in terms of its constitutive dynamic and argues that God's redemptive mission is essential to the integrity of theology. This mission dynamic will be described as consisting of six interacting elements: reign of God, Jesus the Messiah, Holy Spirit, church, world, and salvation. For our purposes here we will consider each in turn. In experience, they are interdependent.

THE REIGN OF GOD

The reign of God, thrust to the center of history in the Christ-event, is the horizon within which God's redemptive mission is being fulfilled.[4] The reign of God *(basileia)* originates with God and expresses God's saving will and purpose. The redemptive power of God is now being guided by a strategy that is being made explicit before the world in the ministry and life of Jesus the Messiah. It is God's will to deliver the creation from the powers of decay and death.

---

[2] F. D. E. Schleiermacher (1768-1834) is usually credited with introducing mission to the modern theological curriculum. He did so by including it under practical theology, a precedent that continued well into the twentieth century. Conceptually, that mode of thinking, the legacy of fifteen centuries of Christendom, remains influential to this day.

[3] See David J. Bosch (1972) for a study of the German systematic theologian Martin Kaehler (1835-1912), who regarded mission as indispensable to proper theological thinking.

[4] It is not our purpose here to consider the much controverted aspects of *basileia*. Scholars in the last generation have moved closer together on its primary meaning and importance. Here we assume as background such studies as Bright (1953), Küng (1967), Ladd (1964), Moltmann (1967), Perrin (1963), Ridderbos (1962), and Schnackenburg (1963). More recent surveys include Viviano (1988) and Willis (1987). These studies divide into two groups: those which closely link or interpret the meaning of *basileia* in relation to the missio Dei, and those which do not. For example, Bright, Ridderbos, Moltmann, and Küng do this effectively. In Viviano's survey of scholarship over the past two millennia, the *basileia*-mission nexus hardly figures. For a Christocentric and missionary interpretation of the meaning of history see Berkhof (1966). For an innovative approach to systematic theology that starts with the rule of God, see McClendon (1994, part 1).

Something extraordinary has been set in motion: instead of *futurum*, ordinary time, a prolongation of the old, the world is introduced to *adventus*, a new beginning. The reign of God is to be realized through the inauguration of a new order—characterized by life, peace, and justice/righteousness—which assuredly will supplant the old order, the reign of death. God wills that life, not death, have the last word.

In spite of its fundamental importance for Christian faith, the church has not kept the reign of God at the center of its life and teaching. Following Jesus' earthly ministry, various interpretations of the kingdom of God emerged. Four views have prevailed: (1) the eschatological, which emphasized the futurist aspect; (2) the spiritual-mystical, which focused on the immortality of the soul and the immaterial; (3) the political, in which an earthly empire is identified with the kingdom of God; and (4) the ecclesial in which church and kingdom are merged (Viviano 1988, chap. 2; cf. Driver 1993, 83-85). Each has exerted great influence in the life of the church, but all are reductionisms that have contributed to the obscuring of the full meaning of the reign of God.

Notwithstanding this partial eclipse of the messianic reality and against a background of hopelessness, oppression, and suffering throughout history, periodic messianic resurgences have reawakened hope by pointing to the promise of the reign of God (Oosterwal 1973; Desroche 1979). One may mention, for example, the Blumhardts in nineteenth-century Germany and their remarkably creative and multi-dimensional influence which was grounded in a renewed emphasis on the reign of God. A full-orbed understanding of mission can only be achieved by embracing this vision of mission as fulfilling God's reign.

The coming of God's reign disturbs the status quo by triggering two reactions. First, because it exposes the egocentric structure of human nature and behavior, it is perceived to be a *skandalon*. This gives rise to *krisis*, the moment of truth that calls for decision in light of the new possibility: "Repent! Turn toward God and be incorporated into the new order." This is both invitation and warning. Those who refuse God's gracious offer will remain in the grips of the old order and its destiny. God's reign challenges human motivation and character at the deepest levels by unmasking the nature of power that is unsubmitted to the will of God.

The reign of God is a mystery we do not grasp fully. Although the whole of Jesus' words and acts was a running commentary on God's will and reign, at no point did he offer a considered definition. Instead, he spoke in parables and performed deeds that brought God's saving power into the lives of people. Nonetheless, surprisingly few caught its larger meaning. Even the disciples who formed Jesus' inner circle did not discern what it was about until after his resurrection and ascension (e.g., Lk 24:25-27, 44-49; Acts 1:3). In the end, the kingdom could be apprehended only through eyes of faith. It is not subject to human control nor can it be manipulated for selfish ends.

The reign of God is the essence of God's mission of redemption. The gospel is rightly termed the good news of the kingdom. This is the animating center of mission and of theology: God as self-giving love coming to the world for the world's salvation through the reign of righteousness.[5] Its meaning must be further elaborated in terms of Jesus the Messiah, who, as servant of God's reign, pioneered the way and demonstrated its meaning (Heb 12:2), the Holy Spirit, who guarantees the realization of the *basileia* (Eph 1:13f.); and the church, which in this interim age lives out God's rule in the world and bears witness to it in light of the eschaton.

JESUS THE MESSIAH

Messianic is the descriptor for the new order because it is actualized through Messiah.[6] The new is signaled in various ways. Most important, God is disclosed to be drawing near and entering redemptively into the human situation. In contrast to the traditional Hebrew reluctance even to utter the name of Yahweh, Jesus is acclaimed as Emmanuel; God is with us by taking on human form and embracing the human situation in the incarnation.

The synoptic gospels link Jesus' baptism, authentication of his messianic authority by the Holy Spirit, the testing of Jesus in the wilderness, and the launch of his public ministry. Jesus began his public ministry with the declaration that God's reign was now breaking forth (Mt 4:17; Mk 1:15). The evident authority that marked his ministry and so impressed his audiences (Mt 7:29) arose from the fact that Jesus identified fully with the reign of God in his person, message and works (Mt 6:10, 26:39; cf. Heb 10:7,9, quoting Ps 40:6-8). Although John's gospel scarcely mentions the Kingdom of God, a motif running through the gospel—which is fully consistent with the reign of God theme—is Jesus' consciousness of being sent by God to carry out God's will so that the world might be redeemed (e.g., Jn 3:16f., 5:30; 17:1, 3, 21, 23, 25) (Comblin 1979, chap. 1).

The parallel passage in Luke 4:16-22 emphasizes both that Jesus stands in the great prophetic line ("there was given to him the book of the prophet Isaiah. . . . 'Today this Scripture has been fulfilled in your hearing'") and that he is doing what has not been done before ("proclaiming the acceptable year of the Lord"). This announcement is the hinge linking two aeons. It signaled that the central prophetic promise to the people of Israel (e.g., Is 61) was now being fulfilled.

Thus the lines of engagement are drawn. The reign of God being manifested in Jesus the Messiah fundamentally contradicts the kingdom of the world. The forces of Antichrist are prodded to action. The axial principle of God's rule runs counter to that of the world. The mission of Jesus the Messiah is to liberate from the kingdom of death. As we follow the public ministry of Jesus, we come upon a series of scenes in which this confrontation is played out as physical, psycho-

---

[5] The one substantial attempt to develop a theology of mission from this viewpoint is that of George F. Vicedom (1965), which grew out of the discussions in the International Missionary Council in the early 1950s. Those discussions were upstaged and derailed by "secular" and "death of God" theologies in the 1960s.

[6] For a fuller exposition of the significance of Jesus the Messiah for our understanding of mission, see David A. Shank (1993). My treatment here is necessarily summary and selective.

logical, social, and spiritual forces under the sway of the old order resist and refuse to acknowledge God's reign now made manifest in the Messiah (e.g., Mt 8-10:1, 5-42). What is of particular import is the way in which Jesus met this challenge.

In Jesus the meaning of redemptive power is redefined. The old order is governed by the myth of redemptive violence and, in fact, is being consumed in the endless spiral of violence (Wink 1993, 13-17). Every attempt to end violence with violence sows the seeds of further conflict.[7] The power of destruction and death that controls the old order operates at both personal and collective levels (Rom 5:8-14). It is the mission of the Messiah to intervene in this reality and break the destructive cycle.

As David Bosch (1991, 108-13) has pointed out, at the start of his public ministry Jesus renounced vengeance as the basis of his messiahship (Lk 4:16-20). Instead, Jesus instituted the new messianic order founded on redemptive love as the direct answer to the spiral of violence. Against the age-old pattern of settling accounts by vanquishing the enemy through multiple forms of "ethnic cleansing," God, through Jesus the Messiah, made peace by "breaking down the dividing wall of hostility" and creating "one new humanity in place of the two" (Eph 2:14b-15). The scope of God's saving purpose cannot be reduced to the personal only. Rather, the personal and the social are intertwined. Reconciliation between erstwhile enemies is effected only through combined personal and social transformation.

By the time of Jesus, the servant *(ebed)* spoken of in Isaiah (42, 49, 50, 52, 53) was interpreted as referring either to the coming Messiah or to Israel itself. References to the servant's suffering and humiliation had been expunged from the official interpretation (Shank 1993, 59f.). According to the party line, if the servant were indeed the Messiah, the anointed one destined to "bring forth justice to the nations" (Is 42:1), he would be a leader who through superior political and military power would vanquish all Israel's enemies. Messiahship was thus cast in conventional political terms and tied to Israel's own fortunes.

Jesus confuted this traditional understanding at two fundamental points (Cullmann 1963, 55). In the first place, he restored the meaning of the covenant God had made with Israel. God's covenant with Abraham and his descendants was predicated on the calling out of this people that they might become the instrument of blessing for all peoples (Gn 12:1-3). Jesus' contemporaries had turned the meaning of covenant inward. They expected the messianic age to bring blessing to Israel and provide them with protection against other peoples. Israel thus had reversed the meaning of God's covenant with Abraham. Jesus the Messiah invited individuals from all classes and clans to repent and submit their lives to God's rule, creating one new people from among the peoples.

---

[7] It was reported in 1993 that some forty wars being waged throughout the world stemmed from ethno-religious conflict. The bitter conflict in the former Yugoslavia can be traced to hostilities engendered six centuries ago. (Most of these conflicts have deep historical roots.) The late Marshall Tito's enforced union of the various factions lasted only so long as maintained by armed force.

The second reversal in understanding had to do with the role of opposition and suffering (Shank 1993, 60; cf. Cullmann 1963). At every step Jesus encountered opposition precisely from the religio-political leadership because his message seemed to undermine their power. His message included strong words that judged them and their abuse of power. The message of Jesus concerning God's new order exposed the sin, corruption, injustice/unrighteousness, and false worship that characterized the religio-political institutions. In the end, these were the forces that combined to put him to death.

From the moment of Jesus' baptism, when God's Spirit came on him in anointing power, he assumed his role as God's servant chosen to bring God's shalom without resort to violence or deceit (Is 53:9). As his ministry unfolds, Jesus appeals to this servanthood as validation for what he is doing (e.g., Mk 10:45). It is a servanthood that leads to his death on behalf of the "ungodly" (Rom 5:6). Instead of the traditional Christendom interpretation of divine power as the power of the *imperium*, the Messiah of God is the crucified God whose sacrifice opens the way to life lived by resurrection power (Moltmann 1974, 190f.; Koyama 1984, chap. 20).

All three of the great Christological passages in the Pauline writings refer to the vicarious redemptive suffering of the Servant (Rom 5:12-14; 1 Cor 15:3; Phil 2:7-8), thereby emphasizing that God's reign is based on self-giving love which accepts and redemptively absorbs the suffering perpetrated by the powers of the present age. Violence may be held at bay and checked by counterviolence, but it can only be transformed by redemptive love. The death and resurrection of Jesus the Messiah are God's final reply to the power of death and the old order. The empty cross signifies the vindication of God's Suffering Servant.

THE HOLY SPIRIT

The Genesis account of creation notes that "the Spirit of God ("wind," NRSV) was moving over the face of the waters" (Gn 1:2b) as God began creating an ordered universe out of chaos. At the beginning of the mission of the Messiah, John the Baptist declared, "I saw the Spirit descending from heaven like a dove, and it remained on him" (Jn 1:32). In both creation and the new creation, God the Spirit is the agent. The parting words of Jesus to his disciples were the promise that the Spirit would come to them, and that coming was linked directly to the continuation of the messianic mission (Lk 24:45f.; Acts 1:8). At Pentecost the disciples experienced what they interpreted to be the fulfillment of the prophet Joel's prophecy. The Holy Spirit was made manifest to them as wind, fire, and prophetic speech (Acts 2). Wind (Hebrew: *ruach*), or breath, represents life. The Spirit is God's breath or life. A special dignity was conferred on humankind at creation when God breathed into Adam "the breath of life." The Hebrew scriptures described the Messiah as the one in whom God's Spirit would be fully present, infused with God's life, anointed by the Spirit.

Scripture also speaks of the Spirit as fire that judges (Mt 3:11), purifies, and blends together disparate parts. At Pentecost the disciples were being tested and prepared for the rigors of witness. To do this they needed to be forged into a unity.

At Pentecost the Holy Spirit demonstrated the new *koinonia* God was creating. Because of its rebellion at Babel humankind was sentenced to live out the consequences of the "confusion of languages." At Pentecost the Holy Spirit reversed Babel. A new people, drawn from the nations, whose linguistic particularity is the means for each to hear about "the mighty acts of God" (Acts 2:6, 11), is called forth. Its unity is expressed neither through culture nor ritual but in worship of the God revealed in Jesus the Messiah (Acts 2:14-36).

As the mission of Jesus the Messiah unfolds, the Holy Spirit is shown to be the leader: at the conception (Mt 1:18; Lk 1:35), Simeon's revelation (Lk 2:25-35), Jesus' baptism (Mt 3:16; Mk 1:10; Lk 3:22) and temptation (Mt 4:1; Mk 1:12; Lk 4:1), inauguration of ministry (Lk 4:18), inspirer and guide of Jesus (Lk 10:21, 12:10; Jn 3:34), the one who enabled Jesus to bring his sacrifice (Heb 9:14), the power by which Jesus was resurrected from the dead (Rom 1:4; 1 Tm 3:16), and the one who accompanies Jesus' disciples in the continuing mission (Lk 24:49; Jn 20:21-23; Acts 13:1-3).[8] At times the Spirit precedes Jesus, while at other times the Spirit follows. Often the work of Jesus and that of the Spirit so intertwine as to be indistinguishable. Always the relationship is one of mutual support in pursuit of a single purpose: realization of God's reign.

Although many volumes of so-called mission theology have been written with little or no attention being paid to the Holy Spirit (Kuitse 1993, 106-10), the New Testament gives a clear model.[9] God's redemptive mission cannot be understood apart from the role of the Holy Spirit. Jesus warned the disciples against attempting to engage in mission without the Holy Spirit ("but stay in the city, until . . . " [Lk 24:49]); he "charged them not to depart from Jerusalem, but to wait" (Acts 1:4) for the Holy Spirit, who is the Spirit of Jesus the Messiah, leader in mission, equipping and empowering for the arduous task of bearing witness in the world where there will assuredly be opposition and persecution (Mt 28:20; 2 Cor 3:8, 4:7-10). "The Anointed One becomes the Anointing One" (Kuitse 1993, 112) as the Spirit of Jesus the Messiah endows the disciple community with the spiritual gifts needed for witness in the world.

---

[8] See McClendon (1994, chap. 4) for a fresh interpretation of the Holy Spirit and mission.

[9] Hendrikus Berkhof (1964, 30) begins chapter 2, "The Spirit and the Mission," with these words: "According to the usual order found in dogmatics, we now expect a chapter about Word and Spirit, about the Spirit and the individual, or about the Spirit and the church. None of these subjects can be seen in the right perspective, however, without a previous consideration of the mission as the first and basic act of the risen Christ. Neither the church nor the regenerated individual would exist without first having missionary witness." In the same chapter he discusses the neglect of mission by theologians, noting that the one exception is Karl Barth (1962), whose treatment has yet to be taken seriously. Berkhof concludes: "Therefore, I regret to say that the highly necessary enrichment of systematic theology by taking in the mission as an essential element in God's mighty deeds is still ahead of us" (33).

In these last days the Holy Spirit holds together the two poles of God's saving action: the Christological and the eschatological. During this interim the Spirit is "the expansion of the divine saving presence over the earth" (Berkhof 1964, 35). The covenant made with Abraham established a pattern by which the divine blessing will be carried to the nations. From the faithful One, the Suffering Servant, through the faithful community the Spirit leads in continual witness to the world of God's salvation until the end of time.

THE CHURCH

After nearly two thousand years it is easy to forget the formal order of relationship among the reign of God, mission, and church. We have already noted the four understandings that have shaped the way Christians have thought about the reign of God, each a reductionism that conceals and suppresses vital dimensions. It is hardly surprising that many of the faithful have not had a vivid sense of the meaning of God's rule for their lives or for the mission of the church. We must, therefore, reassert both the indispensable role the church was appointed to play in the continuing mission of Jesus Christ in the world and the essentiality of mission to the identity of the church.

From a biblical and theological viewpoint the church without mission is inconceivable, and yet for Christendom the operative understanding of the nature of the church did not trade on the notion of mission (Neill 1968, 71-84). At this point two extremes are to be avoided. On the one hand, Christendom held to a view of the church as institution. On the other, we must reject some elements of the instrumental view of the church promoted by the parachurch movement.

Three things must be kept in focus. First, the rule of God is prior to mission. Indeed, mission is the means by which God's reign is being realized in the world. In the second place, as a corollary, we note that mission is prior to church.[10] The church can only be called into being by the preaching of the gospel of the kingdom. Jesus began by proclaiming this gospel and gathering together those who responded. These he taught and then commissioned to continue doing what he was doing. In this age the task of proclaiming the gospel is never finished, for each generation must hear it for themselves. The church becomes something other than a living witness to the gospel when it seeks to preserve the faith through an institution or sacerdotal system. Rather, the church lives out of the gospel by proclaiming the gospel. Third, at Pentecost the Holy Spirit endowed and equipped the disciple community to continue the mission of Jesus Christ in the world (Kraus 1993, chap. 4).

The calling of the church is to glorify the Triune God (1) by faithfully witnessing to the reign of God, and (2) by living as a sign of that reign. To state it differently, the church has a single purpose, which consists of two aspects. These two dimensions cannot be sustained in isolation from one another. They must be held together and allowed to interpenetrate if this purpose is to be realized.

---

[10] Berkhof (1964, 30-31, 38-39) clarifies the Spirit-mission-church relationship.

The legacy that Christendom bequeathed to the church was effectively to reduce it to the status of an institution for the care of the faithful.[11] When missionary witness is reserved for the few who are sent to faraway places, and when Christian existence is understood mainly as ensuring one's own salvation, the ecclesial reality has been distorted and the church trivialized by reason of being disconnected from its raison d'etre.

When the church lives in conscious response to the reign of God, its life is governed by only one criterion. Indeed, the power of the church's witness depends on the extent to which God's kingdom defines and shapes that witness. When the church attempts to make its ministry relevant by rendering "respectable" service, it has adopted an alien criterion and it becomes merely mundane (Yinger 1957, 144f.). Conventional respectability operates by another calculus than the reign of God. It is geared to maintenance of the cultural status quo. What set the ministry of Jesus apart was that his every action and word pointed to God as source of life. To do this requires breaking free from the power system of the dying world order and embracing the reign of God.

The missionary relevance of the church to the world must be modeled on that of Jesus the Messiah. Jesus continually raised the most basic questions with his contemporaries: Whom do you serve? What is your purpose and destiny? Do you live by the power of life or death? His contemporaries did not accuse Jesus of being irrelevant or unrealistic. It was clear that he loved the world more passionately than the self-centered religious and political leaders. His crime was exactly the opposite: he exposed the abuses of power that were destroying life and called people to follow the way of liberation.

The missionary church witnesses by being a "contrast society" (Lohfink 1984, 157-63) or "microsociety" (Miller 1993, 137-45) in which the life-defining features of the larger society are transformed so their destructive power is redeemed. For example, conventional peoplehood based on blood, soil, and culture is transmuted through the regenerating work of the Suffering Servant of God, wherein the meaning of blood, soil, and culture is restored to what God the Creator intended. Indeed, mission combines two fundamental thrusts—the universal and the particular—in one action and one relationship. The universal moves to bring all under the sovereignty of God, thereby relativizing all other loyalties and claims. The thrust of particularity moves toward every people and each person for each bears the image of God. None is excluded from the reach of God's love; all are invited to be reconciled to God.

In the Sermon on the Mount, Jesus used the metaphors of salt and light to describe the way in which the disciple community should live in the world (Driver 1983, 33-36). Several points may be emphasized. First, Jesus' discourse focuses on the importance of the ethical response of the community, for this is what gives concrete expression to the reign of God (cf. Blough 1993). The messianic community's life is shaped by the ethics of the Messiah. The authority of this

---

[11] Ernst Troeltsch explains the emergence of the sect against the background of the church that has "compromised with the world-order" by modifying the moral law of Jesus (1960, 330-43).

stance for the early church is reflected in these passages from Paul: "When reviled, we bless; when persecuted, we endure; when slandered, we speak kindly" (1 Cor 4:12f.). "We are treated as impostors, and yet are true; as unknown, and yet are well known; as dying, and . . . yet not killed; as sorrowful, yet always rejoicing; as poor, yet making many rich; as having nothing, and yet possessing everything" (2 Cor 6:8-10). The church as the messianic community was constituted to embody the message of Messiah, proclaiming through its life and testimony the meaning of the gospel. Its very attitude toward the suffering perpetrated by opposition forces is the result of living in the power of the Holy Spirit in anticipation of God's final triumph at the eschaton.

Second, these metaphors speak to the matter of means and tactics in witness. Both salt and light have a permeative effect, entering into and changing the host environment. Light exposes ruthlessly; it is entirely public. Salt penetrates and transforms.

Third, salt and light become active agents only when they are released into a host environment. They then become life-giving and transforming. Jesus called the disciples to live out their covenant relationship with God as a missionary community characterized by salt and light as transforming agents.

WORLD

Mission and world are indissolubly linked.[12] If there were no world, there would be no need of mission. The gospel of John puts the matter with classic and powerful simplicity: "God loved the world so much that he gave his only Son, that everyone who has faith in him may not die but have eternal life" (3:16, NEB). The world is the scene of God's redemptive action, because it is the world that is in rebellion against God's order.

It is immediately evident that the term *world* connotes different things. The Bible uses *world* in five different senses: (1) the physical universe, (2) the human inhabitants of the earth, (3) the scene of human activity, (4) the forces arrayed against God and God's purposes, and (5) the world as the object of God's mission. John 3:16 refers explicitly to the last sense and implicitly to the fourth. Because of sin the universal problem is that the human heart has rebelled against God, resulting in the alienation of humankind. God's mission is to win back humankind by confronting and overcoming that rebellion with love.

No aspect of the human condition remains untouched by sin. The brokenness and alienation of the human condition is expounded with great profundity by the apostle Paul in Romans, but it is also expounded in countless ways in daily life. The Bible shows God expressing the full range of response to the human community: rage at wanton injustice, wickedness, and rebellion, on the one hand; and tender compassion for the victims of injustice and misfortune, on the other. But God's grace is such that no one, regardless of the scale or depth of personal sin, is beyond the reach of God's power to redeem.

---

[12] See Wilbert R. Shenk (1993, 153-79).

At the beginning of this chapter it was noted that a "primal tension" characterizes the relationship between the disciple and the world. The Johannine writings, in particular, delineate this disciple-world nexus. Three points can be made by way of summary. First, in spite of the world's rebellion and lostness, God's compassion is extended to all peoples and God desires to save humankind. Second, redemption is only possible as men and women allow God to liberate them from their enslavement to Satan, who holds humankind as a pawn in the cosmic battle against God. Third, God sent Jesus to fulfill God's redemptive mission in the world, and Jesus, in turn, commissioned the disciples to continue his mission in the world. The context of discipleship is the world. Service to God is service to the world.

ESCHATON

The New Testament opens with the announcement that in sending the Messiah God's promise to Israel of liberation is being fulfilled. Yet it quickly becomes clear that this is a promise in process of being fulfilled. As Jesus comes to the end of his earthly ministry, he hands on responsibility to his disciples to continue this still-incomplete mission (cf. Jn 20:20f.). Jesus speaks of this mission of proclaiming the reign of God throughout the world as being directly linked to the "end" (Mt 24:14) or consummation. At the ascension of Jesus the disciples were assured that he would return again to claim his victory and to be with them (Acts 1:11).

We are thus confronted with what is usually termed "the already/not yet" of the kingdom. From the earliest days of the church it was understood that Jesus had inaugurated the reign of God but that it would be fully realized only at "the last day" (Jn 6:39, 54) "when all things are subjected to him" and the Messiah himself "will also be subjected to the one who put all things in subjection under him" (1 Cor 15:28). The reign of God has indeed become present in Jesus the Messiah, and in the power of the Holy Spirit the church has continued Messiah's mission. But this is an interim. The forces of Antichrist have not been completely vanquished. The world continues to be under the sway of demonic principalities and powers. Nonetheless, confidence in the final triumph of Messiah nerves the disciple community to remain faithful in witness.

The New Testament is pervaded by this eschatological tension (Shank 1993, 222-26), a tension linked to messianic mission with its notes of judgment, urgency, hope, deliverance, and salvation. On the one hand, the disciple community already is sustained in the Spirit by the first fruit of God's reign. On the other hand, "the sufferings" only heighten the expectation of the final deliverance of God's people from "this present time" (Rom 8:18). Indeed, there are signs everywhere that the whole creation is filled with this longing for liberation, not only because it promises release from hostile forces and death itself but because of the prospect in Jesus Christ of full knowledge (1 Cor 13:2, the reversal of Gn 2:16-17).

The consummation of Messiah's mission thus is presented in the New Testament as being bound up with the missionary mandate Jesus gave to his disciples. The *promissio* of the eschaton is correlated with *missio,* and "the Christian consciousness of history is a consciousness of mission" (Moltmann 1967, 225). The eschaton represents the goal toward which the reign of God is moving. Mission takes its orientation from that ultimate goal.

Jesus spoke of the consummation of the reign of God in terms of a great messianic banquet—the event that the people of Israel believed would inaugurate Messiah's reign. The metaphor of the messianic banquet is rich in meaning: a time when God's people would enjoy shalom through the direct mediation of the Messiah. Jesus reinterprets this banquet, however, by speaking in universal terms about the inclusion of the Gentiles at the banquet table. The guests at this feast will be those who confess their dependence on God, while "evildoers" will be excluded (Mt 7:23; cf. 8:11f.; Lk 13:28f.). God has graciously provided the present time so that men and women can prepare to share in that blessed banquet in the presence of Messiah.

CONCLUSION

The mission of the triune God is to establish God's reign throughout the whole of creation. This is being realized through God's redemptive mission. The character of the mission of God is defined by the ministry of God's messiah, Jesus the servant, whose servanthood was empowered by the Holy Spirit. It is by the Spirit that the church is endowed with spiritual gifts and empowered for ministry as the messianic community. God's redemptive mission will be consummated in the eschaton, but in the interim the promise of the eschaton infuses the messianic community with hope and power as it continues its witness amid opposition and suffering. The interaction of these elements represents the mission dynamic that is the basis of the vocation of the disciples of Jesus Christ in the world.

2

Recovering the Fullness of the Gospel

From time to time the nature of the gospel has undergone redefinition. In the twentieth century the content of the gospel has often been described in terms of a dualism: word and deed, or proclamation and service. This would have impressed earlier generations as a strange construction.

The Bible, for example, contains no discussion of strategies of "social service" or "evangelistic preaching." Nor is there any attempt to contrast one with the other or to establish the primacy of one over the other. We moderns have managed to introduce into our reading of the Bible a distinctly twentieth-century problem.

Missionaries in earlier centuries were not burdened with this formulation. The Vatican throttled the Jesuits in China in the eighteenth century for following Matteo Ricci's lead in adopting traditional Chinese rites as the form for Christian worship, not because Jesuit missionaries taught science to the Chinese intelligentsia with a view to introducing the fruits of Western technology.

William Carey issued his historic appeal in 1792 for missionary action on the basis that Christians ought to use "means" for the spread of the gospel. Carey's phraseology was instinctively broad and inclusive—ranging from direct preaching to agricultural development, Bible translation, and printing, from the founding of local churches to the creating of institutions of higher education.

By contrast, in the twentieth century the problems have arisen primarily at those points where we have insisted on keeping the elements separated and compartmentalized with differing values assigned to the parts. These values have been derived from certain assumptions made by competing schools of thought as they have engaged in polemics against one another.

In spite of the fact that this is a non-issue on biblical, theological, historical, and practical grounds, it has been the center of intense debate in the present century. It is worthwhile, therefore, to examine the origins of the issue. My argument is that the problem of the relationship determines how the church will relate to the world. There are ample grounds for the contention of Richard J.

This chapter was first published in *Missiology: An International Review* 20:1 (January 1993): 65-75.

Coleman that "without malicious intent any congregation, whether Jewish, Roman Catholic or Protestant, could be split over the single issue of social involvement. 'What kind?' 'How much?' 'Direct or indirect?' 'Corporate or individual?' are the dividing questions" (1980, 205). Regardless of where a group positions itself on the theological/ecclesiastical spectrum, one can expect a diversity of viewpoints with respect to sociopolitical strategy. A fully biblical answer will not be arrived at by attempts to strike a particular balance or order of priority between the parts. The only adequate symbol for ministry is the kingdom of God as embodied in Jesus Christ. Nothing less than this can hold together the various dimensions with integrity and coherence.

THE MODERN WORLD

The modern world has been shaped by the intellectual movement of the seventeenth century known as the Enlightenment. No area of life in the West has been exempted from its influence. The Enlightenment celebrated the possibility that humans can arrive at truth through rational processes. It promoted the *scientific method* of inquiry and treated with great skepticism the old verities and dogmas. A new spirit of expectation was in the air. People believed that only a failure of imagination could hold back progress on all fronts. Practical problems could be solved by developing new technologies. Technological innovation spurred scientific advance.

The influence of science was rapidly felt in all realms of knowledge. The scientific method required increasing specialization in each field, while the scope of inquiry expanded steadily. New disciplines continued to be established. The social-science disciplines were founded in the nineteenth century. Knowledge in all areas continued to proliferate at an accelerating pace based on an ever-increasing degree of specialization. The modern world subscribed to the doctrine of evolutionary progress as the birthright of rational human beings. It was widely believed that human society could look forward to unending progress in all areas of life.

Science has been the dominant authority in Western culture for several centuries. Every field of human endeavor has been affected by science. When we wish to validate something, we say it has been worked out according to "scientific principles." Science has dictated methodology and the norms for truth. In spite of the fact that scientists have become increasingly modest in their claims concerning what they know with certainty, in the popular mind the "scientific" remains unquestioned. The story was further complicated when in the nineteenth century *scientism* entered the fray and sought to discredit the miraculous and the transcendent. Not surprisingly, science was perceived to be an antagonist of religion.

Christian scholars had no choice but to come to terms with the challenge of science in biblical studies and systematic theology. It was early assumed that this challenge could be met by adopting the methods of science. Higher critical methods, for example, were devised for the study of the scriptures. Out of concern to make the Christian faith credible in relation to the modern worldview, these scholars rejected the miraculous and adopted an evolutionary vision of the kingdom of God that was being established in the world.

Other Christians were willing to acknowledge the mastery of science in all other areas and gladly accepted the fruits of scientific inquiry, but they refused to concede authority in the religious realm to science. Christians in this group often found themselves the object of ridicule by the scientific community. Furthermore, over time, relations between liberal and orthodox Christians deteriorated so that by the beginning of the twentieth century deepening suspicions appeared. The Vatican censured Catholic modernists in 1906. Between 1900 and 1925 most Protestant churches were wrenched by the modernist-fundamentalist struggle. The modernist wing was subsequently eclipsed by the neo-orthodox movement, which appeared on the scene as a critical reaction to liberalism. The fundamentalists, discredited by their excesses, lost influence as a force in society. Nonetheless, the two extremes, modernist and fundamentalist, left an indelible stamp on succeeding generations. The way all of us think about Christian witness continues to be influenced by this old conflict.

MODELS OF CHRISTIAN WITNESS IN THE TWENTIETH CENTURY

We now turn to the main models of witness that Protestants have espoused in this century. By definition, a model attempts to depict an important reality through deliberate simplification. But it does enable us to make certain observations.

The Social Gospel Model

The social gospel movement grew out of liberal theological assumptions. It became a force in the United States during the last half of the nineteenth century. It never engaged a large number of people and remained primarily a movement of the clergy, but it exerted influence out of proportion to its size. It arose out of pastoral concern for workers tied to the industrial machine whose legitimate grievances were being ignored by management. Walter Rauschenbusch (1861-1918), theological leader of the social gospel movement, hammered out his main ideas while pastoring an immigrant congregation of German Baptists in New York City.

According to Charles H. Hopkins, three ideas defined and united the social gospel: "the immanence of God, the organic or solidaristic view of society, and the presence of the kingdom of heaven on earth" (Coleman 1980, 207). Thus, the social gospel held that the goal of Christian witness was the realization of the kingdom of God here and now. Leaders like Rauschenbusch combined an evangelical emphasis on conversion with efforts to reform the structures of society. Others understood the task largely in terms of social renovation. The social gospel was idealistic and optimistic with regard to what could be achieved through the application of progressive and rational thought.

By the time the social gospel came on the scene, theological liberalism was several generations old. In the minds of fundamentalist critics the social gospel was of a piece with liberalism; but historical accuracy requires that the two be distinguished. H. Richard Niebuhr suggested that liberalism at the turn of the century was living off its spiritual inheritance, a legacy that was largely spent. Liberalism sustained itself by drawing succor from the cultural vision of evolutionary progress that marked the nineteenth century. The basic tenets of Christian conviction were reinterpreted to accord with the modern worldview. In Niebuhr's trenchant characterization of liberalism: "A God without wrath brought men without sin into a kingdom without judgment through the ministrations of a Christ without a cross" (Niebuhr 1937, 193). Rather than revolutionary change through personal conversion, liberalism placed its faith in evolutionary development as promised by the secular vision (Coleman 1980, 206-12). The social gospel was more realistic about human sinfulness, even if optimistic about the potential of social reform. World War I shattered many of the liberal and social gospel assumptions about the innate human capacity for social transformation.

The Individual Conversion Model

Fundamentalism, which was essentially a movement of reaction against the main features of liberalism, as a true child of the Enlightenment, emphasized the individual.[1] In the fundamentalist vision, conversion was a highly individual matter. This effectively undercut the possibility of collective Christian responsibility in the social realm. Fundamentalism was strongly marked by premillennial-dispensational eschatology, which viewed this world through pessimistic lenses. This philosophy of history offered no motive to work for improvement of human welfare in this world. Whereas the social gospel emphasized the realization of the kingdom of God now, fundamentalists concentrated on the "saving of souls" for a future destiny. Whereas liberals took an optimistic view of society, fundamentalists insisted on working with the individual with a view to bringing about spiritual conversion of the individual. Whereas liberals believed in the possibility of using sociopolitical structures to effect change, fundamentalists insisted that the correct strategy was to convert individuals who would then exercise a "converted" influence as private citizens. Whereas liberals depended largely on social action as the form of Christian witness, fundamentalists em-

---

[1] Fundamentalism takes its name from a series of tracts on theological "fundamentals" published between 1910 and 1915. Various conservative evangelicals who sympathized with this initiative did not accept the sharp dichotomy between "word and deed" that became the hallmark of fundamentalism. Many of these groups had their roots in Pietism or the holiness movement of the nineteenth century. The position they took did not lend itself to fervid polemics based on sharply drawn lines of battle. Norris Magnuson's *Salvation in the Slums: Evangelical Social Work* (1990) is a case study of this variety of evangelical, which predated the rise of fundamentalism and, therefore, never accepted fully the normative fundamentalist position.

phasized the priority of proclamation. (At the height of the controversy, during the first two decades of the twentieth century, both sides tended to make the two aspects almost mutually exclusive. Subsequently, fundamentalists have come to acknowledge that service is a part of Christian witness, but always subordinate to proclamation [Marsden 1980, 85-138].)

The Contemporary Model

Both of the foregoing models, forged around the turn of the century in the heat of controversy, have been largely superseded. For lack of a precise descriptor, we will label the alternative to the social gospel and fundamentalist models simply the contemporary model. Its roots lie in the earlier mainstream evangelicalism and the biblical theology movement that arose in reaction to liberal theology. Yet its influence has been felt in conservative circles as well. Whether one turns to the conciliar or the evangelical wings of Protestantism, for the past several decades the usual way of describing Christian responsibility has been in terms of a twofold witness consisting of word and deed, proclamation and service. Sometimes this duality is referred to as the Great Commission and the Great Commandment or the evangelistic mandate and the cultural mandate.

Behind this stands the idea of two basic elements that coexist in a relationship of vital tension. Some argue that these two halves are inextricably linked and that no priority of one over the other can be established. Others say, at least on theoretical grounds, that a logical priority must be given to evangelism. Still another view is that evangelism is clearly the priority, but ministries of compassion are also a legitimate part of all Christian witness.

This model leaves open the question of appropriate strategy vis-à-vis the sociopolitical order. Both the social gospel and the individual conversion models had clear answers. The contemporary model seeks to embrace both the call for personal transformation, because it takes sin seriously, and Christian social responsibility based on the conviction that social structures are also within God's provision for human well-being. It should be noted that this model, in contrast to the social gospel, tends to be more situational than programmatic in its approach to social witness.

TOWARD A RECOVERY OF THE WHOLE GOSPEL

The modernist-fundamentalist contest reached its climax around 1925. For the next fifteen years both movements experienced the strains of readjustment. Indeed, both groups were largely overtaken by events.

As a result of World War II the world system was fundamentally realigned and a new balance of power forged. Budding nationalist movements throughout the non-Western world now burst into flower. The war-devastated countries had to be rebuilt, and the success of this reconstruction effort set the stage for the development movement that sprang to life throughout the less developed coun-tries. The period was punctuated by two further wars in Korea and Indochina.

In this tension-filled and challenging environment Christians of all persua-sions responded concretely. Perhaps the best symbol of this response is the for-mation of relief and development agencies. The conciliar bodies and their re-lated denominations organized immediately following the Second World War. The Korean War was the catalyst for evangelicals to become involved in relief and development. A well-known Youth for Christ evangelist named Bob Pierce saw the plight of Korean children who were victims of the war and founded World Vision. Dozens of other independent organizations were formed during this time to sponsor orphanages and to do relief work in Korea. Many of these agencies appealed to the fundamentalist-evangelical constituency for support. The National Association of Evangelicals organized its World Relief Commis-sion in 1964. What is remarkable is that these children and grandchildren of the fundamentalists, without having altered their credo, became increasingly com-mitted to ministries of compassion.

Conciliar Protestants

Leaders of the conciliar movement among Protestants were strongly identi-fied with neo-orthodoxy and biblical theology. W. A. Visser 't Hooft, founding general secretary of the World Council of Churches (WCC), for example, was an able exponent of biblical theology. By the late 1950s, however, a new current of influence began to be felt. In the following decade the secular gospel made strong impact in conciliar circles. With this came a call, spearheaded by a younger generation of third-world leaders on the staff of the World Council of Churches, to politicize the gospel. This wave of influence reached its apogee in the 1968 Uppsala and 1972 Bangkok assemblies. Although the conciliar movement contin-ued to engage in wide-ranging debate on the form and content of the Christian witness, it had moved away from the perspectives of the biblical theology move-ment and toward greater concern with sociopolitical strategy. The 1982 statement "Mission and Evangelism" by the WCC's Commission on Mission and Evange-lism sought to restore mission and evangelism to the WCC agenda (WCC 1982).

Evangelicals

In 1947 a young evangelical leader threw down the gauntlet to fellow evangelicals. In *The Uneasy Conscience of Modern Fundamentalism*, Carl F. H. Henry challenged the quietist/escapist theological vision that had encapsulated the movement since the 1920s. He staked out a program that has occupied him ever since; namely, joining the classical evangelical insistence on personal trans-formation with a vigorous application of Christian faith and values to sociopolitical concerns. Henry was animated by a sense of the kairos moment. He wrote:

With the collapse of Renaissance ideals, it is needful that we come to a clear distinction, as evangelicals, between those basic doctrines on which we unite in a supernaturalistic world and life view and the areas of differences on which we are not in agreement while yet standing true to the essence of Biblical Christianity. But even beyond this, I voice my concern because we have not applied the genius of our position constructively to those problems which press most for solution in a social way. Unless we do this, I am unsure that we shall get another world hearing for the Gospel. That we can continue for a generation or two, even as a vital missionary force, here and there snatching brands from the burning, I do not question. But if we would press redemptive Christianity as the obvious solution of world problems, we had better busy ourselves with explicating the solution (Henry 1947, 10).

In his introduction to Henry's book, Harold J. Ockenga argued that a comprehensive view of the world's needs and the Christian response arose out of Matthew 28:18-20 "as much as evangelism does. Culture depends on such a view, and Fundamentalism is prodigally dissipating the Christian culture accretion of centuries, a serious sin. A sorry answer lies in the abandonment of social fields to the secularist" (Henry 1947, 14). Both Henry and Ockenga attempted to put distance between themselves and the regnant fundamentalist position of the previous two generations by appealing to the Bible and the precedent evangelical tradition.

Carl F. H. Henry continued his polemic against the social quietism characteristic of fundamentalism. A 1971 collection of essays titled *A Plea for Evangelical Demonstration* shows consistency and continuity with what he wrote in 1947. In an essay contributed to a symposium after the Congress on World Evangelization (Lausanne) in 1974, Henry asserted: "The social implications of the Gospel are integral to evangelistic fulfillment, and social concern is an indispensable ingredient of the evangelistic message." He went on to say, "Social concern cannot therefore be isolated and compartmentalized as a marginal or secondary consideration which the evangelist leaves to others because he has a special calling to evangelise" (Henry 1976, 29). In the background of Henry's forceful comments was an intense debate between those who essentially stood by the fundamentalist formulation of the previous generation, and others, like Henry, who rejected this reductionism. Henry's position has never been as theologically radical or as activist as the Evangelicals for Social Action (ESA) of the National Association of Evangelicals, which came to prominence in the 1970s; but without his lead, the ESA would have had even more difficulty in gaining a hearing for its agenda.

Several recent surveys have traced the course of these developments and the debate they have engendered by analyzing the proceedings of the international congresses convened by evangelicals over the past two decades. Starting with Wheaton (1966) and Berlin (1966), world congresses have been held at Lausanne

(1974), Pattaya (1980), Wheaton (1983), and Manila (1989). These have been augmented by regional consultations on particular themes such as the Consultation on the Relationships Between Evangelism and Social Responsibility (CRESR) held at Grand Rapids in 1982 and attended by some fifty evangelical leaders from various parts of the world representing a variety of positions (see survey by Howard 1983; also see Padilla 1985, 27-33; Nicholls 1985; and Carpenter and Shenk 1990, 203-50.)

This movement among evangelicals has been motivated by at least three things, two of which Carl Henry identified in his earliest writings. The first has been the call to recover a fully biblical vision of ministry. Because of the historical evangelical commitment to biblical authority, the doctrine of regeneration, and the primacy of evangelism, most of the theological development in the area of social concern and responsibility has had to demonstrate fidelity to these essentials while enlarging the scope of the gospel (e.g., Nicholls 1985, 11-61; cf. Yamauchi 1972, 6-8; and Johnston 1978). This first effort has received important reinforcement from the second, namely, the rereading of evangelical history prior to the modernist-fundamentalist controversy of the present century. Nineteenth-century evangelicals were at the forefront of those involved in socially significant innovations (Hardman 1990; Timothy Smith 1957; Marsden 1972, 8-11, and 1980; Moberg 1972; Dayton 1976).

The third impetus has come from the emergence of dynamic leaders of the non-Western churches who have effectively challenged the twentieth-century evangelical formulations. Each of these major conferences has included representation from the churches of Asia, Africa, and Latin America, but the formal "coming out" occurred at Lausanne in 1974. C. Rene Padilla, of Argentina, and Samuel Escobar, of Peru, made particularly compelling statements at Lausanne (Douglas 1975). Without forfeiting fidelity to evangelical essentials, these non-Western leaders were increasingly convicted of the need to interact, in the name of the gospel, with the sociopolitical contexts in which they lived. In the case of the Latin Americans, they were meeting the full force of the challenge of new currents such as the liberation theology movement and the vision of a theology that embraced all of life in the name of the gospel. At the same time they were trying to throw off the burden of an imported Western theology that had been hammered out in Europe and North America and which now appeared increasingly parochial and inadequate to meet the needs of the church outside the West.

These evangelical leaders from other parts of the world were bold to insist that all sociopolitical systems, including capitalism, had to be subjected to theological critique. They also sought to lay on the conscience of the wider evangelical community the crisis of the oppressed and poor masses living under totalitarian systems. This contributed in an important way to raising the consciousness of evangelicals of the North Atlantic region to conditions worldwide. The statements adopted at the Grand Rapids (1982) and the Wheaton (1983) consultations reveal the extent of the influence that the churches outside the West have had on evangelical thought (Padilla 1985, 31).

Has There Been Recovery?

The Grand Rapids Consultation held in 1982 produced a five-thousand-word statement entitled "Evangelism and Social Responsibility." The meeting had been convened in an attempt to find a rapprochement between those who, espousing a position that is scarcely distinguishable from that of the traditional fundamentalists, insisted that evangelism must be maintained as an absolute priority, and those who argued that missiological integrity requires the closest relationship between word and deed. John R. W. Stott and his drafting committee struggled to find a formula that recognized these differences without leaving matters at a stalemate. The CRESR group reaffirmed the Lausanne statement that "in the church's mission of sacrificial service evangelism is primary." This was not totally acceptable to all participants, but it was defended on the grounds that what was intended was a *logical*, not an invariable *temporal* priority (LCWE 1982, 24).

Evangelicals have come a long way, both practically and theologically, in their affirmation of a whole gospel ministry. To this extent they have reappropriated their evangelical heritage.

Whether one turns to conciliars or to evangelicals, both are working with a paradigm that regards the Christian witness as an attempt to balance several components. Debates within each tradition have centered on the extent to which the various elements were recognized and kept in proper relationship, and on strategies adopted for actualizing them in the concrete situation. The goal always is to find the proper balance that leads to equilibrium.

Beyond "Word and Deed"

Our thinking about Christian witness in the twentieth century has been controlled by a paradigm stamped by the Enlightenment. This means we have identified witness in terms of discrete components and then tried to determine the proper balance among them. We noted above that this has precedent neither in the Bible nor in nearly nineteen hundred years of church history.

The ministry of Jesus is notable for its clarity of focus and the flexibility of its response. Jesus responded to people. In that way Jesus allowed the other person to set the agenda. But Jesus always responded out of who he was and what he represented. We know that Jesus both announced the reign of God and embodied the reality of God's new order.

The great irony of the social gospel was that it made the kingdom of God its primary motif but reinterpreted the kingdom to conform to the reigning evolutionary vision of the nineteenth century. The fundamentalists reacted by interpreting the kingdom in entirely future terms. In both cases the vital eschatological tension of the kingdom present and the kingdom coming was lost by reducing its scope.

I submit that the flaw in the "word and deed" paradigm is that it has encouraged us to focus attention on the parts rather than on the *whole,* which is God's *new order*. Once this partial way of looking at Christian witness was accepted, it was impossible to arrive at the whole. We live in the constant frustration of trying to achieve balance and defend priorities. But the whole—that is, God's new order—is always greater than the way we add up the parts. Such arithmetic does not correspond with God's.

When Jesus inaugurated his ministry by announcing the kingdom (Mt 4:17; Mk 1:14f.), he called people into a new reality that had personal and social dimensions and that had both proximate and ultimate implications for their lives. Becoming a disciple of Jesus required immediate and unconditional response; it was the start of a journey that would end for the disciple in the New Jerusalem. Jesus invited men and women to join God's new order for the world. His teaching and his action put the other person in touch with that new order. In Jesus' ministry there was no place for the kind of analysis that segregates and categorizes according to kinds of need. Such a rigid response can only stifle compassion and quench the Spirit. The kingdom perspective out of which Jesus responded had exactly the opposite effect. it awakened faith and brought wholeness.

Jesus' manner of response throws all our rational categories into confusion. It is, of course, quite wrong to read the accounts of Jesus' ministry as unrelated events. This sets us up for a reductionist reading. Each incident and every encounter forms part of a whole, and we fall into the trap of our Western worldview if we proceed to generalize from a piecemeal reading. I have suggested that with Jesus just the opposite is at work. Each part is consistently informed by what is central to his very being; and that dynamic center is the way to salvation. Our "word and deed" perspective continues to fail because it causes us to miss the sense of wholeness that for Jesus was foundational to all else. The fullness of the gospel is God's shalom. Our witness to the gospel ought always to have the effect of pointing to the kingdom of God rather than focusing on the particular expression of ministry in which we are engaged.

PART TWO

THE FRONTIER
IN THEORY AND PRACTICE

Mission is a supremely practical affair—it happens on earth even though its origin and motivation come from beyond. The way mission is conceived and carried out inevitably reflects the historical context in which it is set. Mission leaders in the nineteenth century, influenced by the scientific model, became convinced that to be effective, foreign missions needed a theoretical foundation. They invested considerable effort in developing mission theories and policies.

But there is an in-built tension between theory and practice. The mission movement has been tinctured by activism. Missionaries have been caricatured as individualists impatient with rules and external constraints. The important thing was to get on with the work. In the long run, the development of mission theory has been a desultory affair.

Notwithstanding this lack of systematic reflection and self-criticism, the modern mission movement has been subjected to important modifications over the past two centuries. We can trace various patterns and approaches to mission and compare the differing results. Methods and tactics do influence outcome.

One of the important arenas in which we can evaluate the impact of historical methods is the new religious movement. New movements often have been a response to the attitudes and methods of church and mission in the past. The character of the new movement reveals what was lacking or what proved hurtful in the old. For example, the intellectual and emotional formalism of Western worship has been widely supplanted in Africa by African Initiated Churches that give full vent to the indigenous need for a style of worship that engages the whole person—body, soul, and spirit.

The goal of the Christian mission is people changed through encounter with the gospel so that they are spiritually transformed without losing their cultural authenticity. The emphasis in missiological thought on context since the early 1970s has highlighted the importance of indigenous forms and materials to the Christianization process.

In attempting to understand conversion across cultural boundaries the missionary has relied on a formal Western model shaped by the concept of the autonomous individual and religion as private piety. This is now understood as too tied to one culture. Contextualization theory has provided new lenses through which we study Christian conversion as a complex intercultural process.

3

The Role of Theory in Anglo-American Mission Thought and Practice

INTRODUCTION

Any attempt to study the role of theory in Anglo-American mission thought and practice quickly runs up against certain problems. While the notion of a theory of mission can be traced as far back as the 1820s, the term has yet to gain a secure footing in Anglo-American mission thought. Furthermore, there has always been a certain fuzziness surrounding the concept of mission theory. The key idea in mission theory after 1850 was the concept of the indigenous church, but the supporting theoretical substructure has remained incomplete. Was this because it was simply assumed that the meaning was self-evident and therefore did not require further clarification? Anyone studying the debates of this period cannot escape the impression that there is a great deal concerning mission that remains undeveloped and unresolved.

One might hypothesize that this lack of resolution was due, in part, to the fact that mission studies languished outside the walls of academe. With the exception of two brief periods, at Princeton in the late 1830s and at Edinburgh in the late 1860s and early 1870s (Duff 1868), mission studies were excluded from seminaries and faculties of theology until the end of the nineteenth century.[1] Missions were regarded as a matter beyond the purview of academic theologians. It was left to those directly involved in the missionary enterprise to grapple with a theoretical framework for mission.

This chapter was originally published in *Mission Studies* 11:2, 22 (1994): 155-72. Revised for publication in this volume.

[1] The standard study of the relationship between mission studies and theology is O. G. Myklebust, *The Study of Missions in Theological Education* (Oslo: Egede Institute, vol. 1 [1955], vol. 2 [1957]). As Myklebust's survey amply demonstrates, throughout the Western world the academy either ignored or resisted mission studies until the end of the nineteenth century. Although a number of others prepared the way, Gustav Warneck, the German pastor/mission scholar, generally regarded as the founder of missiology, started his career in mission studies after 1870.

We can suggest other reasons for this state of indecision. Whether or not there was an underlying impatience with theory, the lack of sustained attention suggests it was not valued or was treated with diffidence. This omission has also been attributed to the Anglo-American bent toward pragmatism and disdain for theory (Speer 1902, 45-49). In other words, this reflects a cultural trait that values action over reflection.[2]

THE HISTORICAL CONTEXT

To set the stage for this exploratory study, I offer five observations that characterize the historical context since 1800.

1. The modern mission movement emerged in a historico-cultural context suffused with Newtonian cosmology (Oakley 1961). People assumed that all areas of human experience and learning were ordered by and operated according to "laws of nature." The missionary enterprise, as the key to the working out of God's plan of redemption, was understood to be governed by comparable laws and principles.

2. By 1800 science had become the authority, the standard against which other endeavors were measured. The scientific method was deemed to be applicable beyond the physical sciences. As new fields of study, especially the human sciences, were established in the nineteenth century, they were expected to apply scientific methods in conducting their work.

3. The scientific method, as developed by Bacon and others, was based on a careful and patient gathering of relevant data as the first step in working out inductively the pertinent laws and principles. In other words, the scientist must move from empirical evidence to a formulation of the theoretical framework along with the underlying principles.

4. The missionary enterprise is inherently activist—teleologically guided, that is, toward the New Jerusalem, and eschatologically driven by the urgency of reaching all people with the Christian gospel.

5. The Christian missionary enterprise has been decentralized from the days of the first apostles. Recall that the Roman Catholic Propaganda de Fide was not established until the seventeenth century and was instituted to bring control and coordination, rather than as a center of initiative, to what had been a loose-knit operation. The modern mission movement was predicated on voluntarism, heroism, frontierism.

Undoubtedly there are other relevant observations, but these suffice to suggest elements of contradiction and volatility that have contributed to erratic patterns of development within the modern mission movement.

---

[2] The *International Review of Missions Index, 1912-1963*, included the category "mission theory." When the bibliography was reorganized in 1963, this category was dropped. The cumulative *Index 1912-1990: International Review of Mission* (Smith 1993) does not have "mission theory" as a category. Since 1986 *Missiology* has been publishing a topical bibliography. The section on theory has yet to be produced.

THE RISE OF MISSION THEORY

The single attempt to date to survey the development of mission theory in North America—and so far as I know no comparable study has been made of the British experience—is that by Charles W. Forman (1977) in a sixteen-thousand-word paper presented to the 1976 meeting of the American Society of Missiology entitled "A History of Foreign Mission Theory." In that essay Forman undertook to evaluate the literature produced since 1810, the year of the founding of the American Board of Commissioners for Foreign Missions (ABCFM), the first American mission agency organized to send missionaries abroad. His goal was to test whether missiology, and mission theory as a component, had moved toward "maturity" and "consensus." Forman wanted to know if missiology was evolving a "mediating yet challenging position" that capitulated neither to past practices nor to new trends so as to avoid the fragmentation and polarization that traditionally marked mission thought.

Forman does not give us his definition of mission theory. We can make certain inferences by the way he limits the scope of his inquiry. He excludes from his survey works of history, including histories of mission, and theology. The bulk of the 245 titles he cites falls into the categories of "missionary theology" (as contrasted to academic theology) and "missionary principles and practice." A further clue to how he understands his field appears in his first footnote, where he identifies as the "only historical works on America's foreign mission theory" essays by R. Pierce Beaver (1952, 1966, 1967, 1968) and Charles L. Chaney (1976). He notes "useful sections on mission theory" in historical studies by Elsbree (1928), Varg (1958), and Phillips (1969).

Forman organizes his study into four periods:

1. 1810-1890, during which a fairly constant set of ideas controlled mission theory and less than a half dozen books on the subject were published;

2. 1890-1918, the heyday of American missions marked by a burst of new ideas, rapid expansion in the number of missions and missionaries, and the appearance of a huge new literature;

3. 1918-1940, a troubled era when new ideas regarding mission theory caused intense debate and controversy; and

4. 1940-1952, a culmination marked by a comprehensive statement of mission theory in the National Council of Churches/Foreign Mission Conference study in 1952.

As noted above, theology and history of mission are excluded from Forman's survey. It is valuable, but it neither tells us what mission theory meant in the vast literature reviewed (for example, was its meaning constant or evolving, was there movement toward consensus, or what were points of controversy?) nor how it functioned in the Protestant mission experience since 1810. American Catholic mission thought is virtually absent from the survey, Forman reports, because American Catholics did not write on the subject prior to 1945.

The present study will concentrate on a select group of people who made a direct contribution to the development of the science of missions and its theoretical framework.

- William Orme (1828; 1830)
- Alexander Duff (George Smith 1879)
- Rufus Anderson (1869)
- Henry Venn (1861; 1866)
- Edward A. Lawrence (1895)
- John L. Nevius (1886/1899)
- Robert E. Speer (1902)
- Edward Pfeiffer (1908/1912)
- Godfrey E. Phillips (1939)
- Edmund Davison Soper (1943)
- John Ritchie (1946)

EARLY ATTEMPTS

In his *Memoirs of Urquhart*, William Orme (1828) has the following remarkable passage:

Considering the period during which exertion has been made to propagate Christianity among the heathen, and the number of persons who are employed in the work, both at home and abroad, it is surprising that some work on what might be called the philosophy of missions, has not yet appeared. The only things approaching this character are, the *Hints on Missions* by Mr. Douglas, of Cavers; and the work on *The Advancement of Society,* by the same highly gifted individual. But the former of these productions too accurately corresponds with its title to answer the purpose to which I refer; and in the other, the subject is only noticed as one among many. From these works, however, the germ of a highly valuable essay on the subject of Christian missions to the heathen might be obtained.

What we want is, not an increase of reports of yearly proceedings and of arguments derived from the Scriptures, to persuade us that it is our duty to engage in this good work; but a condensed view of the knowledge and experience which have been acquired during the last thirty or forty years. What appear to be the best fields of labor?—what the most successful mode of cultivating them?—what the kind of agency which has been most efficient and least productive of disappointment?—what the best method of training at home, for the labors and self-denial to be encountered abroad?—whether are detached and separate missions, or groups of missions and depots of missionaries, the more desirable? These and many other questions, require a mature and deliberate answer. The materials for such an answer exist. And can none of the officers whose time is wholly devoted to the management of our missionary societies, furnish such a digest? Are they so entirely occupied with the details of business, as to have no time or inclination left for looking at general principles? Were more attention paid to the ascertaining of such principles, and more vigour and consistency manifested in prosecuting them, there might be less of glare and noise; but, assuredly, there would be a prodigious saving of labor, property, and life; and in the end, a greater degree of satisfaction and real success.

In 1830 William Swan, London Missionary Society missionary to Siberia, wrote a 280-page book entitled *Letters on Missions,* with a 54-page preface by William Orme, by then a secretary of the London Missionary Society. In this preface Orme includes the above excerpt from the Urquhart memoirs and commends Swan's book as a worthy first attempt to remedy this lack of what he calls a philosophy of missions. Orme gives sound pointers toward formulation of a theory of mission.

It is axiomatic that a science requires a supporting theory. In other words, an activity cannot properly be regarded as scientific if it does not have a supporting theoretical framework. Those Anglo-Americans who pioneered a "science of missions" fully intended to meet this standard.

In the natural and human sciences, theory is formulated on the basis of careful observation of the data, whether derived from laboratory experiment or field experience, with a view to explaining the expected outcome of an activity and the most efficient means of attaining it. In popular parlance *theory* means to speculate or conjecture; it denotes that which is unreal or impracticable. But in science a theory is an explanatory framework used to describe a more or less predictable process in terms of its goal, the means of achieving it, and criteria for determining whether or not the goal has been attained. In other words, theory follows observed experience. William Orme assumed that the missionary enterprise needed to be conceived of in scientific terms. Although he did not name it as such, Orme was calling for development of mission theory: careful sifting of the experience of the past generation of missionary endeavor, identifying effective methods and principles, appropriate agencies, selection of fields of labor, selection and training of workers, and setting appropriate goals.

In this regard it is interesting to note the topics that occupied the attention of the London Secretaries' Association (*Records of Missionary Secretaries*, 1920), a body comprised at its founding in 1819 of secretaries of Church Missionary Society, London Missionary Society, Wesleyan Missionary Society, and Baptist Missionary Society, but which gradually grew to include most of the Protestant missionary and Bible societies with offices in London. One of the recurring themes in the association's "off the record" meetings was the working principles of missions. In his centennial review J. H. Ritson (ibid., 30) observes: "We may say that in the earlier years of the Association the subjects were of a general and theoretical character, largely concerned with underlying and fundamental problems and principles. For instance, in 1823 the topic was, 'What are the indications of Providence to authorise either the entering on a new mission, or the relinquishing one already undertaken?' In the following years we note among the subjects discussed, 'What instructions may we derive, in reference to missionary proceedings from dark and discouraging dispensations?' 'What are the reasons why missionaries should not be entirely freed from all inferior occupations, and like the Apostles (Acts vi.) give themselves continually to prayer and

the ministry of the poor?' . . . 'What is the best method of convening gospel
truths to the minds of savages?'" This conveys some sense of the lively ferment
among mission leaders during the nineteenth century concerning the proper foundation for the conduct of the missionary enterprise. We turn now to one notable
example of how mission theory was being forged in the first half of the nineteenth century.

In 1829 the Church of Scotland commissioned Alexander Duff as its first
missionary for service abroad. His commission was to establish a mission in
India using education as the primary means of witness (George Smith 1879,
1:104-9). Rather than being commissioned a bold innovator, Duff's mentors
were asking him to apply in India a methodology of proven effectiveness in
Scotland (Walls 1992, 570ff.). Note how Duff went about working out his as-
signment. Although he was given a blueprint for his work before leaving Scotland, upon arrival in Calcutta in May 1830 Duff launched immediately on a
thorough investigation of the situation. He acted in a proper scientific manner
by:

1. gathering all relevant empirical data,
2. evaluating these materials in light of stated principles and goals, and then
3. developing a rationale and appropriate course of action.

Duff's advantage was that he was coming to a locale where there had been a
full generation of missionary work, including that of the Baptists at Serampore.
He visited every mission and each missionary in the region, paying particular
attention to the schools. He observed and evaluated all the missionary methods
being employed and determined that, in order to avoid the shortcomings of others, he would pursue a different course. Duff's "different course" would henceforth be known as the Scottish educational approach, a distinctive mission theory.
According to Duff, education was foundational to the task of evangelization.

MISSION THEORY

The earliest use in English of the term *theory of missions* apparently occurs in
a sermon Rufus Anderson preached at the ordination of Edward Webb to missionary service under the American Board of Commissioners for Foreign Missions in 1845 and subsequently published as a booklet titled *The Theory of Missions to the Heathen* (Beaver 1967, 73-88).

Anderson was a shrewd and avid observer of the missionary enterprise over a
long period of time; his writings are the most extensive treatment by an Anglo-
American of modern missions in the nineteenth century. He began his sermon
by describing the contrast between conditions in apostolic and modern times.
While modern people have unparalleled resources ("means") for propagating
the gospel, it is no longer possible "to impart a purely spiritual character to
missions among the heathen" (73).

Here Anderson was arguing against the widely accepted idea that Christian
faith was inseparable from Christian civilization. He said: "For, the Christian
religion is identified, in all our diffusion among its professors of the blessings of

education, industry, civil liberty, family government, social order, the means of
a respectable livelihood, and a well ordered community. Hence *our* idea of piety
in converts among the heathen very generally involves the acquisition and possession, to a great extent, of these blessings; and *our* idea of the propagation of
the gospel by means of missions is, to an equal extent, the creation among heathen tribes and nations of a highly improved state of society, such as we ourselves enjoy" (74). The "theory" he sketches out has but two points:

1. "The vocation of the missionary who is sent to the heathen, is not the same
with that of the settled pastor; and

2. "The object and work of the missionary are preeminently spiritual" (75,
77).[3]

Indeed, this concern is central to his writings over a long career.

In the preface of Anderson's most comprehensive treatment of the missionary enterprise, *Foreign Missions: Their Relations and Claims* (1869), he stated:

Some may be ready to regard the theory of missions here described as
being self-evident, seeing it is so very simple. But such an impression
would betray much ignorance of the history of modern missions. It is even
now a controverted point with not a few friends of missions, to say nothing of others, whether civilization must not precede Christianity, or, at any
rate, what is the precise relation of the two. Recent publications show,
also, that the relative place of preaching in the missionary work, as compared with education, is not quite settled, though the difference is perhaps
somewhat more theoretical than practical; and the question seems to have
no great interest beyond the caste-regions of India. Scarcely fifteen years
have elapsed since it was deemed advisable to send a Deputation to India,
with one of its leading objects to persuade the missionaries of the American Board in that country to commence the practice of ordaining native
pastors. There is printed evidence, much of which has not been published,
that the theory of missions advocated by the Deputation when in India,
was substantially the same which is embodied in this work; and the unexpected discussion at the annual meeting of the American Board in 1855, as
to the proceedings of that Deputation, and the holding of a special meeting
to inquire into their proceedings, was in great measure the result of misap-
prehension; as was abundantly shown, at the annual meeting in 1856, by

---

[3] In the volume surveying the first fifty years of the ABCFM Anderson wrote:
"Underlying the theory of missions, as prosecuted by the American Board, is the principle
that the missionary goes forth in the discharge of his own personal responsibility to
Christ. The Board, the churches, are helpers, co-workers in his mission. There is an
implied covenant, and he is one of the parties. . . . Christians at home are indebted to the
missionary only as the missionary is to them. The missionary is doing their work no
more than they are doing his. The Board declared this principle many years ago, as best
comporting with the happiest and most successful prosecution of missions, during a
prolonged period, and on an extended scale" (American Board of Commissioners for
Foreign Missions 1861, 270).

the Report of the "Committee of Thirteen." Yet the numerous columns of the religious newspapers, occupied with this subject previous to the report of that committee, would convince anyone, that the theory of missions was then by no means determined. . . . In point of fact, the principles and methods of foreign missions embodied in the seventh chapter, were wrought out with painstaking, and through much conflict of opinion. . . . The author's aim, throughout, has been to give an honest presentation of what may properly be called the science of missions (x-xi).

At a distance of fifteen years Anderson referred obliquely to the deputation Dr. A. C. Thompson and he carried out to India in 1855 and the resultant "Outline of Missionary Policy" adopted by the American Board of Commissioners for Foreign Missions in 1856, an important and rather controversial statement (ABCFM 1861, 361-68). The "Outline" provided much of the structure for Anderson's statement of missionary principles in his book. This statement was congruent with the policies and principles emanating from Henry Venn and the Church Missionary Society at that time (Venn 1861, 1866).

Anderson and Venn considered their efforts to be tentative, work in progress, with further discoveries ahead. In *Foreign Missions* Anderson commented: "This necessity of a native pastor to the healthful and complete development of a self-reliant, effective native church, is a discovery of recent date. I cannot say, nor is it important to know, by whom this fundamental truth or law in missions was first declared. Like many discoveries in science, it very probably was reached by a number of persons, at nearly the same time, and as the result of a common experience" (Anderson 1869, 111).[4] Although Anderson's emphasis in 1845 on the "spiritual character" of missionary work had shifted to the "indigenous church" as the main focus, he nonetheless continued to grapple with the "Christianity and civilization" nexus.

To summarize, as of 1870 Anderson, Venn, and other leaders in mission shared in a consensus that:
- there is a "science of missions,"
- the essential task is to identity and codify the basic principles of mission,
- this is an unfinished and open-ended process.

The attempt to write a systematic and comprehensive manual of missions lay in the future, however.

MISSIONARY CONTRIBUTIONS

Although they were frequent participants in discussions of missionary principles, missionaries contributed little to the literature on mission theory. John L.

---

[4] Here Anderson paraphrases a passage from Venn's 1867 Letter to the Bishop of Jamaica, in which he expounded the importance of the "native pastor" to the growth and vitality of the church (see Shenk 1983b, chap. 3).

Nevius, American Presbyterian missionary to China, published a series of articles in the *Chinese Recorder* in 1884-85 on his missionary methods, which were designed to ensure the development of indigenous churches, that is, churches truly free of the dependency syndrome the conventional mission methods produced. Nevius had worked to counteract the baleful effects of the conventional mission system in his own ministry. His methodology emphasized the role of indigenous leadership, the dangers of foreign subsidies and institutions, and the importance of involving the local church in evangelization from the outset. These articles were then collected and republished as a small book, *Methods of Mission Work* (1886).[5] Nevius had his greatest influence in Korea. He visited Korea in 1890 as a consultant to the recently established mission, and his advice was taken with utmost seriousness. The Nevius Plan was to exert considerable influence in the development of the Korean Protestant churches and continues to be credited as a significant contributor to the vitality of the Korean church.

Typically, after 1875, the Anderson-Venn "three-selfs" formulation was widely affirmed by missionaries as written law, and it was incorporated into many mission society policy statements; but missionary practice continually compromised this ideal (cf. Williams 1990). As the nineteenth century came to a close, new winds were blowing. In the atmosphere of the High Imperial period, the earlier confidence in the capacity of indigenous peoples to develop independent churches gave way to a renewed emphasis on the needs of colonial peoples to be given protection by the colonial powers.

Edward A. Lawrence

Lawrence was a young Congregational Church pastor in Baltimore who undertook a twenty-month round-the-world journey for the purpose of studying missions in 1891-92. Professor Leonard Woods, his grandfather, was a charter member of the American Board of Commissioners for Foreign Missions at its founding in 1810 and exerted strong influence in the Board for twenty-five years. Following graduation from Yale College, Lawrence studied theology at Princeton followed by studies with Professors Tholuck at Halle and Dorner at Berlin. His book, *Modern Missions in the East* (1895), was more than a recounting of his observations. He intended that it might serve as a "textbook for those who wish to look into the science of missions" (ix).

Summarizing his purpose and methodology, Lawrence said:

> Our swift tour through some of the great, central, critical mission fields of the world is completed. Like a naturalist returned from an exploring cruise, we bring back with us a full cargo of specimen mission facts. But, as in his case, our labor is only begun. It is not enough to dump our load at port and call its total bulk the net gain of our trip. Our collected facts must be analyzed, classified, labeled, organized. Their significance must be found, and, since this is a moral sphere, their applications must be made. . . .

---

[5] See Chao (1991) for a full-scale study of Nevius.

In other words, there is a Science of Missions. By an inductive study of the facts and experiences of the past and present, the near and the remote, it discovers the underlying principles which pervade the whole work. These teachings of experience it compares with the primal impulse of faith, from which the whole proceeds. Assuring itself of their congruence and coincidence, it then reaches the illuminated standpoint from which it may reserve and control the work. With ever-growing clearness it applies to each detail the principles and methods thus suggested by faith and confirmed by experience. The mission undertaking becomes an orderly, continuous, organized appropriation of the world for the Lord Jesus Christ (30).

Thus, he offered the results of his investigation as an introduction to the science of missions.

For Lawrence the essential components of mission included aim, scope, motive, call, fitness, and fitting.

Robert E. Speer

Speer served the Presbyterian Church Board of Missions as secretary from 1891 to 1937, one of the longest tenures in missions administration in history. Speer saw himself as heir to Rufus Anderson and sought to keep alive the Anderson legacy. He breathed new life into the indigenous church ideal through his prolific writing and speaking. His book, *Missionary Principles and Practice* (1902), included extensive discussion of the policy implications for missions of the indigenous church ideal. Speer further defined and refined mission theory and principles by applying them to the total mission process, from the founding of the church to the withdrawal of the mission. Yet he did not produce a manual or a comprehensive and systematic treatment.

Speer was aware that many people were unconvinced of the need for a "science of missions." He observed that there was an "absence of any body of accepted principles governing missionary operations. Here and there a great missionary has worked out some problem and reached solid results, but in a score of other stations other missionaries, not knowing of his results or not willing to accept them, are working out the same problem for themselves" (44). This must be regarded as wasteful and inefficient. Speer argued that a standard body of principles was needed, a science of missions.

Such a science of missions cannot be produced deductively. It must be based on experience. "But now," he said, "after one hundred years of actual experience, of mistake and blunder and success, the time would seem to have come for some sincere attempt to embody the approved results of the best missionary work in such statements as shall clear the ground of much present discussion and save much needless duplication of past painful experience" (45).

Speer asserted that a body of scientific missionary writings was being accumulated. This development was being fostered through such means as the missionary councils, conferences, and consultations that had been held in certain countries, regions, or internationally. Increasingly, one could point to agreement among missions and missionaries as to sound missionary principles and policies.

For Speer, building on Anderson's formulation, a science of missions required a theory that consisted of three main elements: aim, means, and methods or agencies of missions. His discussion of mission theory was based on this formula.

Edward Pfeiffer

Pfeiffer was professor in the Lutheran Seminary at Columbus, Ohio. To him goes credit for writing the first, and until now the only, comprehensive manual of *Mission Studies* (1908/1912) for American missions. His manual depended heavily on Gustav Warneck's five-volume *Missionslehre* (Warneck 1897-1905). Pfeiffer divided mission studies into two parts: history of missions, and theory or principles of missions. He said, "Both lines of study are capable of scientific treatment" (123).

Pfeiffer referred to the ABCFM's 1856 "Outline of Missionary Policy" as a benchmark document that pointed the way in the further development of mission theory. He advocated a threefold division of mission principles:
1. ground or basis,
2. purpose and aim, and
3. means and methods (126).

Pfeiffer recognized that mission studies remained undefined, lacking even an acceptable name for the field of study. He reviewed the various terms that had been proposed—*halieutics, keryctics, apostolics, missionics, propagandics,* and *evangelistics,* among others—and then settled for Warneck's choice, *Missionslehre* or *mission theory.*[6]

Godfrey E. Phillips

British contributions to the theory of mission were infrequent after the nineteenth century. This was the burden of Godfrey Phillips, professor of missions at Selly Oak Colleges from 1939 to 1946. In his book *The Gospel in the World: A Re-Statement of Missionary Principles* (1939), he stressed the importance of

---

[6] The German Catholic missiologist Joseph Schmidlin also drew heavily from Gustav Warneck in his pioneer volume *Catholic Mission Theory,* which was written shortly after Pfeiffer's. Schmidlin is careful to give a comprehensive definition: "Mission theory (or *Missionslehre,* according to the common usage of German scholars) may be defined as the scientific investigation and statement of the principles and rules which govern the work of spreading the faith. As the theory of the missionary art, it seeks to answer the questions as to why, whither, how, and by whom missions should be undertaken. Christian mission theory investigates and discusses, from these theoretical standpoints, primarily the spreading of Christianity. Catholic mission theory thus far has for its special subject the laws which govern missionary activity in its Catholic form" (Schmidlin 1931, 1).

"theory," because among British missionaries "theory is weaker than practice" (preface). He called for the illumination of practice by theory. But he recognized that he was speaking against the prevailing viewpoint. The British had established no professorships in the study of missions, and "there is no study of the theory and fundamental principles or even the history of missions" comparable to Warneck's work in German (26). He warned that if only practice is emphasized there is no basis for self-examination or evaluation. Phillips thought it "premature to speak of a science of missions" (26) and yet the need for it was manifestly clear because missions had a history reaching back to pre-Christian times.

Although a great many excellent descriptive studies were produced by British missionaries and scholars, Phillips's book is the only attempt by a twentieth-century British writer to supply a general treatment of missionary principles. After 1945 a new generation of British interpreters of the Christian mission, including such notables as Max Warren, Stephen Neill, Lesslie Newbigin, and John V. Taylor, came on stage. None of them took up the challenge posed by Phillips.

Edmund D. Soper

Soper is included in our survey because he produced an influential work but did not contribute to clarifying the question of mission theory. Yet Soper's work is more representative of Anglo-American missiology than was Pfeiffer's.

The most comprehensive interpretation of the Christian mission in English in the twentieth century is Soper's *A Philosophy of the Christian World Mission* (1943). In this work Soper never speaks of "theory of missions," nor does he use "scientific" language. This means, if nothing else, that the questions of whether there is such a thing as mission theory, and how it is to be defined and applied in the ongoing development of missions studies were left unanswered. We cannot simply say that Soper used "philosophy" in a way equivalent to "theory." Soper is doing something different. He develops, in large measure, an apology for missions rather than articulating the principles on which missions are to be conducted.

John Ritchie

In 1946 the veteran Scottish missionary to Peru, John Ritchie, wrote a small book entitled *Indigenous Church Principles in Theory and Practice*. Ritchie arrived in Peru in 1906 and was instrumental in the founding of an indigenous church. This experience was the basis for his exposition of "indigenous church principles." Largely self-made and idiosyncratic, Ritchie displayed little historical consciousness. He believed that he and his contemporaries had made an original discovery of these principles "under the leading of the Spirit without the formulation of any theory, concerted plan, or perhaps even appreciation of the revolution which these principles involved" (13). It is evident Ritchie had not

arrived at his theory by studying past missionary experience, but what he advocated was not conceptually original. His vision of the indigenous church was
essentially the same as that of Venn, Anderson, Nevius, and Speer. Ritchie's
contribution was to reaffirm, with clarity and conviction, the centrality of the
indigenous church to the mission enterprise. His book was well timed, for it
coincided with a new wave of concern—stimulated in part by the burgeoning
independence movement among colonized peoples—that mission-founded
churches avoid the dependency syndrome.

DEVELOPMENTS AFTER 1945

Charles Forman ends his survey with the multi-volume report of the National
Council of Churches/Foreign Missions Conference (NCC/FMC) study of 1952,
which R. Pierce Beaver, as director of the Missionary Research Library, had
guided to conclusion. Forman asserts that this marked the culmination of the
development of American mission theory. It is of more than passing interest,
therefore, to note how Beaver (1957), five years after completing the NCC/FMC
study, judged the status of mission theory. In spite of the signal contribution of
Zinzendorf in the early eighteenth century in laying a theoretical foundation for
Moravian sessions, Beaver concluded that German missions did not develop a
theoretical framework until the end of the nineteenth century through the efforts
of Gustav Warneck. Beaver then asserts bluntly: "British and American missions were never given a theoretical basis."

Setting aside for the present the question of whether Anglo-American mission thought had acquired a full-fledged theory, Forman's evaluation seems to
be a fair assessment of the state of play as of 1952: a certain measure of agreement had been reached among mainstream Protestants. But this is not the whole
story. In fact, major new departures were already under way in the early 1950s
that would change the shape of the mission question, including:

- Introduction of the concept of the missio Dei;
- Hoekendijk's attack on ecclesio-centricism;
- Emergence of missionary anthropology, especially through the work of
  Eugene Nida, and the founding of the journal *Practical Anthropology*;
- Publication of *The Bridges of God* by Donald McGavran (1955) and
  subsequent development of the Church Growth Movement[7]; and
- Emergence of "contextualization" as conceptual replacement for "in-
  digenous" through the Theological Education Fund (TEF 1972; Coe
  1976).

The next major thrust in mission was to come from the conservative
evangelicals. Mission activism has never been tied to the availability of a theory.
Mission practice continued to evolve in spite of the lack of a corresponding
development in theory. The last chapter has not been written.

---

[7] To some extent the Church Growth Movement rescued theory in the 1960s from
total eclipse. But the emphasis on methodology in Church Growth thought has been of
only partial help.

REPRISE: MAIN ELEMENTS OF MISSION THEORY

The development of the theory of mission that we have been tracing, starting with William Orme's appeal in 1828, appears to have reached its climax with Robert E. Speer and Edward Pfeiffer in the early 1900s. Speer summarized the theory of mission in terms of three elements:

1. aim/goal,
2. means,
3. methods/agencies.

This formulation was assumed to encompass the entire mission process for establishing indigenous churches, from the founding of a mission to the completion of its task and its dismantling. No one took issue with this notion; neither was it employed in any essential way by succeeding generations. No Anglo-American attempted to write a comprehensive treatment of what mission involves after 1910. As the Forman survey makes clear, there was a dramatic flowering of mission studies during the period 1890-1918, but these were topical and episodic rather than systematic and comprehensive.

While an apparent consensus had been reached concerning the main elements of mission theory by 1910, in practice it was ignored. Indeed, the rhetoric of the "indigenous church" enjoyed a revival in the twentieth century, but no conceptual advance was made beyond Robert E. Speer's restatement of the Anderson-Venn theory at the beginning of the twentieth century. In 1912 Roland Allen (1962) unleashed his probing critique of the traditional mission system. Over the next thirty years Allen and his cohorts in a stream of books, pamphlets, and articles focused their fire on actual missionary practice. To have taken Allen seriously would have involved a review of the theoretical framework of missionary work. The response to Allen was one of paralyzing defensiveness. Indeed, we may posit that the contribution of critics like Allen may have served to divert attention from continued development of a clear theoretical framework. It led to no significant reform among established missions.

CONCLUSION

Several observations concerning the place of theory in Anglo-American missions since 1800 bring this survey to a close. First, the role of mission theory has been ambiguous and erratic. As a concept it had largely disappeared from missiological thought by 1960. Second, this has left missions without a clear framework and a sense of the mission process as a whole, a basis for accountability. Furthermore, much of the writing on mission theory has been partial and parochial. The decline of theory has contributed to conceptual confusion. Third, missions have failed to develop clear criteria for evaluating the evangelizing process. Instead, there has been uncritical dependence on the methods and techniques of modernity.

4

Three Varieties of Mission

Study of the history of Christian missions shows that various conceptions of the task have guided missionaries. The scriptures make clear that mission arises out of God's love for the world and thus represents God's initiative to effect reconciliation with humankind. The scriptures also give us an account of how the earliest Christian disciples, imbued with the Spirit of Jesus Christ, were motivated to continue the mission Jesus had begun. However, the scriptures leave many questions unanswered concerning how the missionary task is to be carried out.

The missionary activity recorded in the Bible gives us little specific guidance as to the conduct of mission in diverse cultures where the missionary must begin by learning a new language, becoming acquainted with an entirely different culture, and coping with a vast array of socioeconomic differences.

The missionary goes forth out of a conviction that a church is to be established among a people where there is no church. In other words, the witness and work of the missionary is expected to result in a new socioreligious reality in the host culture.

Here we shall examine how that process has been conceptualized in three different historical periods. Our purpose is not to criticize certain examples but to observe how particular assumptions and patterns get played out in practice.

THE "INVENTION" OF CULTURE

The way we think about culture has changed greatly over the past two hundred years. We may describe this as moving from a precritical to a critical understanding, and from a critical to a constructive view of culture.

Human beings do not exist apart from culture. The individual is permanently imprinted by the culture and language to which he or she is indigenous. This means that all human beings are conditioned to experience life from within the cultures into which they are born and reared. In the Old Testament the people of Israel defined themselves over against the Gentiles. For the Greeks the *barbar-*

Published in English in this volume for the first time.

ian was a foreigner, someone outside Greco-Roman civilization. The barbarians were the "uncivilized." Terms such as *pagan* and *heathen* describe those who are beyond the pale, religiously and culturally. Linguists have observed that in many languages the word for *human being* refers only to members of that ethno-linguistic group rather than being a generic term for all humankind. By definition, others are less than fully human. This may be termed the precritical view of culture.

Charles R. Taber (1991) has traced the historical development in our understanding of culture. The precritical view described in the preceding paragraph was universally characteristic of peoples' understanding of culture until the nineteenth century. It was normal to assume that one's own culture was a self-evidently correct picture of reality, prescribing what ought to be and how things ought to be done. Naturally, this was the standard by which all other peoples were judged.

In the modern period—that is, from about the seventeenth century—it was not difficult for people in the West to convince themselves that their view of the whole world was correct. They were riding the crest of a wave that continually yielded startling innovations in science, technology, and many other fields of learning. All the signs pointed to the inherent superiority of Western civilization. Yet this very success which produced continuous changes in the means of transportation and communication, led to two unanticipated results.

First, because it enabled Westerners to explore the farthest corners of the globe, it resulted in wide-ranging contacts with peoples of many cultures. Westerners were sometimes taken aback—as when they encountered the Chinese, with their sense of a long history and proud culture—to discover that there were other people who felt in no way inferior to or beholden to the West, notwithstanding its technological and scientific achievements. Over time these contacts caused Westerners to recognize that every people has a culture that is unique and which the people prize. Therefore, it is necessary to think in comparative terms without putting either a positive or a negative value on the cultures of other peoples. The lesson Western peoples have had to learn about culture must be learned by every other group of people. The modern world allows no group to live in isolation from other peoples for long.

Second, this rapid growth in knowledge combined with increased intercultural contact spurred the development of the human sciences. The study of anthropology particularly was simulated by the extensive ethno-linguistic data gathered by missionaries, travelers, and explorers. All of this served to erode the earlier insular understandings of culture. Indeed, it revolutionized the way people everywhere think about themselves and their place in the human family.

The stage was thus set for the shift from a precritical to a critical awareness of culture. "Culture" had been invented; it was now a formal and abstract concept, something to be studied in its own right, based on theories of culture with appropriate methods of research and analysis, and enriched by a growing range of comparative analyses drawn from detailed studies of many cultures throughout the world. Missionaries were already engaged in the study of languages that had never before been written with a view to devising a suitable writing system. Others were learning languages with a literary tradition in order to be able to translate the Christian scriptures into them. All of this contributed to the development of the science of linguistics and comparative studies in language.

Linguistics was an important part, but only a part, of the wider field of studies in culture. People began to think in new terms about cultures. Each one was relative to all other cultures. Increasingly people rejected the earlier notion that one culture could be set up as the standard by which other cultures might be judged. All human beings were of equal moral worth regardless of their cultural particularities. Although many Christians continued to read their scriptures through precritical eyes, the great texts that speak of God's love being extended to all peoples (e.g., Jn 3:16) and God's purpose in Jesus Christ being that of reconciling the Jew to the Gentile (Eph 2) gave theological validation to this critical understanding of culture.

In his study of various conceptions of mission throughout church history, Louis Luzbetak (1988, 64-105) took as his point of departure the basic conflict that emerged in the first years of the Christian movement that is reported in Acts 15 and elsewhere in the New Testament. At every stage this fundamental difference in perspective asserted itself. The way mission was conceived in succeeding periods might be described in new terms, but the underlying problematic remained the same. Another feature remained constant. Until modern times theological debate and critique of missionary approach—in the tradition of Acts 15—was, with rare exceptions, conspicuously absent. Much of the controversy turned on questions of cultural understandings and practices.

We may make several summary observations at this point. First, culture is important theologically because God created humankind to live in culture and to contribute to culture formation. Second, the fact that culture is theologically significant calls for critical evaluation of the issues posed by a particular culture. A culture contributes to the sustenance of a human group, but it also contains elements that oppress and destroy its members. Third, we must abandon the notion that there is a blueprint, a master culture, by which we can engage in evaluation of other cultures. A theology of the kingdom or reign of God establishes God's new order as the criterion against which all human systems may be judged. No culture may be equated with God's reign. Each one is a flawed product of human effort.

This suggests a thesis for our further exploration: a) It is culture rather than theological vision that has been central to formulating conceptions of mission; b) changing conceptions can be correlated with changing understandings of culture as a sociopolitical system; but c) all conceptualizations of mission must be subjected to theological critique if they are to be faithful to God's redemptive mission.

THREE STAGES OF MISSION IN PROTESTANT EXPERIENCE

Protestant missionary experience started in the seventeenth century. The accepted model was that of *replication*. This model was followed until the mid-

1800s when it was superseded by the *indigenous church model* developed by mission leaders in the modern period. The indigenous model survived largely unchanged until *contextualization* was introduced in the 1970s. Even though these three concepts are presented here as chronological developments, it must be emphasized that, in fact, elements of the replication model can readily be found in contemporary missionary practice and not everyone is yet persuaded of the insight contained in contextualization.

It must be stressed again that when we describe these conceptualizations we turn to our understandings of culture for our basic materials. Each model will be characterized in terms of three features: 1) how mission as a process is understood; 2) who controls the process; and 3) the view of culture assumed.

Replication Model

Key features:

1. Mission is a process through which the missionary seeks to replicate or reproduce a church in another culture patterned carefully after that of the church from which the missionary originated. Protestant missionaries in the seventeenth and eighteenth centuries were from what is known historically as Christendom— Christianity as it had become intertwined with European culture.

2. The missionary as representative of Christendom is charged with responsibility for the success of the outcome.

3. The view of culture is precritical and ethnocentric.

The seventeenth and eighteenth centuries form an important prelude to the modern mission movement among Protestants. Although missionary work during this period was carried out on a modest scale by a few scattered missions in India, Sri Lanka, the East Indies, the West Indies, and North America, it determined the model of mission that was to characterize Protestant missions until well into the nineteenth century. In the background of Protestant missions from the beginning was the concept of Christendom. Early Protestant mission pioneers combined basic concepts they borrowed from the Catholic "Christendom" mission tradition with their Protestant convictions to forge a model they claimed as their own. But its main distinguishing feature was that Protestants from the beginning assumed that the scriptures must be made available in the vernacular languages. This reflected continued Protestant defiance of the authority of the Roman hierarchy rather than special insight into the meaning of culture for the transmission of the Christian message. Like Roman Catholics, Protestants were firmly committed to Christendom, the historical synthesis of the Christian religion and European culture, as the standard by which they measured their results. Given their precritical view of culture, there was no other way they could view their task.

One of the most widely publicized missionary enterprises in the seventeenth century was that founded in 1632 by John Eliot at Roxbury, Massachusetts, among the Iroquois. Eliot was of the Puritan tradition. In addition to translating the Bible into the "Moheecan" language, Eliot took a cue from Roman Catholic missions and gathered his converts into "praying towns" as a way of protecting them from the influences of their indigenous culture. Eliot understood Christianization to require inducting the Indian convert into Christian culture and erasing as much as possible of the indigenous culture.

Although largely ignored by mission historians, Thomas Mayhew, John Eliot's contemporary, carried out his missionary work among the Indians on Martha's Vineyard, an island off the Massachusetts coast, along different lines. In an important respect Mayhew should be recognized as a precursor of a later variety of mission. Mayhew showed a deep respect for Indian culture and sought to incorporate aspects of Indian folkways and ritual into their expression of the Christian faith. But it was Eliot's example that was emulated far and wide by other missionaries. Mayhew's critical view of culture was out of step with the prevailing precritical view, which called for a mission to "produce after its own kind," culturally and ecclesiastically.

Mission as replication is based on two premises. First, it is assumed that there is such a thing as a Christian culture. This is definitive ecclesiastically and culturally. Second, since Christendom represents the "original," the mission task is to reproduce or replicate this original. To propagate the gospel is to invite people into this definitive culture. This missionary approach was promoted from the seventeenth century onward under the banner of "Christianity and Civilization." In the nineteenth century a third "C"—for commerce—was added. These three C's were shorthand for replication.

The main point of debate about this variety throughout these two centuries was whether civilization was prerequisite to Christianization or not. Some argued that a Christian civilization had to be created before indigenous peoples could hope to become Christian, while others were equally firm in asserting that the gospel was the starting point for faith and for creating a Christian civilization. But there was no doubt that Christianization required its corresponding civilization or culture.

Late in the eighteenth century a small group of Christians became concerned about the iniquitous slave trade and launched a campaign that was to continue for more than fifty years. The first goal was to abolish the slave trade; subsequently, slavery itself became the target. The struggle culminated in 1834 when the British Parliament enacted a law outlawing slavery throughout the British dominion. Many of these activists were also involved in promoting Christian missions. Not content to treat only the symptoms, they sought a remedy that would make this "illegitimate" trade unattractive. They urged that legitimate trade be developed as a counter-force. It was argued that a thriving "legitimate" economy was the best means of routing the slave trade. Thus a powerful moral motive impelled advocates of commerce to add it to the other two C's. When David Livingstone gave his famous valedictory in 1858, he said: "I go back to Africa to make an open path for commerce and Christianity." At that moment the slave trade in East Africa was in full swing, and Livingstone's call was, in part, an appeal for continued struggle until slavery was put to an end.

Replication assumes that the only way to ensure faithful reproduction of Christendom is through careful tutelage by a representative of Christendom. New adherents to the Christian faith had to prove their authenticity as Christians by being "culturally circumcised." This approach makes few concessions to the host culture (see Mbiti 1976, 6-18). Throughout this period one does not encounter theological critique of mission methods or approaches; neither was there conceptual development of mission theory.

Indigenization Model

Key features:

1. The indigenization process is expected to reproduce Christendom in another culture by drawing on the people and materials of the other culture, but the script is provided from outside. This approach attempted to make adjustments to the new culture but essentially did this by changing the cast of players without rewriting the script.

2. The missionary is the primary agent for deploying and managing all the resources.

3. A differentiated view of culture is assumed, with cultures ranged along a continuum from primitive to the most highly developed (or "civilized"). Culture is evolving.

The modern mission movement was launched around 1800. From the start it held that the goal of a mission was the founding of an indigenous church. By the middle of the nineteenth century, with more than a generation of experience behind them, the leading missionary societies were beginning to face a new set of questions. They now could begin to see the results of the methods they had employed. Of special concern was the fact that the churches founded by these missions were not as vigorous and self-reliant as the idealistic founders had anticipated. Instead, these new churches showed signs of an unhealthy dependency and a lack of rootedness in native soil. It was obvious something was wrong.

Many mission leaders wrestled with this problem. It was during this time that calls for a "science of missions" began to be sounded. There was growing frustration at what appeared to be only modest success and rather signal failures in missions. A rigorous critique of past methods and practices was advocated in order to arrive at a more productive approach.

By 1850 a new formulation was at hand; it soon became "the indigenous church" or the "three-selfs" principle. This formulation is generally associated with two mission administrators, Rufus Anderson (1796-1880) and Henry Venn (1796-1873), and, in the next generation, the missionary John L. Nevius (1829-93). In fact, the raw materials, and even the phrasings, had been around well before this time (Shenk 1990). The distinctive contribution of Anderson and Venn was to synthesize these elements into a coherent formula: a church could be judged to have become indigenous when it was self-financing, self govern ing, and self-propagating. Generally it was believed that the indigenous church would emerge as a result of following a scheme consisting of several stages of development starting with missionary control, moving to shared control or leadership, and then to indigenous control. Only rarely were these transitions from stage to stage negotiated successfully. The missionary found it difficult to relinquish control, and the indigenous people were frustrated by this evident reluctance to entrust this responsibility to the church. Nevius added to the debate the authority of field experience. In China he developed a program of evangelization and church development that he believed to be consistent with the indigenous church ideal. This required that local people be drawn into leadership in the new church as early as possible. The Nevius Plan found its greatest acceptance in Korea, where it was made foundational to the Protestant movement. It has been credited as the basis for the rapid growth of the Korean church.

Anderson, Venn, and Nevius all helped to make the concept of indigenization the dominant concept in missions for the next century. Anderson and Venn worked with their missions to devolve responsibility for churches and institutions on indigenous leadership. During Anderson's tenure with the American Board of Commissioners for Foreign Missions the mission-founded churches in the Sandwich Islands became independent. In the 1840s Henry Venn set in motion a process in Sierra Leone that culminated in the transfer of responsibility to local leadership of churches and schools by the 1860s. These two examples from the nineteenth century demonstrate the possibilities and limits of the indigenization idea. Some successes could be claimed for it; but it generally proved difficult in practice to implement, as Nevius's experience in China illustrates. Nevius never won the respect and cooperation of his colleagues in China. His fame rests on the fact that his ideas were accepted and followed in Korea.

The indigenization approach was viewed by its advocates as correcting and superseding the concept of replication. But it remained tied to the Christendom model. It modified the replication model at certain points, but it was not a radical departure from it. Control of the process remained largely in the hands of the outside agency: the missionary and the missionary society. As noted above, most missions got stuck in stage one, frustrating the success of the mission and development of the church.

By 1850 the human sciences were in their infancy. The conceptual foundations for sociology and anthropology were being laid. There were still few tools at hand for critical study of culture. Occasionally intuitive insights concerning culture would break forth, as in Henry Venn's instructions to outgoing missionaries June 30, 1868. This was at the time when evolutionists were putting forward their novel "scientific" theories of race. Thoughtful Christians were exercised by the implications of such views, and Venn had expressed his disagreement with these notions. On this occasion of sending out another contingent of missionaries he offered his missionary colleagues this advice:

1. Study the national character of the people among whom you labor, and show the utmost respect for national peculiarities.

2. . . . race distinctions will probably rise in intensity with the progress of the Mission.

3. As soon as converts can be gathered into a Christian congregation, let a native church be organized as a national institution.

4. As the native church assumes a national character it will ultimately supersede the denominational distinctions which are now introduced by foreign missionary societies.

5. The proper position of a missionary is one external to the native church (Venn 1868, 316-18).

In this statement Venn correctly anticipated the tensions that would continue to mount if missionaries did not develop a deeper and more sensitive appreciation of the host culture and allow the new church greater freedom in expressing its faith in its own cultural idioms.

Anderson and Venn came to the ends of their careers just as the high colonial period was dawning. The ideals they expressed through their many pronouncements, policies, and administrative decisions were largely ignored by their own missionaries in the field and then eclipsed by events in the next generation. Nevertheless, the issues they sought to address did not disappear. Their successors only postponed the inevitable. In the end, the missions had to come to terms with problematic aspects of the indigenization concept.

Whereas the replication approach focused on the correct reproduction of the "original," indigenization emphasized finding the functional equivalent within the other culture for the "original." That is to say, the goal of indigenization was to find the symbols and forms in the host culture through which the Christendom view of religious life might be expressed. Venn's statement of 1868, if pushed to its logical conclusion, would have stretched the concept of indigenization to the breaking point. What he was intuitively reaching for could not be achieved by following the approach to which he was committed. Most proponents of indigenization assumed Christendom continued to furnish the norm by which they were to judge their work. The goal of indigenization was to see that norm reproduced, albeit dressed in indigenous clothes.

One of the sharpest critiques on missionary methods in the modern period was that of Roland Allen (1868-1947). As a missionary to China, Allen was an eyewitness to the Boxer Rebellion of 1900. His first book was an account of that episode. He was profoundly disturbed by the foreignness of the mission-founded church in China. Allen attributed this result to the mission system.

Roland Allen's critique was based on his reading of the experience of the apostle Paul and the early church (Allen 1962). He argued that Paul's conception of mission contrasted sharply with that assumed by the modern mission movement with its elaborate institutional system and stages of development. Allen did not approach his subject sociologically but rather historically and theologically; yet it is clear that his vision of the process of establishing new churches could not be achieved through mission as indigenization. He did not propose a new theory of culture, but he argued that the church can take root in every cultural context and there become a faithful representation of the body of Christ.

The modern mission movement of the nineteenth century may well be viewed as the last great thrust outward of the old Christendom (Shenk 1984; cf. Latourette 1970, 7:413). What it produced instead was a new church spread round the world that increasingly demanded freedom from the foreign cultural forms that mission brought. The old structures of Christendom simply could not contain this new reality that had entered diverse cultures and had to adjust to various political systems. The two variant approaches to mission produced by Christendom— replication and indigenization—looked more and more like attempts to outfit a youthful David with Saul's armor. Neither model solved the problem of control by agents and agencies from outside the culture.

Contextualization Model

Key features:

1. Contextualization is a process whereby the gospel message encounters a particular culture, calling forth faith and leading to the formation of a faith community, which is culturally authentic and authentically Christian.

2. Control of the process resides within the context rather than with an external agent or agency.

3. Culture is understood to be a dynamic and evolving system of values, patterns of behavior, and a matrix shaping the life of the members of that society.

Seldom has a major conceptual shift been made with such apparent suddenness as the change from the indigenization to contextualization. The new model made its debut in the 1972 report of the Theological Education Fund, *Ministry in Context*. In explaining the difference between indigenization and contextualization, TEF director Shoki Coe maintained that because *indigenous* derived from the natural world, it had a static, even past-oriented character (Coe 1976, 20-21). What was needed was a concept that suggested dynamic interaction with the diverse living contexts in which the churches are found today, enabling them to engage the vital issues of life and death for the people in each society. A fundamental difference between the two models was that responsibility for contextualizing the message of the gospel no longer was seen as resting with individuals from outside the culture; rather, that responsibility lay with the church and its leaders from within the culture.

What was now being assayed and proposed as a formal model of mission had in fact been anticipated in the experience of certain new Christian movements that sprang up in the wake of Christian missions. These movements were distinguished by the fact that they were indigenous from the beginning. They instinctively rejected foreign forms and experimented with indigenous alternatives. An early and outstanding example of this was Uchimura Kanzo (1861-1930), a man of great intellectual ability and personal piety. Uchimura insisted that rather than causing him to surrender his Japanese character because he was a Christian, his faith in Jesus Christ had made him more authentically Japanese. He rejected the denominational church form brought from the West and formed the Mukyokai (No-Church Movement) based on Japanese cultural patterns. He struggled to grasp the relationship between Christian faith and Japanese culture at a deep intellectual level (Lee 1989, 24-30).

Shoki Coe argued that this emphasis on context should lead to a changed understanding of the process of theological development. "This dialectic between contextuality and contextualization indicates a new way of theologizing. It involves not only words, but actions" (Coe 1976, 22). He believed this approach would overcome the persistent dichotomy between theory and practice that has marked academic theology. Whereas the TEF initiative was directed at changing theological education, the searchlight was rapidly turned on the whole mission enterprise. It soon became common coin to speak of a contextual approach to mission.

This is not to suggest that ideally the church should be slavishly or uncritically identified with a culture. On the contrary, it means that the church must be culturally valid precisely in order to bring a radical critique to bear on culture. Uchimura did not believe it was a contradiction when he insisted that his Christian faith made him more authentically Japanese. Rather than a contradiction this represents the tension that must characterize faithful Christian discipleship. And this is the true issue of missionary witness.

Because mission as contextualization is of recent origin, we have had little experience in working out this variety of mission in the field. Although a sizable literature on contextualization has been produced in the past two decades, further theoretical work is needed.[1] People are still struggling to understand how it can be implemented. It does appear that much more attention has been paid in the literature to the theological basis for contextualization than was the case for replication or indigenization. But this needs to be combined with deeper understanding of culture as a system of meaning and values.

We have reviewed these three varieties of missionary approach as three discrete developments within precise historical periods. This, of course, oversimplifies actual experience. For example, as was pointed out with regard to the concept of indigenization, during the High Imperial period there was widespread apostasy and many missionaries, in practice, reverted to replication.[2] Indeed, today one can readily find examples of all three varieties being followed.

Missionary practice is not necessarily informed by the learnings of previous generations. As Charles R. Taber (1991, 132) reports with regard to the way

---

[1] To cite only a few of the recent important books: Conn (1984); Gilliland (1989); Kraft (1979); Luzbetak (1988); Schreiter (1985); and Shorter (1988). All contain further bibliographical suggestions.

[2] A thorough study of what happened in Henry Venn's own society in the following generation is now available in C. Peter Williams, *The Ideal of the Self-Governing Church* (1990). While the Church Missionary Society held to the Venn ideals until the end of the nineteenth century, the missionaries consistently failed to apply them. Ultimately, the CMS itself abandoned the Venn ideals.

missions have drawn on the human sciences, it is difficult to demonstrate that the availability of growing and unparalleled opportunities for cultural studies has meant appreciably better relations between missionaries and the people among whom they minister. At the same time we cannot escape the fact that the way we go about our work makes a great difference as to outcome.

CONCLUSION

This study of three conceptions of mission has emphasized how these constructs are historically and culturally conditioned. None of the three discussed here has drawn directly on a particular theological vision. Nevertheless, it is necessary that missionary efforts be subjected to theological critique. Indeed, it is dangerous to act as though we are dealing with a matter that consists only in finding the correct method, technique, or approach. To reiterate Taber's implied warning: the availability of greater knowledge—in this case knowledge of culture—does not guarantee greater effectiveness or faithfulness in mission. The goal of mission is to bear witness to God's love as revealed to us in Jesus Christ. Prior to everything else there must be a transformation of a missionary's own mentality into Christlikeness. The missionary's task is to be an instrument of ongoing transformation in the world. If the missionary's being and work are to be an instrument, this suggests that someone else is in control.

The example of the Word becoming flesh, the incarnation of Jesus Christ, is the baseline against which we must evaluate all our missionary efforts. Can replication or indigenization or contextualization be equated with incarnation? The incarnation is foundational to mission (Jn 1:14). The example of God's action in Jesus Christ has crucial things to say about the nature of the power that is to be used (i.e., agape), who controls the process (i.e., messianic servanthood), and the view of culture that underlies it (i.e., God comes to all people within their own cultural context). This offers a new horizon of missionary obedience, but it also calls for a deeper penetration into the meaning of both gospel and culture than has been achieved thus far. In this, God's sending of Jesus Christ points the way forward for all who aspire to be his disciples.

5

New Religious Movements and Mission Initiative: Two Case Studies

The modern mission model has been challenged repeatedly. The earliest and most enduring of these challenges has been that posed by what has been described variously as *independency, independent churches, spiritualist churches,* and *indigenous churches,* among other terms. All of these designations are problematic in one way or another. In this chapter we shall refer to this phenomenon as New Religious Movements (NRMs). These movements have arisen in direct relation to the Christian missionary enterprise and can be found throughout the world. Four preliminary observations may be made:

1. NRMs are a fruit of the modern mission movement. They would not have happened apart from the coming of the cross-cultural missionary. These movements, as Harold W. Turner (1981) has pointed out, combine in a new form elements of the religion the missionary brought and traditional indigenous religious forms and ideas. It is thus genuinely new. It is recognizable as combining Christian elements and traditional religio-cultural elements. These NRMs range across a spectrum from those that disavow any intent to identify themselves as a part of the Christian faith family, notwithstanding the elements that may have been borrowed from Christianity, to groups that see themselves as moving fully within the Christian orbit, albeit with indigenous forms and thrust.

2. Although these movements were long ignored or misunderstood by missionaries and mission-founded churches, they have become a permanent presence worldwide. In the nineteenth century NRMs cropped up in widely scattered places. Some did not last long, and most did not grow to any appreciable size. No one in the nineteenth century observed that these groups were appearing throughout the world, always in direct relation to Christian missionary activity. Toward the end of the nineteenth century the movement gathered momentum, and by the beginning of the twentieth century a few missionary statesmen and scholars began to take the phenomenon seriously. But generally these groups

Published in English in this volume for the first time.

continued to be viewed by missionaries and churches as threats to be overcome. This attitude prevailed until well into the 1970s in many areas. Even today NRMs are not well understood, although they are treated with much greater respect.[1]

3. Much of the earlier prejudice was the result of ignorance. Through the pioneering studies of scholars like Bengt Sundkler, Efraim Andersson, Harold Turner, F. B. Welbourn, and David Barrett, public perception has changed. Scholarly study has led to numerous personal contacts, and contacts have resulted in relationships that have ripened into friendships and deepening spiritual fellowship. Accurate information has enabled the outsider to understand a group in the light of its self-understanding. Those that do not wish to be classed as "Christian" must be respected, while those that desire to be accorded full membership in the Christian family are increasingly so recognized.

4. As has been emphasized, these NRMs are the fruit of cross-cultural mission, but they are an unintended fruit. Often they have emerged as a result of deep conflicts and misunderstandings that have left scarred memories. It is incumbent on us to ask: What does this experience of NRMs tell us about mission assumptions, methods, and approaches? What can we learn that will enhance the missionary's effectiveness in the future?

We will seek answers to these questions through two case studies: the United Evangelical Church of the indigenous peoples in the Argentine Chaco, and the Dida Harrists of Côte d'Ivoire (Ivory Coast).

THE UNITED EVANGELICAL CHURCH

The Tobas are one of the largest of a number of indigenous ethnic groups located in the Gran Chaco of Argentina and Paraguay. From the sixteenth century onward the Tobas began encountering non-Indian peoples and their cultures. The first encounter was in the form of military expeditions into the Chaco, followed with visits by explorers, Roman Catholic missionary priests, various kinds of entrepreneurs, and, finally, politicians. Virtually all of these outsiders were Europeans representing European culture and interests.

By the twentieth century the situation of the Tobas was deteriorating seriously. They were experiencing deprivation in the form of loss of possessions, status, and worth. As a people whose traditional way of life was based on hunting and gathering, they depended on access to wide expanses of territory, guided by the availability of fruit, honey, fish, roots, berries, and game. Each facet of the encounter with Europeans had introduced a further encroachment on that traditional way of life. The Tobas were indeed being deprived of their traditional territory, and with this loss went their very way of life.

The Tobas had not responded positively to the earlier Catholic missionary work. The church was perceived to be one element in the growing foreign encroachment. The first Protestants arrived in the region late in the nineteenth

---

[1] The extent of this global phenomenon can be most readily grasped by turning to the continent-by-continent six-volume bibliography of these movements prepared by Harold W. Turner (1977).

century. Others came during the following decades. They relied on conventional missionary methods that attempted to replicate among the Indians the particular denominational tradition from which the mission came. Although the missions increasingly paid lip service to the notion of indigenization, they did not truly understand or respect Indian culture. A great chasm stood between the two cultures—missionary and Indian. Existing theories of mission did little to help build bridges between the two worlds.

In spite of this history of hurtful relationship with outsiders, the Tobas correctly perceived that this foreign presence had become permanent; it was something they had to adjust to. In return, the Indians increasingly desired acceptance as persons by the dominant society.

In 1924 the Toba community sustained a severe crisis. The people's confidence in their shamans was shattered when the attempt by the shamans to curb further incursions by outsiders resulted, instead, in the massacre of Toba men, women, and children by the Argentine police. The Tobas began to look elsewhere for a source of authority. They were to find this alternative source of authority in the church. In the wake of this crisis, several Tobas traveled to Buenos Aires, where they came into contact with certain Pentecostals. Subsequently, Pentecostal representatives visited them in the Chaco and Formosa provinces and made efforts to establish a Pentecostal church. This did not prove entirely successful, but it did provide new ingredients for what was about to happen under indigenous leadership.

Around 1940 a religious movement began to percolate among the Tobas. It drew inspiration from the Pentecostals but tapped deeply into indigenous Toba spirituality. In the words of Elmer Miller (1967, 31), "The religious movement referred to represents a syncretism of traditional views on health, disease, spirits, witchcraft, and general cosmology with modern Pentecostal emphases upon healing, speaking in tongues, and other forms of spirit possession." This NRM arose in the wake of the collapse of the traditional way of life. It represented a new religio-cultural synthesis that could provide authority and coherence to the Tobas as they sought to cope with the demands of their drastically changed and changing environment. To a remarkable degree this was to prove effective. By the 1980s Toba population had grown to twenty-five thousand people—at a rate more rapid than for the general population—and the majority of the Tobas were related to the United Evangelical Church. Outside observers have been impressed by the progress the Tobas have made in the intervening years in stabilizing their community in spite of the fact they have continued to suffer discrimination at the hands of the larger society. It is generally asserted today that the church has been a primary source of cultural cohesion for these people.[2]

---

[2] Several investigative reports have been written on the situation of the indigenous people of the Gran Chaco over the years. The most recent was done by a German development agency in the mid-eighties: Volker von Bremmen, "Moderne Jagd-und Sammelgruende: Entwicklungshilfeprojekte unter Indianern des Gran Chaco" (Argentinean, Paraguay, Bolivian), epd-Entwicklungspolitik: Materialien, vol. 3. It is available in German and Spanish.

We now turn our attention to the way missions have related to the Tobas since the 1940s. For our purposes we outline the main features of the strategy adopted by one mission working in the Chaco and Formosa provinces of Argentina, namely, the Mennonite Mission. Other missions have pursued other strategies.

The Mennonite Mission, which began working in Central Argentina in 1917, sent workers to the Chaco in 1942, shortly after the start of the religious awakening among the Tobas. Thus these missionaries arrived at a time of considerable ferment among the people. As the Mennonite missionaries surveyed the situation, they concluded that what was required was a program that would help to stabilize and fortify the Indian community—economically, socially, and spiritually. The Mennonites were not sympathetic to the indigenous religious expression because of the way it combined traditional cultural features with what appeared to be Pentecostalism—something incompatible with what the missionaries were accustomed to.

The Mennonite Mission proceeded to develop a conventional mission program consisting of store, school, clinic, and chapel, each symbolized by a building that housed an area of program concentration designed to contribute to the transformation of Indian life. For example, the missionaries correctly perceived that the Tobas did not function within the money economy in an acceptable manner. They decided that it was important that the Tobas learn how to participate in this kind of economy. The Mission helped families establish bank accounts to be operated, in part, as savings accounts. After a time this was abandoned, as it produced misunderstanding on both sides. The Indians suspected the missionaries of taking advantage of them through the accounts system, and the missionaries were frustrated at the inability of the Indians to understand and appreciate the values this system held for them. This points to the larger clash between Toba and missionary value systems. Two worlds were colliding without either group understanding the other.

The Mennonite Mission found its efforts frustrated repeatedly. By the early 1950s, ten years after starting, serious questions began to be raised as to the efficacy of the whole approach. In 1954 the Mission engaged Dr. William D. Reyburn, linguistic consultant with the United Bible Societies in Latin America, and Marie Reyburn, anthropologist, to study the situation and recommend a course of action to the Mission. Out of the Reyburns' consultancy came a drastically changed approach and the strategy that was to guide the Mission's work over the next decades. In effect, the Reyburns counseled the Mission to abandon predetermined and traditional program blueprints, to get in touch with the Indians and their culture, and to respond at those points where Indian-defined needs appeared.

First, the Mission recognized that the indigenous church was an authentic part of the body of Christ in which the Holy Spirit was manifestly at work. Indeed, this indigenous church was culturally attuned while also reaching out for help in deepening its faith and nurturing its membership as the body of Christ in that place. If the indigenous church is the goal of mission, then why not start, as in this instance, with the fact that an indigenous church already exists—even though under straitened circumstances—and contribute to its strengthening?

Second, the Mission disposed of store, clinic, school, and chapel buildings. None of the Mission's efforts to make these serve the Indian community had proved effective. On the contrary, the institutions had been a source of misunderstanding and conflict. It seemed wise to abandon these well-intentioned but ineffective programs. The missionaries moved to nearby towns where they were readily accessible to the Indians.

Third, the Mission committed itself to the translation of portions of the Christian scriptures into the Toba language, something that had not yet been done. This meant working in close collaboration with a Toba counterpart.

Fourth, the Mission became an advocate for the Indians in their struggle to gain legal recognition for their indigenous church. According to Argentine law, a religious group could be considered legitimate only when it has been granted legal registration. Previous attempts by the Indians to register their church had been rebuffed by the authorities. The Mennonite Mission became involved in this process in the late 1950s by initiating contacts with the government, through the appropriate departments, and pursuing this initiative until the government of Argentina in 1961 recognized the United Evangelical Church as a legal religious body. In 1962 a copy of this registration was delivered to each congregation.

A fifth feature of this strategy was that the Mennonite Mission declined to establish "development" programs for the Tobas. The Mission concentrated its efforts on Bible translation and making available the fruits of Bible knowledge and on the training of church leaders. Missionaries had no formal or official position in the United Evangelical Church. They attempted to maintain relationships with all the leaders. The mission staff followed the practice of visiting local congregations, but gradually, as the church grew, it became impossible to stay in touch with all.

Throughout the years since the mission underwent this "conversion," there have been numerous occasions for soul-searching as to the correctness of the strategy. Always present was this considerable cultural distance that separated missionary from Toba; also present was the abiding conviction that collaboration was possible, that indeed it was God's will that the UEC and Mission should work together. The Tobas have at times criticized the Mission's strategy because it has not delivered to them certain material benefits that have come to be associated with missions. But standing behind this resolve was the observation, arrived at with the help of William and Marie Reyburn, and summarized by Elmer Miller:

> The singular failure of Protestant Missions to function among the Tobas as originally designed is of interest, particularly when seen against the background of Catholic Mission failure. More significantly, however, in spite of the disintegration and final abandonment of institutional ties between the Toba and the Missions—Emmanuel, Mennonite, Go Ye, Beams of

Light, Grace and Glory . . . and finally, Church of God Pentecostal—the
congregations in Toba communities continue to grow and prosper under
aboriginal leadership (Miller 1967, 107).

Not only has the UEC grown among the Tobas, it has also attracted into its
membership the Mocovi and Pilaga as well as many Argentines who could claim
some European ancestry. Beginning in the early eighties many people from the
Wichi (Mataco) tribe have also affiliated with the UEC. These erstwhile Angli-
cans are from another linguistic family. More recently, Gypsies have been converted—through the witness of the UEC.

In summary, we can identify three principles of action that have emerged out
of this experience. First, many of the intercultural conflicts that have arisen in
the past have centered on sources of power, such as institutions and programs,
and the way these have altered patterns and relationship in the local community.
Therefore, the mission must seek to avoid contributing to conflict within the
indigenous community over sources of power by not introducing institutions or
programs; rather, the mission should work to enhance indigenous forms and
institutions.

Second, the mission should seek to contribute to the advancement of the
indigenous community those things which (1) are being sought by them, but (2)
they have been denied because of their weak position in society. Legal registration of the church has proved to be of enormous consequence in terms of self-
confidence and identity, but the indigenous peoples were virtually impotent in
the face of official bureaucracy and discrimination to get their church regis-
tered. The church desired the Christian scriptures but had no educated people
who could undertake the translation task on their own. In the case above, the
Mennonite Mission was in a position to assist in both areas of need.

A third principle is that the mission must avoid competing with indigenous
leadership or being drawn into a position where it is responsible for the welfare
of the church. This does not mean that the mission must feign disinterest in the
church. On the contrary, the most fundamental proof of the mission's commitment to the church is its willingness to continue being available long term to
serve without taking control.

THE DIDA HARRISTS

The Dida are an ethnic group located in southcentral Côte d'Ivoire. Historically, they have been exploited in a variety of ways by more powerful neighboring peoples. And they bore more than their share of the heavy burden imposed
by the French colonials during their long occupation of the country.

In 1913-15 the Liberian prophet William Wadé Harris made his way across
southern Côte d'Ivoire preaching a simple but powerful message. It is estimated
that more than 100,000 people were baptized by Harris in Côte d'Ivoire before
the frightened colonial authorities banned him permanently from the colony. In
this instance a NRM was instituted through an African, himself a first-genera-

tion Christian, who earlier in his life had been involved in the political struggle in his country. While serving a prison sentence for fomenting political rebellion, Harris saw a vision in which God directed him to quit politics and begin to preach the gospel.

The Dida were among the first Ivoirians to hear and respond to Prophet Harris, a point of pride to them to this day. As an ethnic group they have been oppressed and generally denied access to modernization. If their youth went away to school, they seldom returned to live in Dida country. Only now are the Christian scriptures being translated into Dida. Because few of their church leaders were sufficiently fluent in French to be able to draw freely on the Bible, even in French, they could not depend on the scriptures for nurturing faith to any significant degree. So how has this people sustained their faith as an indigenous Christian group?

In the early 1980s the Didas invited a Mennonite missionary couple to live in their area to provide training for their church leaders who had had no opportunity for any formal Bible training. James and Jeanette Krabill arrived in Dida country in 1982 feeling they were rather on trial since their going to the Dida was frowned on by the national Harrist leadership. At the same time the Krabills were attracted by the obvious sincerity of the Didas and the opportunity to relate to a group of Harrists among whom was still to be found a handful of people baptized by Prophet Harris himself. It seemed to be an unusual opportunity to make contact with individuals who had living memories of the prophet's ministry and message. But this was an opportunity that would not last much longer. Along with launching a full-scale Bible study program, the Krabills set out to collect and preserve these fragments of memories. No written documents survived. All depended on oral tradition. Oral tradition must, of course, be handled with great care. Memories are fallible, and what one hears must be checked against the perceptions and memories of other contemporaries. Only after much patient sorting, checking, and corroborating can one begin to have confidence in what has been distilled.

Out of this process eventually could be formed some impression of how it was possible for a people to have kept alive a faith ignited by a brief but intense contact with this man from Liberia some seventy years earlier. What has been the content of the preaching and singing over the years (Krabill 1990)?

The Krabills noticed early how important singing was to the Dida churches, who hold daily worship services. The music at each service is led by a choir drawn from a particular age group. Three choirs regularly participate on a rotating basis: the older women and men, the middle aged, and the youth. Furthermore, it was discerned that the music used by each of the groups was distinct. The senior-age group sang songs in a language rapidly becoming archaic and increasingly unintelligible to the youth. The middle-aged choir used songs composed during its members' own youth, while the current youth were composing and singing contemporary songs.

James Krabill concentrated particular attention on the music of the senior-age group, because it was recognized that with their passing an important part of Dida cultural and religious history would be lost. The Dida tradition held music in high esteem, and certain women had long been recognized for their gifts, both as composers and performers. Prophet Harris himself had counseled the people to preserve their indigenous tunes but to find words that bring glory to God. The music sung by the senior choir in the 1980s was the fruit of this initial period of sifting and reworking.

This is of special interest missiologically because of the way Harris sought to "redeem" traditional pre-Christian music, turning it into an important resource for the nurture of faith in Jesus Christ. It is noteworthy that Harris was critically aware of the need to respect the culture of the people while bringing it under the reign of Jesus Christ. In this he was acting consistently with his vision of the coming of the kingdom of God, the key note in his message.

As these songs were translated into contemporary language, the themes from the early years of the Harris movement among the Didas became evident: although the people were suffering political and spiritual oppression, God would deliver them. Thus, these songs provide commentary on the sociopolitical situation of the people and how they viewed their circumstance in the light of Harris's message to them. Each generation of songs, it was observed, reflects this combination of the sociocultural context in dialogue with the claims of faith.

Some one hundred of the more than five hundred extant songs were eventually recorded and transcribed in both Dida and French. Several cassettes of these songs have been sold back to the Didas at affordable prices. This step has stimulated in the people a new appreciation for their heritage and the way their faith has enabled them to cope with the vicissitudes of history. The composing of new music continues unabated among the Dida.

This case suggests several points. First, it is possible for a Christian group that has been deprived of access to the Christian scriptures and other means of nurture drawn from the experience of the wider church to keep faith alive by a dynamic worship that includes music composed in context. In this case only a few theological themes were recalled from the prophet's preaching, but they were essential and helped guide the people in worship.

Second, it is important not simply to record and preserve these songs as historical and cultural artifacts but to return them to the people in forms (translated and on cassette) that will enable them to continue to draw on their faith heritage. This action affirmed the value of their cultural as well as their spiritual heritage.

Third, this suggests that an important mark of an indigenous church is that it is creating its own hymnody. To do this a people must remain vitally rooted in its soil while also possessing a clear vision of what the gospel means in that context. A people who cannot sing its faith is a people in exile spiritually, emotionally, culturally, historically. In contrast to an NRM like the Dida Harrists, mission-founded churches typically must struggle to find their indigeneity. This case suggests that an important means of achieving this sense of "at homeness" culturally may be found in indigenous art forms.

In contrast to mission-founded churches, NRMs have been spared the risk of appearing as something alien to their culture. The criticism that has been directed against them from the beginning, often by those who themselves were not indigenous to that particular culture, has been that they were *too* culturally adapted or syncretistic. What is at issue is the basis for judgment. Do the cultural forms accredited by "Jerusalem" furnish the criteria, or is what the Holy Spirit is doing at "Caesarea" definitive? Is a group guided by a sense of following the reign of God, or is it preoccupied with its cultural identity?

The role of the missionary outsider is, in part, to act as a representative of the wider Christian movement, mediating insights from scripture and history that will serve to enrich the faith of an indigenous community. But the missionary can also validate the efforts of the indigenous community to be culturally authentic as well as authentically Christian. For the Didas this was an especially important juncture. Over the previous seven decades they had had many encounters with outsiders, both Ivoirian and European. Virtually none had been affirming of the Didas as a people. They had been deceived, exploited, physically abused—especially when forced to work on road-building crews—and generally treated with indignity. Among the many encounters was a series of attempts by Christian missions of many stripes to bring the Dida Harrists under their sway. Usually this was done by depicting the Dida church as inferior and not fully Christian. While this had the effect of steeling the resolve of the fiercely independent Didas to maintain their freedom, it also left them with feelings of inferiority. Thus, to find their culture, especially as represented in their music, valued and affirmed was an important step in creating a positive climate for the Didas to see their own church as an authentic part of the whole body of Christ while beginning to draw more fully on the Christian scriptures.

CONCLUSION

At the beginning we observed that NRMs have produced a new and alternative paradigm. This new paradigm may be seen as an extended comment on traditional mission assumptions, methods, approaches, and the role played by missionaries.

Outsiders regarded Dida and the Toba cultures as inferior. In spite of this attitude of contempt both groups clung tenaciously to their indigenous traditions. Although they suffered various losses due to the encroachments of the larger society, they refused to surrender their cultural values. Missionaries who sought to relate to them for the purpose of introducing Christian faith and the benefits of modernization found themselves unable to penetrate Dida and Toba defense mechanisms. It would be quite wrong to interpret this to mean that both groups were simply trying to avoid contact with the outside world. On the contrary, they were seeking to establish relationships but on terms that would not be injurious to their cultural values and way of life. They wanted to be respected and to be allowed to make the critical choices concerning their future.

For both the Tobas and the Didas the Christian faith furnished the matrix within which to make sense of their rapidly changing worlds—from a highly traditional culture to one increasingly accommodated to modernity, from a closed society to one inexorably becoming interdependent with the political economy of the nation. But the Christian faith became functional only when it was in the cultural idiom of the Tobas and the Didas. It had to be allowed to engage them at the points of greatest contingency: being able to respond to spiritual forces that dominate their lives, finding answers to health and healing, and listening to God speak through dreams and visions. In particular, this called for worship that helped these communities create a new sense of order and coherence amid a situation where the old center no longer held things together.

In both cases, over the years numerous attempts were made by missionary groups to relate in what was perceived to be proper ways of doing missionary work. In the end, at least in the examples studied here, the mission itself had to undergo fundamental reorientation.[3]

---

[3] One set of reports that describe recent initiatives to relate to NRMs by mission agencies, combining description of program and missiological analysis, is contained in *Ministry of Missions to African Independent Churches,* ed. David A. Shank (Elkhart, Ind.: Mennonite Board of Missions, 1987). This brings together a valuable collection of papers presented at a conference of people from various parts of Africa presently engaged in Bible teaching and other programs in relation to NRMs.

6

The Contribution to Missiology of the Study of New Religious Movements

INTRODUCTION

According to John G. Gager,

A curious irony emerges from the titles of two important works in the field of social anthropology. Peter Worsley entitles his study of cargo cults in Melanesia, *The Trumpet Shall Sound*, and Kenelm Burridge's work on millenarian activities bears the title, *New Heaven, New Earth*. Both titles are direct quotations from the New Testament, yet neither author mentions early Christianity except in passing. Indeed, one searches the abundant literature on millenarian movements almost in vain in an effort to ascertain whether anthropologists regard early Christianity as fully, substantially, or tangentially related to millenarian activities in more exotic parts of the world (Gager 1975, 20).

A parallel curious irony is found when one sets out to establish a connection between the study of new religious movements and missiology. There is but scant recognition by one field of the other. Here we wish to examine this relationship and suggest ways missiological studies might be enriched through closer attention to the study of new religious movements.

Religious studies have flourished during the past two decades. Just as the final triumph of secularization and secularism seemed assured, scholars began noticing religious stirrings that suggested surprising vitality. To be sure, certain varieties of Christian faith—or of Judaism, or Islam, for that matter—seemed to be losing out, but these losses were usually more than offset by movements of renewal and innovation that were releasing new energies within the community. Furthermore, new religious movements of immense variety were emerging. Such

First published in A. F. Walls and Wilbert R. Shenk, eds., *Exploring New Religious Movements* (Elkhart, Ind.: Mission Focus Publications, 1990), 179-205. Revised for publication in this volume empirical evidence pointed to a future in which religion would continue to play a vital role.

This unexpected turn is now forcing a reappraisal within the religious studies field. But scholars seem ill-prepared to cope with the new opportunity. Philip E. Hammond has noted that the scientific study of religion has remained tied to the theoretical constructs of the founders. In the thought of Marx, James, Durkheim, Weber, Freud, Malinowski, and H. R. Niebuhr secularization was assumed to be irreversible and inevitable. Hammond (1985, 1-6) argues that the time has come to reexamine this model in light of the new data and its apparent inadequacy.

Today we are confronted with an embarrassing wealth of materials for the study of all varieties of religious phenomena worldwide. But there are major problems to be resolved. The reductionism that has characterized the "scientific" study of religion is one of these issues. Walter H. Capps has called on religious studies "to develop the methodological apparatus to trace, discern, and understand new religion" (Capps 1978, 101; cf. Hargrove 1978, 257-66). Without new models and more adequate methods the new data will be forced through the old grid, resulting in the same unsatisfactory results.

Missiology has experienced a similar sort of lag in theoretical development. The theoretical foundations laid by Anderson, Venn, Speer, Warneck, and Schmidlin in the nineteenth and early twentieth centuries remain largely intact. In spite of a steady flow of critical studies of the philosophy and methodology characteristic of missionary work since 1800, and notwithstanding calls for new paradigms, we are still dependent on that original inheritance.[1]

The study of missions has exhibited ambivalence toward religious studies as well as new religious movements, and that with good reason. The missiologist has generally felt the criticism of colleagues in the social sciences and religious studies over the supposed lack of scientific rigor, objectivity, and detachment from the material being studied. Whether such criticism was justified is not our question at the moment.

Missiologists have fared little better in relation to new religious movements. A perusal of the standard missiological journals turns up relatively few articles on this theme; equally few books have been published. Yet missionaries and scholars closely related to the missionary movement have been among the pioneers in the field. Generally, their point of departure has been to produce an objective scholarly study within the confines of an academic discipline. We should note several studies that attempted to build bridges between disciplines.

The volume edited by David J. Hesselgrave, *Dynamic Religious Movements* (1978), presented twelve case studies of rapidly growing religious movements drawn from various parts of the world. As Hesselgrave points out in his introduction, the writers kept essentially one question in mind: Why is this movement growing? Other critical questions were bracketed.

Hesselgrave had a clear missiological objective. He was suing for the attention of those concerned about the mission of the church and challenging them to think

---

[1] Cf., among others, Walbert Buhlmann (1976, 383-94), which describes the changing world situation and consequent need for further theoretical development.

about processes of growth by learning from religious movements that were gaining adherents, regardless of whether these were counted in Christian ranks or not.

A quite different pioneering effort is Gottfried Oosterwal's theological critique entitled *Modern Messianic Movements* (1973). Oosterwal demonstrated great appreciation for the movements he had known firsthand in the field. He urged the wider Christian community to appreciate the authenticity of the quest in which many of these groups were engaged. But he also pointed to questionable elements that had to be judged by a Christological norm. He underscored the importance of a missiological approach that took full account of the eschatological dimension—the dimension which all too often had been lacking or distorted in the missionary message, but which these movements were poised to hear.

No one has seen the relationship between new religious movements and missiology more clearly or worked with greater perseverance to get the attention of the missiological community than Harold W. Turner.[2] Combining appreciation for these movements with an understanding of the phenomenon worldwide and its manifold interfaces with the historical Christian churches, Turner has attempted to lay on the conscience of the Christian community its responsibility to come to terms with the complex features of modern missions that exerted far-reaching positive influence as well as pursuing policies, practices, and attitudes which proved to be counterproductive (cf. Turner 1973, 47-65; 1984, 111-13). He also urged new openness to relate to these movements missiologically. Turner has made important contributions to scholarly understanding of these movements by demonstrating their importance to the fields of the history and phenomenology of religion, on the one hand, while participating in initiatives to secure the human rights of adherents of these movements on the other.

MISSIOLOGY

Missiology is both old and relatively new. In his survey of the development of missiology as a discipline, Johannes Verkuyl demonstrates that though there was some awareness of the need for formal study of missionary action early in the nineteenth century, it was not welcomed and given a place until the twentieth century (Verkuyl 1978, chap. 1). Despite advocacy by prominent mission leaders, it long was a sickly plant that had difficulty taking root. The mission agencies invested scant resources in the formal study of the science of missions, as it was called in the nineteenth century. When they did sponsor missionary training institutions, they insisted on emphasizing the practical aspects, since theory was considered to be largely irrelevant.

But it was equally difficult to find a place for mission studies in the academy. This difficulty stemmed from causes both internal and external. This period was not noteworthy for its theological productivity. Furthermore, ideas about the theological curriculum were rather fixed. Innovation was resisted. Toward the

---

[2] Several of his essays on this theme have been collected and republished as a section in *Religious Innovation in Africa* (1979, 255-93). He was guest editor for the January 1985 issue of *Missiology* with the theme "New Primal Religious Movements."

end of the century a few intrepid figures, led by Gustav Warneck of Germany, managed to win a toehold for the academic study of missions.

Thus, missiology as a discipline suffered from this double bind. It was held at arm's length by the practical-minded missionary societies, and it was only grudgingly granted a place on the margin of the theological faculty in the university.

Verkuyl offers a multifaceted definition of missiology, reflecting to some degree its hybrid character as a discipline:

> Missiology is the study of the salvation activities of the Father, Son, and Holy Spirit throughout the world geared toward bringing the kingdom of God into existence. . . . [It is] the study of the world-wide church's divine mandate to be ready to serve this God who is aiming his saving acts toward this world. Missiology's task in every age is to investigate scientifically and critically the presuppositions, motives, structures, methods, patterns of cooperation and leadership which the churches bring to their mandate (Verkuyl 1978, 5).

Such an enterprise requires various tools and involves intersections with several disciplines, including the science of religion. According to Verkuyl: "Without a phenomenology of and history of the current religions, proper dialogue with and missionary approach to these religions are impossible" (Verkuyl 1978, 10). It should be noted, however, that Verkuyl here has in mind the major religions of the world. New religious movements do not come within his purview.

To recapitulate, a functional definition of missiology includes the following features:

1. History of the Christian movement, especially its expansion;
2. Normative content, foundation, and motivation for Christian mission;
3. Contemporary situation, including the religious, which shapes present context; and
4. Trends that will influence the future course.

The discipline of missiology then will draw on biblical and theological studies, church history, and the human sciences.

NEW RELIGIOUS MOVEMENTS AND MISSIONS

The phenomenon of new religious movements usually is divided into two major groupings. The first includes movements in the industrialized Western world, which generally have appeared since 1945. The second group comprises movements that have sprung into existence outside the West. These movements are the product of the encounter between a powerful external influence and a primal society. In general, new religious movements arise as a result of upheaval and clash. But the one variety occurs primarily intraculturally, while the other results from intercultural contacts.

Little attention has been paid to the interface between these two groups or to what they have in common vis-à-vis culture change. The fact of the persistence of religion worldwide—and indeed its vitality and intensity of innovation—puts a new set of questions to all students of religion. Earlier theories about the future of religion in the face of secularization offer little help. These new movements seem to reaffirm that religion requires a certain intensity of experience if it is to shape values and compel loyalty.[3]

One of the key observations students of new religious movements in primal societies have made is that the emergence of these movements can be correlated with the presence of Christian missions. In his study of this phenomenon in Africa, David Barrett asserted:

> It is in fact the case that schisms from foreign mission bodies in Africa have been taking place for the last hundred years on a scale unparalleled in the entire history of the expansion of Christianity. . . . Most of these movements have emerged spontaneously in areas that have been subjected with intensity to Christian missionary activity for several decades (Barrett 1968, 3).

Numerous studies can be cited to substantiate Barrett's contention. Here we only wish to establish the genetic link between the missionary movement and the emergence of new religious movements in primal societies worldwide. As Turner argued in his study of the Native American, this fact ought at least to force missiologists to begin seeking the flaw in a missionary approach that produced these results (Turner 1973, 62). We should be able to ask these critical questions without condemning wholesale everything done in the past or appreciating the scale of achievement of the modern missionary movement since 1800.

It would be fruitful indeed to pursue an investigation into a theme that relates directly to a specific Christian initiative carried out over a long historical period in diverse circumstances which has produced a widespread but unintended result. Even at this late date such information would be valuable. Several benefits might accrue from such scrutiny.

A generation ago Max Warren drew on Martin Buber's concept of "I and Thou" to develop a theology of relationship and attention, for "real life is meeting." Studying groups that arose in reaction to the coming of Western missions, we will see mirrored in them the mission project sponsored from the West. In other words, people of the West will see themselves, both their strengths and foibles, through the eyes of others. It will also open up new vistas on peoples who have both selectively appropriated from the Christian revelation and rejected parts of historical Christianity as represented by the West. In other words, the act of respectful and sympathetic study can open the way for meeting and mutual understanding.

Another gain would be the challenge to greater integrity in the message. Jean Guiart and Mircea Eliade were of one mind in asserting that missionaries in the

---

[3] Cf. chapters by Dick Anthony, Thomas Robbins and Paul Schwartz, and John Coleman (in Coleman and Baum 1983, 1-16). For a critical overview see Eileen Barker (1985, 36-57).

South Pacific failed to recognize the fullness of the Christian faith and consequently did not appreciate the responses of the indigenous peoples. In other words,
the Melanesians could hear authentic notes in the Christian message to which
the missionaries, conditioned by Western culture, were tone deaf. Primitive
Christianity was millennial, a theme that the missionaries could not wholly sup-
press in their preaching. The Melanesians were especially sensitive to this motif
and interpreted much of what they heard and saw demonstrated by the missionaries as being a down payment of what was yet to come. In their historical situation they felt themselves to be a victim people and yearned for liberation from
oppression and injustice. They heard in the gospel a promise of release and a
new life of peace and prosperity. The irony was the missionaries shared many of
these perspectives, but the vocabulary they used to get their agenda across failed
to communicate to the local peoples (Guiart 1970; Eliade 1970). Ultimately,
disillusionment set in as these millennial expectations were not fulfilled—and
cargo-cults emerged.

A genuine meeting would have opened the way for a more reciprocal sharing
of the message, with the missionaries understanding why the Melanesians were
attracted by the millennial theme and the Melanesians being given opportunity
to hear why to the missionaries other accents were important.

Essentially, the charge that has been brought against the modern missionary
movement is that it has been but another attempt to universalize something that
was profoundly particular and parochial, namely Western civilization. And this
is experienced as the ultimate effrontery: that one culture or people arrogate to
itself the role of determining and managing the destinies of other peoples.

None of this is new; it has been attempted repeatedly throughout history in
both religious and political terms. The early Christian church faced such a situation. The Judaizers wanted to insist to Gentile believers that they accept the
Jewish laws as the condition for their admittance into the Christian family. This
conflict led to the conference held in Jerusalem reported in Acts 15. That conference decision affirmed the validity of both Jewish and Gentiles cultures but
declared that neither had salvific significance; neither was to be elevated to the
level of a universal determinant binding on all peoples everywhere.

The situations of the early church and the modern missionary movement dif-
fer in important ways, however. The early church comprised a community that
was socially marginal and powerless. The modern mission movement has long
been viewed by critics as simply the religious dimension of a massive and powerful Western movement to colonize and dominate the world. The early Christians were numbered among the persecuted and suffering, while Western Christianity has been seen as the religion of the powerful. To some extent this is an
unfair caricature, but not entirely unfounded.

WHAT MISSIOLOGY CAN LEARN
FROM NEW RELIGIOUS MOVEMENTS

Missiology itself evolved as a tool to rationalize and make more efficient the
Christianizing process. Among the pioneer missiologists were those who devel-

oped critical perspectives on missionary methods and policies. And there are shining examples of missionaries who were keenly aware of the social or political plight of the people among whom they were living and sided with them in their struggle for justice. But pragmatism was the keynote of missionary thought and practice.

In the first part we have argued that missiology does indeed need the contribution a study of new religious movements in primal societies can make, especially those movements that identify themselves as being in some sense Christian, since these groups have emerged in response to Western missions.

We turn now to an exploration of six facets of that contribution: contextualization, theological reformulation, religious innovation, economic and cultural development, church growth, and ecumenical relationships. The vocation of missiology is to be the science of the *oikoumene* in the service of God's redemptive mission to the world. A respectful listening to and learning from these movements will foster development of a more self-critical and positive missiology.

1. Precursors to Contextualization

From its earliest days the modern missionary movement was marked by multiple perspectives. On the one hand, mission promoters frequently depicted the task to be done as a fairly simple process of presenting the Christian message in a straightforward manner to peoples sunk in darkness and despair, peoples who consequently would respond gladly and quickly. On the other side was the growing group of missionaries in the field, who knew firsthand how complicated the process was. As foreigners they had to master a strange language—often before it was written—and try to understand a highly intricate culture with quite another worldview. Learning the new language and culture were requisite to any effective communication of the Christian message. As the complexity of the task became more apparent, mission theorists moved through several stages as they sought to conceptualize the task.

The great theoretical breakthrough in missions thought in the nineteenth century was identification of the indigenous church as the goal of mission. Other theoretical and policy developments were largely embroidering on this basic theme.

Prior to the enunciation of this principle around 1850, missions were conceived as an act of carrying out Christ's last command. A variety of motives were invoked to stir the faithful to give and to go. But clarification of the indigenous church as goal of mission offered what seemed to be a coherent and measurable goal toward which missionary efforts could be directed. Mission societies developed strategies and policies to achieve this goal. This concept continued to be the linchpin of mission thought for the next hundred years.

Notwithstanding the theoretical tidiness of the indigenous church concept, it became evident early on that missionary practice fell short of the ideal. A cursory review of the literature shows that periodically books were published that criticized missions practice, and the indigenous church ideal was restated. For example, John L. Nevius wrote a series of articles for the *Chinese Recorder* in 1885, later issued in book form, which set forth his alternative to the missionary practice he saw around him. Roland Allen first gained notice with his book *Missionary Methods: St. Paul's or Ours?* (1912/1962), a stern attack on contemporary missions. Similar works followed. The World Dominion movement emerged in the 1920s as gadfly to missions, its central concern being to encourage the development of indigenous churches.[4]

The political climate was undergoing important change throughout this period. Nationalist movements were springing to life in all of the countries colonized by the European powers. Frequently Christians joined their compatriots in these movements for political independence.

In *The Philosophy of the Christian World Mission* Edmund D. Soper asked: "Has Christianity demonstrated in the modern world, as it did in the two previous periods of achievement, that it can be a part of the life of all kinds of people, differing in race, nationality, and location? . . . Can Christianity become truly 'indigenous' to the culture and life of a people?" (1943, 125). Later Soper notes: "At the present time indigenization is a most pressing matter. Just as there is a British, a German, and an American type of Christianity, so there is a demand that the Christianity of Japan be distinctively Japanese" (ibid, 266). Soper demonstrated the importance of expressing the Christian faith through the art forms, architecture, and cultural customs of a people rather than with what is imported.

At about the same time another movement was being launched that was to promote the application of cultural anthropology to missionary work and Bible translation. Through the creative leadership of scholars such as Eugene A. Nida this movement quickly gained influence. Books continued to be produced during the 1940s and 1950s expounding the indigenous church theme, including John Ritchie's *Indigenous Church Principles in Theory and Practice* (1946).[5] A Pentecostal missions administrator, Melvin L. Hodges, wrote a small book, *The Indigenous Church* (1953), that enjoyed wide influence. Hodges restates the classical nineteenth century "three-selfs" formula but shows no historical awareness, and the influence of the newly emerging missionary anthropology is conspicuously absent. T. Stanley Soltau had served in Korea, where the Nevius Plan had been implemented effectively. In his *Missions at the Crossroads* (1954) he advocated the indigenous church as "a solution for the unfinished task."

Several threads run through the literature from Nevius to Soltau. First, there is an implicit criticism of contemporary mission practice that failed to live up to the ideal. Second, despite disclaimers along the way, the controlling assumption is that the outcome depends largely on mission leadership. Third, there is virtually no conceptual development during these six decades. Essentially the same patterns and programs are advocated in 1954 as in 1900. The blueprint has not been altered. Fourth, insights from indigenous cultures are not appropriated in

---

[4] Perhaps the best-known pamphlet published by World Dominion was *The Indigenous Church,* by Sidney J. W. Clark, which he originally wrote at the request of the National Christian Council of China at the conclusion of an extensive survey of missions in China in 1913.

[5] Ritchie was a long-time missionary to Peru who was serving with the American Bible Society when he wrote his book.

the service of more incisive analysis. The focus seems to be obsessively set on mission structure and administration. Fifth, despite the implicit critique of mission practice, the closest anyone came to a thoroughgoing evaluation was Roland Allen; and he stirred deeply negative reactions, so that his insights were not widely appreciated and applied.

Viewed in the perspective of the foregoing summary, William A. Smalley's brief critique of the indigenous church in *Practical Anthropology* in 1958 takes on added importance as a harbinger of what was to come. He pointed out that the "three-selfs" were quite inadequate as diagnostic tools. He suggested "that the three 'selfs' are really projections of our American value system into the idealization of the church" (Smalley 1958, 51-65). He sketched out a more dynamic and creative role for the missionary as a source of cultural alternatives to aid the new church in making choices.

Undoubtedly, the contribution of the cultural anthropologists found ready acceptance both for their fresh insights and new tools and because of the influential writings of Stephen Neill, Max Warren, Walter Freytag, and others who put the state of the mission movement in the broader historical and theological perspective. The International Missionary Council played a key role in organizing conferences around timely themes that encouraged lively debate and continuing missiological ferment.

The next decade was a time of identity crisis for missions, culminating around 1970 in the call for a moratorium on the sending of missionaries from the West to other parts of the world. This demand by some younger churches for full autonomy coincided with the granting of political independence to virtually all colonial possessions by the European powers.

The year 1972 marks an important shift for theory. A new term was introduced into the lexicon of missiology: *contextualization.* Though lacking linguistic grace, it changed the angle of vision on a range of issues. Fundamental to all else, however, was the way it shifted the locus of attention to the host culture. It built on the notion—by now widely accepted—that every culture can be a vehicle for the gospel. In contrast to the theory of the indigenous church, for which no theological foundation was ever developed, proponents of contextualization appealed to the incarnation as the basis of missionary witness.

While Protestant missions from the beginning emphasized the importance of translating the scriptures into the vernacular languages, Roman Catholic practice adhered to another tradition, which largely kept the Bible locked up in a holy language. In this regard, Vatican Council II signaled an important shift by approving the use of vernacular languages for worship and encouraged the reading of scripture by all members of the church. For both Roman Catholics and Protestants the introduction of the concept of contextualization offered a new theoretical construct for understanding the communication of the Christian message, as well as a framework for evaluating the effectiveness of missionary practice.

Although new religious movements began emerging more than a century ago wherever missions went, few people asked what these movements might have to teach.[6] One of the outstanding features of new religious movements was, of course, their indigenous character. By definition, these groups emerged out of a particular culture with all its distinctive features and idiom. And they were not dependent on external sources for financial support or leadership.

These groups have typically arisen in response to a crisis experience of an individual or group indigenous to that culture. Frequently, a charismatic leader has appeared as a catalytic agent bringing about resolution in a time of crisis in ways culturally appropriate to that group.

That is not to say that a new group accepts only those elements and materials indigenous to their own group. A movement may borrow and adapt elements from various sources but ultimately the outcome is one suitable to and understood by the people of that culture. Thus, the result rings true in that place and time.

For example, the Church of the Lord (Aladura) in Nigeria adopted a liturgical structure which superficially reflects the Anglican tradition out of which the founder and first members came. But the original liturgical form has been transformed by the Church of the Lord (Aladura) so that it is Yoruba in flavor and style.

Furthermore, the theological agenda of these new religious movements indicates that it is genuinely theirs rather than that of an outsider. They are free to emphasize those themes most important to them in worship—joyous spontaneity, the use of indigenous musical instruments and forms—and to give a different balance to the Christian message than would be typical in the West. For example, many of these movements give priority to healing, deliverance from evil powers, and prayer.

Thus, long before the term *contextualization* came into vogue in missiological circles, these new religious movements were living laboratories of that which had to come about if the churches in the non-Western world were to take root and survive. Because these movements had arisen outside the control of Western influences, from the outset they exhibited a contextualized religious response to what they had heard in the Christian message.

2. The Re-visioning of Theology

With the passage of time it became increasingly clear that failure of the church to take root in Asian, African, or Latin American soil—that is, the failure of the indigenous church program—was due, in no small measure, to the nature of Western theology, which was no more exempt from cultural particularism than liturgy, architecture, clerical raiment, or what constituted social gentility.

---

[6] See the fascinating study by Janet Hodgson (1984, 19-33) on a movement going back to 1815. A group of scholars (Bond, Johnson, and Walker 1979) has rejected the notion that these movements are a response to a clash between outside influences and indigenous dynamics. Rather, they see these African churches as expressions of. indigenous forces in continuity with their religious past. A sophisticated analysis and critique of the crisis/response model is that of Robert S. Ellwood Jr., "Emergent Religion in America: An Historical Perspective" (1978, 267-84). Ellwood offers the "emergent" model instead—each emergence arises out of latent religious elements.

In the 1950s K. A. Busia, later prime minister of Ghana, asserted: "For the conversion to the Christian faith to be more than superficial, the Christian Church must come to grips with traditional beliefs and practices, and with the world view that these beliefs and practices imply" (Baeta 1971, 20). A decade later another well-known African scholar, Bolajui Idowu, charged: "The Church in Africa came into being with prefabricated theology, liturgies, and traditions. In the matter of Christian ethics, the converts found themselves in the position of those early converts before the Council of Jerusalem (Acts 15)" (Idowu 1968, 426). Idowu had already made these same points forcefully and with eloquence in a little book entitled *Towards an Indigenous Church* (1965). Both Busia and Idowu called for a deepened appreciation of indigenous culture and a theology adapted to the pastoral needs of their peoples.

Busia and Idowu stood in a long line of leaders who saw the need for a fresh understanding of theology if the new church was to be given the help needed in fully appropriating the faith. For example, Hendrik Kraemer and J. H. Bavinck advocated the reformulation of theological education in Indonesia in the 1920s in order that seminarians might study *theologia in loco*. At that time Kraemer and Bavinck were voices crying in the wilderness. Books written during the period on "indigenous church principles" emphasized the importance of thorough training for church leaders, but it was assumed that such training would be Western (cf. Rowland 1925, 147-56).

By the late 1960s it was increasingly understood that how theology is conceived and transmitted powerfully shapes a church, with the potential of making it exotic or indigenous. The quest for indigenous theologies quickly gained momentum. John S. Mbiti conceived of the task as that of holding in tension the universal kerygma and many provincial theologies (1976, 6). Mbiti suggested that genuine theology could emerge only out of deep experience. The mission-founded churches had been inhibited from serious theological engagement with their own cultures by overly protective missions. The result was retarded development. Thus, Mbiti looked for an alternative source. He regarded the independent churches as "ultimately an expression of theological protest," even though they were not the direct result of church-mission controversies (ibid, 16). In their "protest" they had developed authentic African responses to the gospel.

What approach should be taken in developing theologies in context? E. W. Fasholé-Luke has suggested that a theology for Africa be developed tapping four sources: the Bible, traditional religions and philosophy, the Western theological inheritance, and the experience of the independent churches (Fasholé-Luke 1976, 141-44). Although the latter seldom have a formal written theology, they have dressed important biblical themes in African garb and freely danced and sung of their faith in Jesus Christ.

Indeed, it is precisely this informal style that has raised questions about what constitutes theology. Is a faith tradition built and nurtured through the traditional pedagogy of recital any less authentic? Can not theology shaped through encounter with spiritual forces in prayer and pastoral ministry have an integrity of its own?

The question of how theology develops may well turn out to have quite another answer when the culture under consideration is oral (cf. Hollenweger 1980, 68-75). In oral societies the collective memory is stored in stories and songs. It is quite wrong to impose artificially on such a society an approach to theology that demands tomes of systematic theology written in a foreign language for a totally different people in another period of history.

In an important study of the contribution of independent churches in Africa to the development of an African theology, M. L. Daneel pays particular attention to Christology (Daneel 1984, 76-88; cf. Bediako 1983, 81-113). Despite a lack of written theological reflections, one can discern in their lived experience and in the biographies of leaders a vital awareness of the suffering Christ, who has transformed life. "A study of the historic development of the Independent Churches illuminates the change from 'oppressive suffering' to 'redemptive suffering'"(Daneel 1984, 80). As did Jesus, these disciples have identified with the oppressed, resisted the oppressor, and preached hope.

But Christ the Victor also plays an important role in dealing with the powers and in healing. The independent churches have understood the work of Jesus through the paradigm of the traditional healers. In drawing on the familiar they have also transformed it by attributing the insight that comes to them in diagnosing illnesses to the presence of the Holy Spirit. These churches also recognize the Lordship of Christ in cultivating among their members an awareness of the divine presence in worship and especially during the eucharist. But Jesus also commissions his followers to go out as ambassadors (Daneel 1984, 86ff.; cf. 1980, 105-20).

Through the study of these religious movements we gain further perspective on this fundamental fact. Each movement produces a formal structure of belief, doctrine, or creed. Typically few of them have elaborate frameworks, and fewer still have even begun to produce a systematic theology. But each has a self-conscious thought structure.

The structures or patterns are identifiably the product of the culture of origin and represent the response within that context. This development, as depicted in new religious movements, demonstrates that theology must be dynamically contextual. This means that theology may be constructed in modes other than Hellenistic philosophical categories. Furthermore, it suggests that orthopraxy is as important, especially among preliterate peoples, as orthodoxy. And it suggests that theology is a dynamic, living, growing interpretation of the faith in response to a changing environment. If it fails to respond to that environment, it will become irrelevant.

The way we think about theology today in the West has been directly affected by the experiences of churches in the non-Western world. And that experience has been influenced by the examples of the new religious movements.

3. Primal Societies as Seedbeds for Religious Innovation

It has been recognized for some time that new adherents of the Christian faith, following the initial Jewish phase, have been won almost exclusively from primal societies rather than the major religions of the world. New religious movements furnish several lessons in this respect.

The peoples of primal societies are highly vulnerable in the face of stronger and dominating cultures. The peoples of primal societies seemingly are easily overwhelmed by the stronger cultures. Representatives of Western cultures in particular have tended to treat these primal societies as inferior and to patronize them by offering the supposed benefits of "civilization." Westerners have failed to respect them by prescribing rapid acculturation to Western culture as the best path for them.

But primal culture has proved to be amazingly resilient. Forced acculturation has usually done nothing more than push primal features underground, only to have them then reemerge in times of crisis, often in quite unexpected forms. Indeed, we can find abundant examples of such resurgence of primal religiosity in the West as well. The flowering of witchcraft and magic in nineteenth-century France, in spite of a national program of secularization, is but one example.[7]

The study of new religious movements in recent years has demonstrated the importance of taking seriously and understanding sympathetically these primal forms as a prerequisite to knowing religious reality in any society. Any such study will force us to ask in relation to a given culture what conversion means. It will require us to inquire into the nature of religiosity of a particular people. It calls us to come to terms with the worldview of which this religiosity is an expression.

4. Religion as Ally of Cultural Change and Development

Hundreds of years ago in the West religion was considered indispensable to civilization, for it was the source of cultural innovation and anchor for all of life. Beginning with the Renaissance, religion in the West began to lose this special status. From the Enlightenment onward, religion came into disrepute. It was characterized as reactionary and an impediment to social progress. Marxist theoreticians and many intellectuals have seen religion as a drag on human advancement.

The period since 1945 has been marked both by the gaining of political independence by former colonies of the European powers and a concerted effort to modernize the less developed nations. The development movement has been dominated by rational planning, the application of scientific technology, and

---

[7] Cf. Thomas A. Kselman, "It is somewhat puzzling that the forces of 'modernization' seen as producing outbursts of religious enthusiasm in other centuries and cultures are generally seen to have no similar consequences for the nineteenth century. The number, significance, and visibility of miracle cults and prophetic movements in France, with Lourdes as the leading example, suggest that our understanding of France's modernization must be revised" (1983, 195). In an older study Geoffrey Parrinder (1963), sought to demonstrate similarities and continuities between traditional cultures in Africa and Europe.

major infusions of capital. The development literature is notable for its disdain for religion. This attitude is reflected both in the dismissive attitude assumed by most development experts toward religion and the meager amount of literature devoted to the religion-development nexus. Even in Christian circles little has been done to challenge this highly tendentious attitude (von der Mehden 1986, esp. chap. 1).

The Swedish economist Gunnar Myrdal concluded from his massive three-volume study *Asian Drama* (1968) that the major obstacles Asian nations faced in their development efforts lay in the realm of values and worldview rather than in the organizational and technical spheres. Two decades later it is increasingly acknowledged that religion is indeed a vital force—both positive and negative—in national development; it cannot be ignored.

The new religious movements have been quite unaware of these strictures against religion. On the contrary, new religious movements have turned to religion as a source of development and change. They have done this, first of all, by drawing instinctively from religion those values that are prerequisite to progress. Many of these groups, for example, have insisted on an ethic of self-restraint and thrift. They have taught the importance of personal discipline and integrity and insisted that their adherents be industrious and set goals. By offering their people liberation from evil powers, they have desacralized the material and political world. In addition, these groups frequently have encouraged a spirit of self-determination and self-responsibility. All of these are significant components in human development (Turner 1980, 523-33; 1982).

These movements have been important in another way. In numerous cases they have fostered new forms of social organization that helped their followers to cope with dysfunctional aspects of their former way of life. The Aiyetoro community in Nigeria adopted a communitarian form of organization that for a period of time enabled members of the community to reach a new level of productivity and well-being. The Korsten basket weavers of Zambia are another case where a marginal group of people organized themselves into an effective economic unit that benefited all its members.

From the beginning of the modern missionary movement it was assumed that there was an intimate connection between the Christian message and personal and social development. The symbol of this understanding was the compendious three-volume report by James S. Dennis, *Christian Missions and Social Progress* (1897-1906), published at the turn of the twentieth century. This is a veritable catalog of the changes wrought in non-Western lands through the influence of Christian missions. Dennis's work appeared at the time when the Social Gospel movement was in full flow. World War I shattered much of that optimism, and missions went on the defensive as the nationalist movements gained momentum. Thus the attitude shifted from one extreme to another. A careful study of new religious movements will help restore a more balanced view of the role of religion in human development. Missiology may once more have a positive contribution to make in this field.

5. Understanding the Processes of Church Growth

At the beginning of this chapter we noted the role that power played in the movement of Western peoples to other parts of the world. Christian missions have also been stamped by the various forms of power on which they depended in the carrying out of the mission. What we ought to recognize is the impact this has had on mission-founded churches, their relationship to the missions; and those groups that arose in reaction to, but independent of, the missions. This needs to be understood both in terms of historical process as well as relationships. This can be expressed in terms of a dialectic moving from thesis to antithesis and then synthesis.

Thesis. The Western mission enters the scene bringing several things, including a new religious message and an alternative worldview. But the mission also represents a dominant culture that demands submission to it. In the course of time a church is formed, but one that is tied to the mission and the church which sent it. This involves the rejection by the new adherents of their own culture at a deep and crucial point, namely value system, family loyalties, communal solidarity. The result is an alienation between the new adherents and their own people.

Antithesis. At some point a reaction to the initial stage sets in. The reaction may be encouraged by a nationalist political movement or by some other religious form. But at the heart of the reaction is a rejection of "mission" Christianity. The people may continue to cling to the kernel of the Christian message but seek to throw off the husk in which it was brought to them.

One way of dealing with such a situation is to call for a moratorium in an effort to break the pattern and system by which outside power has controlled the development of the church.

New religious movements, of course, have had complete autonomy from such outside influences by virtue of their spontaneous emergence. They are nonetheless also an antithetical statement about "mission" Christianity.

Synthesis. The preceding stage can be resolved only when there is a synthesis opening the way to the establishment of new relationships based on equality and interdependence. The weakness of the classical indigenous church ideal was that it suggested that the ultimate stage for the new church was achieved when it had absolute autonomy and no longer looked to the mission for relationship. Both theologically and sociologically this is untenable. The church has come into being precisely through this outside influence, and the relationship cannot be denied. Once the dysfunctional elements in that relationship have been overcome, both on the part of the dominant mission and the subservient church, a satisfying partnership can be effected.

A mature relationship will recognize the integrity of both parties and their mutual need of one another. A part of that acceptance will involve recognition by the mission of the strength of a theology and liturgy that are more thoroughly contextual and appreciation for the way in which this contextuality can become a gift to the church universal.

Thus the study of new religious movements can provide an alternative model for understanding how the church grows. Churches that have never experienced a period of mission tutelage have less need to be reactionary and are more spontaneously indigenous in their faith expression. But they also suffer lacks—interaction with other Christian traditions both contemporary and historical, access to the scriptures and leadership training, a sense of acceptance by the wider Christian community.

6. Ecumenical Challenge

The study of new religious movements, if carried out in a sympathetic, sensitive, and appreciative attitude, is a first step in ecumenical recognition of the validity of new forms of Christian life. Interaction with these new religious movements has shown several things. First, those new religious movements with a Christological orientation are usually reaching out for fraternal relationships and seeking to understand their place in the wider Christian history and tradition. Far from rejecting other Christians, they want to understand and be understood.

Second, the ecumenical dimension is not simply a call to relationship. It also implies an acknowledgment that these groups emerging out of the interaction between Western and non-Western forms have produced a new genre of Christian thought and practice that can enrich the life of the church universal.

Third, this is a call for mutual submission. It invites Western Christians to submit their orthodoxies to the scrutiny of the new religious movements. It opens the way for adherents of the new religious movements to submit their orthopraxies to scrutiny in the light of Jesus Christ. Together both Western church and new religious movement will discover new dimensions of what it means to follow Jesus Christ—the one who alone holds all together.

7

The Wider Context of Conversion

The first condition of ultimate success was to secure the good will of the chief; and, fortunately for the missionary, the chief had many reasons to compete for his presence if not for his doctrine. To the powerful and well-informed ruler, like Mutesa of Buganda or the Nyamwezi chief Mirambo, the fact that he was a European was of supreme interest. Both these rulers had had enough contact with the outside world to know that the friendship of a new class of foreigners was worth cultivating as a diplomatic counter-weight to the class they knew already.
    —Roland Oliver, *The Missionary Factor in East Africa*

Christian missionaries were the vanguard, but barely, of the larger European coming to the interior of East Africa. The first missionaries arrived in the mid-1870s, following the death of David Livingstone in 1873. Arab traders had been present on the coast for a long time and were beginning to move aggressively inland in pursuit of trade, at the center of which was trafficking in slaves. Livingstone and others laid on the conscience of the West the slave trade being conducted by the Arabs. Several British missionary societies organized to send missionaries to the region, and Cardinal Lavigerie opened the way for Roman Catholic missions.

The indigenous peoples of the region were a mixed multitude. Some groups were nomadic; others moved in response to the threat from more powerful neighbors or the need for improved food supplies. By the late 1800s East Africa was rife with geopolitical machinations. Foreign interlopers were on the increase, and newcomers were weighed in terms of what they brought to the political-military balance of power: Egyptian incursions from the north, Arab traders from the coast, varieties of European missionaries and explorers from several sides. The "old gods" appeared impotent in the face of these new realities, and the traditional way of life seemed doomed (Oliver 1952, 16).

This chapter is the revision of a paper presented at Workshop on Conversion in Africa, Center for the Study of World Religions, Harvard University, Cambridge, Massachusetts, May 13-15, 1988.

From the beginning all missionaries had to confront the ambiguities of the situation. They realized their presence would be used by the king and chiefs to bolster their political ambitions. This brought to light the differences of understanding concerning conversion. The Catholic and Calvinist missions set about developing educational and social institutions for the benefit of the community. "Civilizing" was seen as a necessary step in evangelizing the people (Oliver 1952, 23f.). In this view the initial incorporation of people into the Christian community would be followed by catechism and education in the Christian way. British and German evangelical Protestants, on the other hand, decried reliance on *preparatio evangelica*. They held out for a definite experience of conversion. A generation later evangelicals had come to accept the school as foundational to evangelization in East Africa, while maintaining the rhetoric about conversion as personal "rebirth" or "change of heart."[1] Neither theory, however, could escape the sociopolitical dimension of conversion in Africa. Becoming a Christian, or Muslim, was as much a communal act as an individual one.

Studies of conversion have been concerned with the religious and moral reorientation of an individual that results from a decisive personal crisis or external challenge. This recentering is expressed in terms of a reformulated worldview and new affiliations. Conversion understood as individual change will continue to be basic to the study of this phenomenon, but it is not the only model.[2]

My argument here is that to understand conversion[3] in Africa or Asia, relative to the modern mission movement, we need a model that, in addition to considering the individual, also takes account of the sociopolitical context. Whatever the relationship between the missionary and other personifications of Western influence—explorer, trader, soldier, colonialist—the peoples of Africa, Asia, and

---

[1] That there was no easy resolution to this difference of approach is reflected in the difficulties all churches faced with superficial or nominal adherence. Cf. Oliver: "If missionaries found that belief in Christian doctrine came easily to Africans, they soon discovered also how difficult and foreign was the practice of Christian morality" (1952, 208). All denominations faced this dilemma.

[2] Lofland and Stark (1965) develop "a model of the accumulating conditions that appear to describe and account for conversion to an obscure millenarian perspective" (874). Conversion is precipitated when a person (1) experiences sustained and acute tensions (2) "within a religious problem-solving perspective, (3) which leads him to define himself as a religious seeker; (4) encountering the D[ivine] P[recepts] at a turning point in his life, (5) wherein an affective bond is formed (or pre-exists) with one or more converts; (6) where extra-cult attachments are absent or neutralized; (7) and, where, if he is to become a deployable agent, he is exposed to intensive interaction" (ibid.). The first four points can as readily be applied to stereotypical evangelical conversion (e.g., Augustine, Luther). With some modification, five and six may be used by mainstream evangelical Christianity.

[3] The way *conversion* is interpreted varies from one Christian tradition to another. Even within a tradition its meaning may change over time. Ronan Hoffman (1968) demonstrates the changing understanding of conversion among Roman Catholics and notes that the term has been avoided in Catholic documents in recent years.

Latin America perceived the Christian project largely as the religious dimension of Western expansion. It will become clear that what the missionary understood as conversion was frequently quite different from the understanding of the Baganda, Igbo, or Javanese.

TOWARD A MODEL OF CONVERSION IN THE WIDER CONTEXT

To illuminate conversion of the individual in relation to the wider sociopolitical context, a model must be based on those salient features that influence the process. The term *world system* was introduced in the 1970s to describe the way the world has become increasingly interdependent through a series of subsystems: communications, financial, educational, political, religious, technological. At the heart of this system is a world economy held together by technology, which enables it to react to stimuli with great speed.

This system has been developing over the past several centuries. The flowering of technology and industrialization in the West coincided with the spread of Western influence and modernization throughout the world. As the case of East Africa shows, modernity and colonialism affected the cultures, politics, and religious outlook of the peoples of that region. The concept of the world system underscores the interdependent nature of the modern world. Even people on the periphery soon feel the pulsations generated elsewhere in the system. Five dimensions of the wider context are identified here.

1. Contingency and Human Existence

Life is universally overshadowed by a sense of contingency manifested in tragedy, injustice, illness, catastrophe, and, ultimately, death. Subliminally, each human being senses the ever-present threat of chaos should order break down. Indeed, from time to time crisis does overtake the social and political order with disruptive consequences. One function of culture is to construct the means of coping with contingency by describing the order of the universe and the powers that impinge on human existence. A culture shapes the way a people understands and responds to these forces. In traditional cultures, people seek the blessing and benefit of benign powers through worship and sacrifice. When faced with adversity, they attempt to mitigate evil forces by appeasing or deflecting them. The sense of contingency is intensified as the world system becomes ever more closely bound together.

Religion is integral to worldview. Geertz has defined religion as:

(1) a system of symbols which acts to (2) establish powerful, pervasive, and long-lasting moods and motivations in men by (3) formulating conceptions of a general order of existence and (4) clothing these conceptions with such an aura of factuality that (5) the moods and motivations seem uniquely realistic (1973, 90).

If this symbol system is destabilized because the universe in which it operates is being undermined and rendered incoherent, the sense of contingency will be intensified and lead to crisis.

> *Postulate: So long as a people's worldview provides coherence and reassurance amid life's vicissitudes, they are unlikely to convert to an alternative worldview. Conversely, rapid cultural change or social crisis is a sine qua non of conversion on a wide scale.*

2. Cultural Systems

Cultures may be classified according to scale, degree of homogeneity, religious complexity, economic base, and political disposition. We identify three basic groups:

1. Small-scale, ethnically homogeneous, usually agrarian/subsistence based, no differentiation between religion and culture;

2. Large-scale, multi-ethnic nation-state, dominant world religion(s), traditional society, inward-directed (for example, India, China);

3. Large-scale, multi-ethnic nation-state, dominant world religion(s), technological-industrial economy, expansively outward-directed (for example, Western nations).

Each culture moves along its particular historical trajectory at its particular pace. The way a culture responds to change is determined, in part, by that pace and by the coherence of its worldview and its ability to control its destiny. Small-scale ethnic societies have had difficulty withstanding influences from more powerful societies—whether economic, political, or religious. On the other hand, large-scale societies vary markedly in their capacity to control conversionist movements sponsored by foreigners. Here China and Japan in the nineteenth century present important contrasts. Whereas Japan was able to reorganize its government and forge a unified national policy, throughout the nineteenth century the Ch'ing Dynasty was moving slowly but inexorably to its denouement and overthrow in 1911. Until 1949 China continued on a turbulent and chaotic course. Japan took a different path. By 1880 Japan had settled on a deliberately chosen program of modernization while maintaining a high degree of social control. Conversionist movements have made relatively little impact on Japan, whereas China has absorbed both religious and ideological conversion movements on a large scale.[4]

---

[4] Richard H. Drummond (1971) emphasizes the near-mania among Japanese for the artifacts of Western culture, including openness to Christianity. Yet a profound ambivalence was always present: "This mood was rooted not only in the continuity of ancient hostility and the fear of the *Kirishitan*. It was also intimately connected with the deepest levels of ethnic awareness, national pride and loyalty, which in an earlier period were expressed in a rather unreasoning anti-foreign policy but which, as the nation in the 1800's came to a new sense of its power vis-a-vis the countries of the West, emerged in the form of a resolve to reassert both Japanese political independence and the unique cultural traditions of the land" (196f.).

Postulate: The capacity of a cultural system to exert control over its populace is a key determinant of the extent to which an externally-sponsored conversionist initiative will succeed.

3. Colonialism

The first extensions of Western power took the form of economic or military expeditions, sometimes accompanied by missionary intentions. This was followed by the establishment of entrepôts. In the nineteenth century the Western powers greatly enlarged their spheres of influence by colonizing most of Africa and substantial parts of Asia. This was the basis for special relationships between a European power and its colonies in Asia, Africa, or Latin America and resulted in a dialectic between metropolis and colony, core and periphery, with the metropolis dominating its dependent colonies. This shaped the sociopolitical context in which conversion, as a religious phenomenon, has taken place outside the West in the modern era. However, colonial policies differed markedly among the various colonial powers. The leading colonial powers in the nineteenth century (Great Britain, France, Netherlands, Germany) all pursued policies that were perceived as adverse to mission societies. In the twentieth century a measure of cooperation was established. But the colonized peoples experienced the foreign presence—colonial and missionary—as one based on coercion.

Postulate: Conversion in the colonial context became stereotyped as "religious change under duress." The coercive dimensions were frequently not overt but were nonetheless real: becoming a Christian in a colony was perceived as ensuring one's economic or professional security; in other instances, refusing to convert was a way of demonstrating one's loyalty to the nationalist cause.

4. Modernization

Except for Islam, religious conversionist initiatives in the modern period have generally followed in the wake of the worldwide process of modernization. Christian conversionist movements have been integrally linked with this larger movement of modernization—at times critical of that movement, at other moments regarding themselves as allies in a "manifest destiny." The encounter precipitated by the modernizing movement—that is, between traditional (both primal and large-scale) and industrial-technological societies—has induced crisis for all traditional cultures. The challenge posed by the forces of modernization has called into question the adequacy of traditional cosmologies. This has elicited several types of response.

a. *Large-scale movements of conversion to Islam or Christianity among primal peoples.* After several generations of contact with modernizing influences in the South Pacific, the symbolic way of describing conversion was to speak of life versus death. Among the churches of New Caledonia the key word describing religious experience is "the word of life" (Guiart 1970, 131ff.). This reflects the growing sense of despair, helplessness, and impotence of indigenous peoples at the hands of colonizers, which eventually was resolved through conversion—not infrequently on the grounds that this would unlock the secrets concerning white power. The traditional way of life was increasingly experienced as a cul-de-sac, the way of death. Conversion promised life.

b. *Selective accommodation to Islam or Christianity but without significant conversions.* This has been true in a large-scale society like Japan, which was able either to blunt or actually to control outside influences through social sanctions.

c. *Intensive efforts to withstand conversionist initiatives through the traditional religio-cultural system—for example, India—accompanied by revitalization of the traditional religion.* Hinduism with its elaborate socioreligious controls was able effectively to withstand conversionist efforts among Hindus. But by the same token Hinduism was unable to prevent wide-scale response to these conversionist initiatives directed toward the Harijans of India. Those classes, traditionally excluded by Hinduism, turned elsewhere when they saw the possibility of being liberated from their low estate.

It is not, however, sufficient to inquire into the impact of modernization as measured by the number of conversions. By 1850 Western culture was already far down the road toward becoming a culture dominated by technology and industrialization. Modern culture is characterized by differentiation. Daniel Bell (1976) describes industrial society as consisting of three spheres: techno-economic (organization of production and allocation of goods and services); polity (social justice and deployment of power); and culture (symbolic forms—arena of expressive symbolism, including religion). Each sphere is subject to its own axial principle, and the three spheres tend to operate conflictually with one another. The role of religion in this cultural system contrasts with that in a traditional society, in which religion is integral to the whole. The authority of religion in modern culture was palpably eroding by 1850.

It is this truncated understanding of religion that the Christian missionary took to other parts of the world. The powerful cultural forces that reshaped the West in modern times pushed religion to the margin or forced it underground. By contrast, one of the noteworthy features of traditional societies is that religion remains a constitutive element. One can only speculate as to what might have been different had there not been this disjunction. Suffice it to say that by the 1980s Western peoples were described as worshiping "fragmented gods" (Bell 1976, 10ff.). Each sphere of life had its own cosmology, without a means of bringing coherence and integration to life as a whole.

Postulate: For traditional cultures under threat from Westernization and modernization, the Christian message proclaimed by the missionary contributed to the sense of personal and social fragmentation. As the nineteenth century progressed, the missionary's message increasingly reflected

*the fragmentation of Western culture and conversion became focused on
the "spiritual."*

5. The Multiple Facets of Conversion

As the case of East Africa makes clear, the missionary's focused understanding of conversion contrasted with the African's. The message of the evangelical missionary centered on sin and salvation. While some hearing the gospel for the first time undoubtedly were searching for answers to personal questions, justifiably many others responded out of social, economic, and political motives because these were the pressing issues they faced. In retrospect it is possible to describe how these multiple facets combined to foster a large-scale movement into the church. But the evangelical preoccupation with conversion did not prepare the missionary to understand the multiple dimensions of the situation in East Africa.

Postulate: A conversionist message will appeal to a variety of motives. While some motives may be rejected, motives that arise out of sincere yearning for life change can be used as bridges into a comprehensive application of the Christian message to the needs of converts.

Summary

These five variables indicate the complex factors that come into play when one places the process of conversion in a wider perspective. This need not devalue the experience of personal conversion that for many individuals marks a basic change of allegiance and the adoption of a new worldview. But all these experiences can be better understood when placed within a wider context. Furthermore, for the many peoples who have changed religious affiliation without a vivid religious experience—and yet have matured into devoted adherents—seeking to appreciate their pilgrimage within this wider framework lends validity to their experience.

CASE STUDIES

These brief case studies include a restatement of the evangelical understanding of conversion followed by a series of reactions that provide further illustrations and commentary on the model presented above.

1. The Evangelical Mission

The motor propelling the modern mission movement was the evangelical vision of a world enslaved to sin, from which only the offer of salvation through Jesus Christ offered deliverance. Conversion was at the heart of the evangelical vision, in which individuals acknowledged their need for salvation, professed faith in Christ, and thereupon experienced a transformation and personal reorientation. The focus was on the individual, yet the wider social implications were not overlooked.

In dedicating his book *Missionary Labours and Scenes in Southern Africa* to Prince Albert in 1842, Robert Moffat wrote "that all methods of effecting the civilization of Africa, apart from the Gospel of Christ, have hitherto proved abortive; but it is presumed that the present Narrative will demonstrate, that, in every instance where the gospel has been introduced, it has effected a complete revolution in the character and habits of its people." Then Moffat added grandiloquently, "Philosophy must eventually confess her impotence; the pride of science be humbled; and the fact be universally acknowledged, that the Gospel of Christ is the only instrument which can civilize and save all kindreds and nations of the earth" (Moffat 1969, ii). Moffat's statement reveals three things representative of the evangelical outlook. First, he emphasizes the centrality of conversion. It suggests both his fundamental theological premise and the key to his strategy. Second, his statement accurately reflects the comprehensive scope of the gospel as understood by evangelicals at that time. In the third place, this statement shows Moffat to be a representative of his culture. On the one hand, this is Moffat's personal response to the "civilizing versus Christianizing" debate. He votes in favor of "Christianizing."[5] On the other, he is also conscious of the criticisms leveled against the Christian faith and its missionary vocation. At the same time Moffat subscribes to the "civilizing" mission of which the West is steward on behalf of the world.

The evangelical conversionist vision, which Robert Moffat embodied, was capable of rather broad application. Speaking as leader of an evangelical missionary society, Josiah Pratt in 1804 instructed the first contingent of missionaries the Church Missionary Society sent to Sierra Leone:

> You will take all prudent occasions of weaning the Native chiefs from this slave traffic, by depicting its criminality, the miseries which it occasions to Africa, and the obstacles which it opposes to more profitable and generous intercourse with the European nations. But while you do this, you will cultivate kindness of spirit towards those persons who are connected with this trade. You will make all due allowances for their habits, their prejudices, and their views of interest. Let them never be met by you with reproaches and invectives, however debased you may find them in mind and manners (Stock 1899, 1:83-85).

Far from avoiding sensitive sociopolitical questions, Pratt enjoined on his missionaries the duty to oppose the slave trade by inculcating a conscience against it and advocating alternatives.

---

[5] "Much has been said about civilizing savages, before attempting to evangelize them. This is a theory which has obtained an extensive prevalence among the wise men of this world; but we have never yet seen a practical demonstration of its truth" (502).

A successor to Josiah Pratt, Henry Venn, effectively held together this evangelical emphasis on the essentiality of conversion and the widest possible implications of the Christian message. He asserted that "the real foundation of association in the true Church is the conversion of the sinner to Christ, the radical renewal of the individual" (Venn 1861, 187). Still, Venn's understanding of the Christian gospel was all-embracing. He insisted that the essential strategy for bringing about personal and social transformation had to be based on conversion of the individual, yet he exerted great personal effort to promote industrial and commercial development in Africa as a means of ending the slave trade and advancing Africa's fortunes. Nonetheless, he kept a close rein on his missionaries lest they become involved in political action.

And herein lies the weakness in evangelical ideology. Because it stressed so forcefully the role of the individual, it couched all its thought about strategy and tactics in individual terms. It was asserted repeatedly that the converted individual would ensure social and political change. Collective action by the church qua church was ruled out of bounds. Evangelicals, therefore, found concerted effort in addressing social issues difficult to contemplate.

2. Reactions to the Evangelical Conversionist Movement

Responses to the conversionist program outlined in the preceding section may be viewed from two angles: that of the peoples to whom the missions were sent, and that of the missioners charged with putting the program into action.

The Missionized

Reactions to the coming of missions were not uniform. Responses ranged from the warm welcome, on the one hand, to sustained effort to block entry, on the other.[6] Whatever the response, it was never made in a vacuum. Local peoples keenly and quickly sensed the power implications of such intrusion. Chief Daapa invited the missionaries to work in Pondoland early in the nineteenth century, and what opposition there was remained local and unofficial. The fact that the missionaries were British was in their favor, since British troops helped the Faku fight their dreaded enemies, the Tshaka. Later the missionaries advised the chiefs in their affairs with the British government. The Pondo perceived them to be their allies in coping with hostile forces (Wilson 1961, 353).

China largely succeeded in keeping the missionary out until the unequal treaties were forced on her in the mid-nineteenth century. In Nigeria and Southern Africa, where nation-states were not yet organized, one chief might welcome the missionary and another forbid entry. Whatever the reaction, the missionary was perceived as a representative of another cultural-political system that posed a challenge to the host culture (Isichei 1973, 99f.). Even when the missionary

---

[6] Elizabeth Isichei writes: "Initially, the rulers of Ibo states always welcomed the advent of trade and missions" (Isichei 1973, 101); she suggests that the Onitsha welcomed missions because of political vulnerability (1970, 211).

did not arrive in the wake of the colonial powers, the missionary came as representative of a powerful culture. In the case of China the outsider was regarded as a cultural inferior, but China repeatedly suffered the ignominy of military defeat at the hands of these inferiors.

In the colonial situation many local leaders chose to cooperate with the colonial power and the missionary. Since these invasive forces were perceived to be beyond the power of the local rulers to remove, it was the better part of wisdom to accommodate to the inevitable. One type of collaborator has been termed the *manipulator*. Recognizing that they were helpless to overthrow the colonial power, this type chose to ally themselves with it in order to gain some advantage. The second type of collaborator was the *improver*. This group sought to take advantage of the opportunities posed by the coming of the outsiders by getting an education, entering the civil service, church, or professions (Isichei 1973, 176-78).

It has been widely noted that in numerous cases the earliest converts to Christianity were individuals from the margins of society, including those from the slave class in places like Nigeria. In terms of systems analysis, this is not surprising. The marginal elements saw the promise of improved status through a shift in allegiance. Christianity became stigmatized as the religion of inferiors or outsiders and failed to make serious inroads into the culture in the first several decades. From the founding of the first mission in Yorubaland in 1846 until 1905 the missions gained converts largely—but not exclusively—among socially and politically marginal peoples, including those who had returned from Sierra Leone (Isichei 1973, 88, 104).[7] The political unification of Nigeria under British rule in 1906 triggered a crisis that affected all realms of life in the country. A colonial power intent on creating a central authority forced social and political realignments throughout Nigerian society, thus disrupting traditional lines of authority and power. The religious reaction was rapid. Almost immediately a period of sustained growth in adherents began—growth sustained by all classes of society.[8]

An outstanding example of conversion among dispossessed peoples is that of the Harijans of India. Already in the early sixteenth century there had been large-scale or group conversions to Christianity. From the nineteenth century on, the number of such group movements increased. By the twentieth century it was observed that where major accessions to the church had occurred in India these had been among the aboriginals or outcasts. These were the peoples who had no recognized place within the Hindu religion and were disenfranchised by society. In J. Waskom Pickett's pioneering study of this phenomenon he examined the motives behind these conversions through a series of case studies. One of the

---

[7] Isichei notes: "As in other missionary contexts the missionaries drew their converts mainly from the rejects of Ibo society" (1970, 212).

[8] Cf. Willis (1977) who investigated the large-scale religious movement in Indonesia ca. 1965-71 using as his framework the sociopolitical upheavals through which the country passed at that time.

themes in the responses is that as a people they were oppressed by the landowners. In the power dialectic of Indian society, these peasants were trapped on the
periphery. Moral support by the missionaries and pastors emboldened the peasants to sue for their rights. As Pickett reported in his study of these movements,
the landowners were forced to show respect:

> "Why did you become a Christian?" we asked a young man in Vidyanagar
> who had been baptized less than a year before. "All of us in this village
> became Christians together," came the quick response, and it was recorded
> that he had followed the crowd. "But you didn't have to become a Chris-
> tian because these others were doing so." "No, I wanted to be a Christian."
> "Why so?" "So I could be a man. None of us was a man. We were dogs.
> Only Jesus could make men out of us" (Pickett 1933, 158).

Another motive for conversion reported by Pickett was the sense that the traditional religion was no longer efficacious in dealing with evil spirits. The traditional cosmology seemed unable to provide a satisfactory answer.

The Indian case illustrates how a traditional worldview broke down under the
impact of an oppressive sociopolitical situation. Interaction with representatives
of an alternative worldview who offered concrete alternatives set the stage for
conversion. The political implications of the Harijans' situation remain highly
sensitive in India up to the present.

One further variety of response is what Clifford Geertz has called "internal
conversion." In this instance, a socioreligious group, in response to challenges
posed by outside influences, undergoes important changes within its religious
life and structures by borrowing and adapting modes and techniques observed in
the external sources of threat. The Balinese have been Hindu for many centuries,
but Balinese Hinduism has maintained no ties with the rest of the Hindu world
and has existed as a traditional—in contrast to a rationalized—religion. For a
long time the Balinese have felt threatened by the Muslim majority in Indonesia;
and it was the Muslim leadership that pressured the government not to grant
official status to Balinese Hinduism as a religion. Geertz reports that over time
the Balinese responded to this external threat through an intensification of religious life and significant rationalization (including efforts toward an explicit
theology and dissemination of literature about Bali-ism; reform of congregational life; and efforts to win government recognition as a religious body) (Geertz
1973, 179-89).[9]

The Missionary

In the field situation missionaries came to realize that if they were to succeed
in converting people through the Christian message, they had to adapt their communication to the cultures in which they worked. They realized they were up

---

[9] Cf. Isichei (1970, 221ff.). Many other examples of such religious resurgence resulting from intercultural contact can be cited. An outstanding one is that of the Ahmadiyya.

against cultural forces that they had to come to terms with as best they could. Robert Moffat describes his struggle to understand the worldview of the Africans in order to find the appropriate analogies by which to introduce the Christian message. He hails the Acts of the Apostles as a model for all missionary communication and asserts that the missionary "will find it necessary to adapt his discourses to the circumstances of the people among whom he labours" (Moffat 1969, 301).

A contemporary of Moffat's, Methodist missionary William Taylor, who also served in South Africa, declared: "We did not simply proclaim the truths of the gospel to them, for the work of an ambassador for Christ embraces much more than that, but followed St. Paul's method." Taylor goes on: "In preaching to the Jews, he based his arguments on the clearly defined prophetic Scriptures, which his hearers admitted. In preaching to heathens he went directly down into the regions of their own experience" (Taylor 1867, 390). Taylor then reproduces, as an example of his attempts at adaptation, a sermon he preached to a group of people who were not Christian. In it Taylor deals with the evangelical essentials but tries to communicate by using culturally suitable metaphors and images.

Critique

Gabriel M. Setiloane has scrutinized closely the efforts of Moffat, Casalis, Giddy, and other early missionaries to understand the Sotho-Tswana. Setiloane concludes that they failed to engage the Sotho-Tswana on every important point. He declines to speak about missionary "success" but then reluctantly concludes that

> in so far as missionary endeavour in the land of the Sotho-Tswana, once launched, did not die out and close down, but has remained and given birth to a Church with its accompanying organization and institutions, schools and hospitals; inasmuch as the membership on the roll-books of the churches increases annually, as it has done over the years, and people feel sufficiently identified to write on Census Return forms that they are "Christian"—even though they pay a visit to Church to worship only once or twice a year—then it must be conceded that the missionaries who first brought the Gospel to the Sotho-Tswana have "succeeded" (1975, 123).

Others have made the same observation. John V. Taylor noted that Anglican missionaries in Buganda faithfully preached traditional evangelical doctrine.[10] What the Baganda heard and what became the foundation for the church in Buganda was the message about "the transcendent God" who was Creator and Sustainer of life and with whom they could now have direct relationship (John Taylor 1958, 252). Here one feels keenly the contrast between a defensive and embattled Victorian evangelicalism encountering a people whose traditional worldview was beginning to crumble.

---

[10] The same point, albeit from various angles, has been made many times over. Ranger (1972, 5ff.) offers an interesting example.

As Setiloane and Taylor show, the process of intercultural communication is exceedingly complex and subtle. Nonetheless, in both Southern Africa and Buganda the encounter, despite apparent flawed communication, resulted in fundamental religio-cultural change. Perhaps more important than what the missionaries said was how they said it and how they comported themselves among the people.

It is evident that the missionary movement cannot be accurately evaluated only in terms of which side it identified with. It influenced various parts of a complex system. At times its importance as a symbol of modernization-cum-religious change far outweighed its actual influence at the local level.

Critical Importance of Timing

As discussed in chapter 5, the Toba Indians of the Gran-Chaco traditionally were a semi-nomadic people who survived by hunting and gathering. They encountered European intruders throughout the period from the sixteenth to the nineteenth centuries. These intruders fell into three classes: military/politician, explorer/entrepreneur, and priest. All of these intruders were of European background, and all agreed as to the objective to be pursued vis-à-vis the Toba: pacification and civilization. By the twentieth century the Toba situation had deteriorated seriously, and the Tobas resorted to armed rebellion. The last of these rebellions, in 1924, resulted in a large-scale massacre by the Argentine police. Several years later a Toba *cacique*, or chief, made contact with a Pentecostal evangelist/pastor, and by the early 1940s a mass movement was under way, led by *caciques*. Elmer Miller concludes that had the Pentecostal message arrived a hundred years earlier, however, it would have been no better received than was Catholic teaching then or Anglican and Protestant missions later. The crisis in Toba society, especially the widespread sense of deprivation and the loss of authority of the traditional leaders and worldview, coincided with the arrival of the Pentecostal message. By the 1960s the Tobas were largely affiliated with the church and their religious life provided the source of authority and cohesion in Toba life. Their religious and community life retained important features of their traditional culture.

Whether the missionaries were evangelical or Roman Catholic, they shared the conviction that the people to whom they went needed to be converted. What is notable in the responses of the missionized is the absence of priority on the message per se. Typically, they were marginalized or oppressed or experiencing a severe cultural crisis and responded to that which offered concrete help: an ally against malevolent forces, refuge from social ostracism, freedom from fear of unfriendly powers, educational opportunity. Each of these represents an appeal for empowerment and security. In accepting what the missionaries offered, such people also accepted, at least to some degree, new values and new elements which altered their worldview.

A Case of Conversion Aborted

In 1964 the Evangelical Presbyterian Church of Ghana, together with its counterpart North American mission agency, launched a mission in Northern Ghana led by an American missionary, Alfred C. Krass, and two Ghanaian colleagues from the south. Krass left Ghana in 1970. The mission was located at Chereponi among the Chokosi (or Anufo), Konkomba, and Komba peoples. By 1970 twenty-two new congregations had been established. In several cases entire villages had been baptized, while in others extended family systems had come into the church. This movement of rapid conversion seemed to portend continued accessions to the Christian church. Instead, a decade later the church had no leadership, church attendance was low, and indeed, numbers of people had reverted to their traditional religion or had become Muslims.

In seeking to understand this surprising turn, Krass noted how the coming of the mission in 1964 seemed to coincide with peoples' readiness for modernization (Krass 1983, 49-59). The people were becoming more mobile and their "world" was rapidly expanding as local youth went away to study or to enter the professions. The traditional religion seemed quite incapable of helping people make the transition into the modern world, and Islam seemingly did not offer much help. Krass did observe that the people who responded most readily were from among the "despised majority," who were under the domination of the royal clan and Muslim traders. Thus they were seeking help in coping with this domination. The mission instituted a large development program to assist the people in improving their lot.

It is evident that the South Ghanaian and American missionaries did not understand the Chokosi culture as thoroughly as they assumed. They failed to realize the extent to which the power struggle between the dominated majority and the royal and Muslim classes preoccupied Chokosi life. Catholic missionary Jon Kirby, who came to Chereponi to work several years after Krass left, confirms this (Kirby 1985, 15-25). He observed that Islam offered two things that were indispensable to the people. First, Muslims controlled the trade routes. Thus, they had it in their power to offer benefits to those who cooperated with them. Second, Islam presented positive alternatives to traditional religion, whereas Christianity seemed to ignore traditional religion. Indeed, Kirby argues that the Chokosi never understood Christianity as a religion at all. In their view, to qualify as a religious alternative Christianity would have had to prove itself as a problem-solver at three levels—community, household, and individual. In contrast, Islam had established itself as capable of solving problems. When crises arose in the lives of Christian converts, they typically resorted to traditional means of solving their problems, whereas Muslims turned to their religion.

Looking back, Krass admits: "I was as much a missionary of a secular world view as of Christianity." The Chokosi clamor for modernization bespoke deeper concerns. By directing missionary efforts at meeting the people at the technical level, the Chokosi did not encounter the Christian message as something that spoke to their need for a cosmology that gave coherence and security in life.

3. The Role of the Mission System

In one of his trenchant criticisms of missions, Roland Allen said in 1912: "Our missions are in different countries amongst people of the most diverse characteristics, but all bear a most astonishing resemblance to one another" (Allen 1962, 142). The observations about the missions system that so exercised people like Roland Allen were not new. The 1860 Conference on Missions at Liverpool heard major addresses, "On Native Agency in Foreign Missions" and "On Native Churches." The minute passed following the first address stressed the importance of preparing local people to carry responsibility for evangelization and church leadership:

> The European or American missionary, who, in obedience to Christ's command, bears the Gospel in some heathen country, is a stranger and a foreigner there: his work is temporary; his position is exceptional; and when Christianity becomes localized, his peculiar functions and duties come to an end. Christianity must be embodied in a living form in native churches; and the outward services it demands must be performed by native pastors and native missionaries of all grades (*Conference on Missions* 1860, 227).

In response to the address "On Native Churches," the Rev. Behari Lal Singh observed that there were fifteen thousand Christians in Bengal and missionaries had commented on the superior intellectual and moral gifts to be found among them. Then Singh asked: "Why are not such distinguished men appointed pastors over native churches?" (*Conference on Missions* 1860, 292f.). Singh pointed to the fact that a large portion of these Christians were poor peasants who lived at a subsistence level. Support of a paid pastoral ministry would be difficult to provide. Singh also cited an external fact that was retarding self-support. He called this "the false position in which a European missionary is placed by continually retaining the pastorship over the native church" (293). With power and discipline kept in the hands of the pastor, this creates "a cringing disposition . . . in the native flocks." With his superior financial and social position, inevitably the missionary was seen in the community as a prime source of charity. This created an unhealthy dependence.

Among missionaries it was widely recognized that the missions system itself was a problem, and yet no one seemed capable of bringing about reform. They acknowledged that it overpowered the local church and community by injecting an element of coercion and control that overshadowed the missionary's message and made voluntary response difficult. The role of the missions system bulks large in any attempt to understand the intercultural dynamics of the conversion process.

China offers a classic case study of the difficulty of adapting the missions system. The system was the largest missions establishment in the world and highly organized. The leitmotif running through the missionary conference held at Shanghai in 1877 was the question of how to use this system effectively. It was generally agreed that the mission organization was foreign and temporary. The unresolved question was how to foster development of a self-supporting indigenous church through the instrumentality of this foreign system. It was insisted that Christian converts must be taught stewardship and responsibility for meeting the needs of the poor. "It is beyond dispute that only in this way can a genuine native church be developed," said S. L. Baldwin (1878, 284). He went on to assert that "only a self-supporting church can demonstrate to the heathen the genuineness of native Christianity. A church dependent on foreign funds will ever be looked upon with suspicion" (284). These latter words were indeed prophetic in light of what took place after 1949.

At each succeeding conference in China discussion revolved around this matter: the unqualified requirement that the church be indigenous, the distortions and dependence resulting from the system, and the dilemma facing the missions (cf. Hood 1986). The frustration was not only on the side of the missionaries, of course. In 1906 the first independent Chinese church was founded in Shanghai by the Rev. Yu Kuo-chen. In subsequent years a growing number of such autonomous and fully indigenous churches were started in China.

Most Chinese Christians maintained their membership in the mission-founded churches, but by the 1920s these Chinese Christians were deeply frustrated and increasingly vocal about it. At the 1922 National Christian Conference held in Shanghai, both missionaries and Chinese spoke about the indigenous church. Yet their viewpoints stand in sharp contrast. Chinese leaders said:

> We wish to voice the sentiment of our people that the wholesale, uncritical acceptance of the traditions, forms and organizations of the West and the slavish imitation of these are not conducive to the building of a permanent genuine Christian Church in China. . . . The rapidly changing conditions of the country all demand an indigenous Church which will present an indigenous Christianity, a Christianity which does not sever its continuity with the historical churches but at the same time takes cognizance of the spiritual inheritance of the Chinese races (Rawlinson, et al. 1922, 502).

It seemed self-evident that only Chinese leadership could complete this conversion of Christianity into a religion that was authentically Christian and Chinese.

The missionary side of the equation responded only by tinkering with the system rather than attempting an overhauling or standing aside and allowing the Chinese to take the reins into their hands. This was essentially the stance they maintained until 1949, when the torrent of events overwhelmed them and carried the old system out to sea.

One of the charges brought against the church in China by the communists in the post-1949 period was that it was foreign and supported by foreign funds. Christian leaders, therefore, took steps to declare in unequivocal terms their loyalty to the new government in *The Christian Manifesto* published in 1950. Built into the manifesto was a description of the church as characterized by the "three-selfs": self-supporting, self-governing, and self-propagating. The Protestant church became known officially as the Three-Selfs Patriotic Movement.

In the aftermath of the Cultural Revolution (1966-76) it has become clear that the Christian movement in China not only has survived but has in fact grown substantially. All of this has happened under straitened circumstances and with only Chinese in leadership. To this day the theology and patterns of church life in China bear the mark "made in the West," but the Chinese have dealt with this issue in their own way. Without apology, the Roman Catholic Church continues to conduct the Mass in Latin. The new Protestant hymnal published in the early 1980s includes some 150 hymns brought to China by missionaries, but the Chinese church leaders are free to insist "they are ours, too." The old saw about the "foreignness" of the Christian faith has faded away because the churches in China have proven that they are authentically Chinese and Christian.

The Toba experience has much in common with that of the Chinese. What is crucial is where responsibility is lodged rather than form. The Toba *cacique* borrowed freely from the Pentecostal movement and fashioned a new synthesis that responded to the needs of the Toba people. But the Toba have successfully fended off each outside attempt, including that of Pentecostal groups, to get control of the Toba church. The church in China arrived at its position of self-governance by an entirely different route, yet it has been equally important for the selfhood and integrity of the Chinese church to have become self-governing. Movements of religious independence throughout the world point to the crucial importance of this point. Transformation resulting from the interplay between two religio-cultural systems is not complete until leadership and control are fully in indigenous hands.

CONCLUSION

Christians and Muslims alike understand their faith to enjoin missionary witness. During the past two centuries Christianity and Islam have grown steadily through missionary action. In Nigeria alone an estimated thirty-five million people have converted to Christianity since 1846; an equal number have become Muslims during the same period. Neither Islam nor Christianity has won significant numbers of adherents from other world religions. The vast majority of all conversions have taken place among small-scale ethnic societies and those marginalized by a powerful majority society, such as the Harijans in India.

The context of these large-scale conversionist movements has been the dynamic modern period during which Western influence was being extended throughout the world and the world system emerged. Two observations should be noted. First, converts were drawn almost entirely from cultures in which decision-making is communal. Personhood is defined in relation to one's group: "I belong, therefore I am." Second, the emerging world system intensified feelings of vulnerability for whole societies. Traditional folkways were being overrun by colonialism and modernization. The evangelical missionary message was directed to the individual, but that message was received through eyes and ears that responded corporately, by a community that felt itself besieged.

Inevitably, the question arises: Was this conversionist effort successful? Scholars studying such movements are eager to pose this question. J. D. Y. Peel has wryly observed that even sociologists and anthropologists who themselves profess no religious allegiance show an unusual proclivity to judge a conversion movement on how fully the new religion has been adopted (Peel 1967-68, 121).

The case studies considered above point up the ambiguities of this history. In East Africa Roman Catholics and Calvinists adopted one model, while evangelicals advocated another. Regardless of which model was followed, within a generation the results were in hand; there was no appreciable difference in outcome. By the early 1900s Catholics and Protestants alike were frustrated by the widespread nominality that characterized the Christian community (cf. Oliver 1952, 172-202).

Neither model seriously engaged with cultural realities on the ground. The missionary was sent out armed with instructions as to the desired results and the methods by which the goal was to be achieved. Western peoples had unbounded confidence in correct formulae and methodologies. Missionaries and their sponsors completely underestimated the intractable and complex nature of culture. The insertion of Western missions into African and Asian cultures was indeed a catalyst for far-reaching change, but it was change that proved difficult to channel and control. Ironically, the outcome—which missionaries had hoped to avoid— turned out to look a lot like European Christendom.

Two main conclusions can be drawn from this investigation. First, conversion is a considerably more complex process than is usually described. That complexity is compounded when one introduces the influence exerted by the multiple dimensions of the wider context. Yet this step must be taken if we are to have a more realistic understanding of what conversion entails. All the missionaries who worked in East Africa shared the goal of establishing Christian churches made up of committed disciples of Jesus Christ. The fact that nominality appeared in the churches so early poses many questions. Second, this study indicates that, along with more complete descriptions of the process, we need adequate criteria for evaluating conversion. Rather than starting with imported models and assumptions, the assessment must begin within the sociopolitical context in which conversion is taking place: What impact has conversion had on the context, and what impact has it had on the converts? Has it resulted in changed moral and ethical behavior at the individual as well as social levels? What was the motivation for conversion in this instance?

At a minimum, these findings suggest that conversion has played an important role in religious history in the modern period. We need to revisit this history. It holds promising fresh insights that can expand our understanding of conversion.

8

Missionary Strategy

STRATEGY IN MISSION STUDIES

Strategy is a recurring themes in the history of missions thought and practice.[1] It focuses on how mission has been carried out and the numerous attempts to form plans for world evangelization (Barrett and Reapsome 1988).

Ambivalence toward Strategy

A certain ambivalence has characterized discussion of strategy in relation to missions. There is good reason for this ambivalence. In the first place, strategy originated as a military concept. *Strategy* derives from the Greek *strategos* or "general." The role of the general of an army is to form a comprehensive plan for conducting a campaign in order to win a military objective. This involves the art and science of assembling all necessary resources—political, economic, psychological, and military to support execution of a strategy. Once a plan is adopted, it is assumed that what remains is to implement this strategy by rigorously following this predetermined plan. In a military campaign the "other" is an enemy who is to be forcibly subdued through whatever means necessary. Neither the goal nor the means employed in a military operation is appropriate to Christian mission. Second, the very term suggests calculation: a careful weighing of alternatives, searching for the most efficient means based on empirical data. How does such a stance relate to the work of the Holy Spirit? If missionary obedience involves discerning and following God's will, then a considered tentativeness ought to mark our most carefully laid plans. The history of missions contains many surprises which remind us that, at best, we "know in part" only.

While much has been written over the past two centuries about mission strategy, one is hard pressed to find biblical and theological explications of strategy

First published in James M. Phillips and Robert T. Coote, eds., *Toward the Twenty-first Century in Christian Mission* (Grand Rapids, Mich.: Wm. B. Eerdmans Publishing Co., 1993), 218-34.

[1] Special thanks to colleagues Roelf S. Kuitse and David A. Shank for reading a first draft of this essay and offering important suggestions.

(but see Shank 1973; Wagner 1971, 15-47).[2] The failure to provide such theological guidance must be reckoned a serious default.

Strategy Culturally and Historically Conditioned

A strategy always reflects the culture and historical moment in which it is
formulated. Just as the way a people wages war is shaped by its culture—in
particular its values, worldview, and technology—strategy becomes a projec-
tion of the culture of the strategist. Modern mission strategy has been molded by
two outstanding features of Western culture.

First, mission strategy has been informed by the philosophy of pragmatism
and a concomitant confidence in technique. One of the hallmarks of Western
culture in the modern period has been the use of the scientific method. This
powerful methodology has influenced the ways people in the West study and
think. Western people have been schooled to believe that all phenomena can be
investigated by rigorous application of the critical tools of scientific analysis.
Such investigation has been carried out in order to expand human knowledge
but also for the purpose of gaining control and effecting a solution. This approach to problem-solving is applauded when it is employed to conquer a dread
disease. But not all areas of human experience can be reduced to empirically
verifiable categories. Social scientists have been warning of the price being paid
in Western culture as a result of an uncritical acceptance of the scientific method;
the price is the profound alienation found in modern society. In the words of
Theodore Roszak, "While the art and literature of our time tell us with ever more
desperation that the disease from which our age is dying is that of alienation, the
sciences in their relentless pursuit of objectivity raise alienation to its apotheosis
as our only means of achieving a valid relationship to reality" (1968/1969, 232).
Uncritical confidence in the scientific method has led us to believe that whatever is amiss in human affairs can be reduced to a manageable problem, and a
problem is there to be solved. This reductionism not only distorts reality but it
fosters the illusion of omnipotence.[3]

In the second place, the Western approach to strategy has emerged out of a
linear view of history, particularly its faith in evolutionary progress. This view
of history is now under attack precisely in the West, where it has long been
regnant (Trompf 1979).[4] The conviction that progress is inevitable and open-

---

[2] See J. Herbert Kane (1976, 73-85) who discusses "Paul's Missionary Strategy." He
cites Roland Allen (1962) and Michael Green (1975) who argue that Paul had no thought-
out strategy. Without discussing or rebutting Allen and Green, Kane proceeds to identify
nine elements in Paul's "strategy." This hardly adds up to a strategy. Kane indicates
possible principles of action we may deduce from Pauline practice rather than a strategy.

[3] For a preliminary probing of the American penchant for technology, see A. F. Walls
(1990a).

[4] Every vision of history can produce distortions and lead to disillusionment. The
linear view is no exception. When it loses direction, it forfeits its goal. The biblical
vision is linear, with history moving toward its culmination in the kingdom of God.

ended is now widely perceived to be misguided in light of the major wars fought in this century at the initiative of peoples who are heirs of the Enlightenment. The continuing threat of military confrontation in many parts of the world and the way our burgeoning technology menaces the ecosystem daily remind us that all human progress is ambiguous in its outcomes.

BIBLICAL PERSPECTIVE

The starting point for thinking about a biblical approach to strategy must be a consideration of God's missionary initiative. Genesis 1–3 forms a prolegomenon to the rest of scripture by tying together creation, mission, and redemption. Several themes stand out: God is the subject. The whole of creation is an expression of God's grace and is therefore "good." Man and woman are created in God's image and appointed to share in the stewardship of God's creation. The coming of sin into the world does not alter God's intention for humankind and the created world. God is committed to redeeming the world from its bondage to sin. Even though humankind was expelled from Eden, God entrusted to the human couple a mission (De Ridder 1983, 173-75). God's redemptive mission is advanced through the prophetic promise of a Messiah. The New Testament reports and interprets the Christ-event as the fulfillment of the messianic promise (Mt 3:2-3; Lk 2:22-32; 3:4ff.; 4:1-19, Jn 3:16).

God's strategy may be summarized in terms of three stages: (1) The election and sending of Abraham so that "by you all the families of the earth shall bless themselves" (Gn 12:3), along with the covenant binding Israel to be the instrument of salvation for the nations. (2) The sending of Jesus Christ (Jn 1:14), the divinely appointed Messiah, who continues the strategy of *pars pro toto* (the one for the many). (3) The sending of the church as an extension of the mission of Jesus Christ (Jn 17:18; 20:21). Each "sending" is from a position of vulnerability and weakness in obedience to God's call to bring healing and salvation to all peoples (cf. Dt 15:15; 16:12; 24:18; 26:5; Phil 2:5-8; Jn 17:18).

Several additional observations may be made about the messianic strategy as seen in the self-understanding of Jesus and the apostles. Jesus insisted that he was sent only to the lost sheep of the house of Israel (Mt 15:24; 10:5ff.) in spite of the fact that his mission was to the entire world. In line with this the apostles Paul and Barnabas preached first to the Jews and then to the Gentiles (Acts 13:46-47). As Paul and others moved out in cross-cultural witness, they followed the Jewish Diaspora, and this took them to the urban commercial centers throughout the Mediterranean basin. The Holy Spirit thus used the Diaspora to further God's redemptive purpose.

THEOLOGICAL FRAMEWORK

The biblical materials suggest a fivefold theological framework for thinking strategically.

1. God's Redemptive Mission: The Source

Mission has its source in the nature and purpose of God. God the Creator is none other than God the Redeemer. God's saving purpose can be traced through the calling of Abraham and his descendants to enter into covenant relationship for the blessing of the nations. This saving purpose is expressed supremely in the sending of God the Son to be the savior of the world. God's redemptive strategy stands over all history (Vicedom 1965; Berkhof 1966) and points to the goal, the kingdom of God. Certain statements of God's redemptive mission have been indispensable in sustaining faith in God's purposes and hope for the consummation. Isaiah projected this vision—"For the earth shall be full of the knowledge of the Lord as the waters cover the sea" (11:9) and there will be "new heavens and a new earth" (65:17; cf. 2 Pt 3:13). John's Revelation depicts the outcome of God's redemptive program—that is, shalom—in which the unity the peoples of the world could not achieve is now realized through God's gracious provision in Jesus Christ (Rv 5:9-10; 7:9-10). The picture is filled out in Revelation 21:1-7. These vision statements contain both present and future dimensions. The Christ-event demonstrates and fulfills God's mission.

2. Jesus Christ: The Embodiment

The Old Testament introduces the notion that God's redemptive strategy is tied to the coming of the Messiah (Is 11:1-9; 42:1-4, 53; 61:1-3). The synoptic gospels emphasize the continuity between Old and New Testaments—that which was promised is now being fulfilled (Lk 4:16-21). When the incarnate God enters the human scene, it is as a helpless baby (Jn 1:14), signifying both identification and vulnerability. Jesus inaugurates his public ministry by proclaiming the reign of God (Mt 4:17; Mk 1:15) and embodies that reign, demonstrating its power and interpreting its meaning for the lives of his listeners. That embodiment projected a new way of being. He came as one who serves and who was self-emptying (Phil 2:5-8), but his was a transforming presence. "From his ministry emerged a new people from and in the midst of all nations," observes David Shank. "Through that strategy of persuasion through his suffering Servant, God created a like-minded people who are servant to all peoples for their blessing and salvation. The strategy of Christian mission is nothing more—nor less—than participation in carrying out God's own strategy. Its shape is that of a cross" (Shank 1973, 1). The risen Christ commissions "like-minded people" to continue the mission of redemption in his name (Mt 28:18-20; Jn 20:19-22). They will take their strategic clues from their Messiah leader.

The coming of the Messiah results in crisis and calls for decision. Stephen represented to the religious leaders the Christ-figure. They rejected Stephen's witness and martyred him for it (Acts 7:54-60). Later Paul would interpret his own *metanoia* in light of that martyr witness to Jesus Christ (Acts 22:17-21).

3. Holy Spirit: The Power

Building on the work of Roland Allen, Harry R. Boer (1961) demonstrated how central the Holy Spirit is to mission. The Spirit is the primary agent of the mission of the Messiah. Missionary obedience is first of all an act of submission to the leadership of the Holy Spirit. Strategic thinking ought to begin and end with the prayer "Your will be done." Within this ambit there is ample space for the hard thinking involved in strategy-making, but it will be held in check by the awareness that the Holy Spirit is sovereign. Because mission is the will of God, the Holy Spirit is the driving force in mission. The primary purpose of the Spirit is that the messianic reign be actualized. In our strategizing we can depend on the Spirit to discard all that is unworthy of Christ.

4. Church: The Instrument

At each stage the sending is for the purpose of bringing blessing to the nations. In his life and ministry Jesus Christ has modeled all that it means to embody the life of God. It results in a new community that is characterized by shalom and a passion to extend life to the nations across lines of race, class, sex, and nationality. Thus the church continually draws on that model for its own ministry. Whatever does not build the new community must be rejected. Actions that produce alienation or bondage are contrary to the gospel.

Throughout history, mission has been fulfilled by those communities for whom the Christ-event was normative and spiritual vitality was expressed in discipleship. In these groups the Holy Spirit has found openness to the reordering of congregational life for mission. It is in these groups that the priesthood of all believers began to be recovered together with the full range of Spirit-given charisms.

5. Cultures: The Context

Strategic thinking that is consistent with the other elements of this framework will respect the varied contexts of mission. All human cultures are equally the means through which people hear the gospel "in their own tongue." The apostle Paul insisted that he was prepared to "become all things to all people" in order that they might hear the gospel. Strategic thinking based on master plans far removed from a particular context must be treated with great suspicion. Vincent Donovan's attempt to reach the Masai by abandoning the conventional missions system in favor of a strategy attuned to Masai culture points us in the right direction (Donovan 1978). Other examples can be found in the history of missions, where missionaries rejected "cultural diffusion" in favor of finding ways to "translate the message" into the language and culture of a people (Sanneh 1989).

STRATEGY IN EARLY CHRISTIAN HISTORY

Primitive Christianity has been the scene of fresh and creative scholarly investigation in recent years. That the early church grew and extended itself on a surprising scale is a matter of agreement. But scholars remain divided as to the causes of this growth. What can be said is that there was no grand strategy and no central command (Kreider 1990). In a perhaps too categorical statement, Robin Lane Fox insists that "we cannot name a single active Christian missionary between St. Paul and the age of Constantine" (Lane Fox 1986, 282). Yet the faith spread—by sheer force of its inner logic and dynamic. It had captured the loyalty-to-the-death of the rank and file, and it was they who were the vanguard of evangelization. The early Christians believed themselves to be the community of the Holy Spirit, in which gifts of ministry were given for missionary witness.

As already noted, the New Testament gives us no basis for speaking of strategy in conventional terms. The Great Commission defines how the church is to understand itself in relation to the world: the church is to be a sign of God's reign and a witness to the world of the full scope of God's redemptive purpose in history. Yet it does not instruct the church concerning strategy and tactics for fulfilling this mandate.

In addition to the overarching theological strategy noted above, an implicit ecclesial strategy can be found in Acts 11:19-26 and 13:1-3. The first passage is remarkable for the fact that it can report that "a great number" and "a large company" had "turned to the Lord," but there is no honor roll informing us of the leaders who masterminded this astonishing result. In response to the martyrdom of Stephen and the persecution of the church that ensued in Jerusalem, believers had scattered to places like Antioch, imbued with a passion to tell the news about Jesus Christ. This apparently resulted in growth from the grassroots by a process of cell division. The Holy Spirit inspired these disciples to tell family, friends, and neighbors of their faith so that the church grew.

Acts 13:1-3 introduces a contrasting pattern. The Holy Spirit instructs the Antiochene church to "set apart" two leaders who will lead the church in cross-cultural mission. Paul subsequently describes his apostolic calling as being directed to "the Gentiles" (Acts 15:12) in order "to bring about the obedience of faith . . . among all the nations" (Rom 1:5).

These strategies arise out of a pneumatically empowered ecclesiology. The two patterns are complementary; neither is complete without the other. In the recorded history of the church the second claims the bulk of attention—focused as it is on a select group of intrepid figures undertaking daring expeditions and crossing geographical and cultural boundaries. But there are periods in the history of the church when the spread of the faith depended entirely on the unsung faithfulness of ordinary folk doing what the first believers at Antioch had done. Even in periods such as the nineteenth century, when commitment to cross-cultural mission was renewed and missionaries went "to the ends of the earth," much of the work on the ground was done by local evangelists, catechists, and lay people speaking and acting the gospel.

By the late fourth century A.D. the position of the church in society had undergone important changes. It had been transformed from a marginalized and persecuted minority into the religion favored by the state. With this had come a new understanding of the nature of the church. Instead of taking the incarnation and the cross as the model for strategizing, the church now looked to the political-military realm. And the nature of mission changed accordingly. It was as though the church presumed to take the Holy Spirit captive. The effects of this shift are well illustrated by the way Charlemagne went about conquering and Christianizing the peoples of Europe, drawing his inspiration from Augustine's *De Civitate Dei* (Latourette 1953, 355; 1970, 2:102f.). The forced conversion of the peoples of Europe posed no difficulties for Charlemagne and other so-called Christian rulers. Their strategy was dictated by the military model. This model continued to exert pervasive influence on strategic thinking in Christendom.[5]

THE QUEST FOR STRATEGY IN MODERN MISSIONS

The influence of modernity on Christian missions is evident in the emphasis given to strategies and methods. Missions were largely in the hands of voluntary societies that had to raise funds and recruit workers from a committed but limited constituency. The pressure to meet program needs was constant. Wise and careful strategy was seen as the way to ensure program effectiveness, and Enlightenment concepts of rationality were early applied to program development and administration. Economy and efficiency had to be emphasized. The goal was to ensure maximum return on resources invested.

William Carey and Rufus Anderson

An early example of the quest for effective mission strategy is adumbrated in the title of William Carey's 1792 manifesto, *An Enquiry into the Obligation of Christians to Use Means for the Conversion of the Heathen* (Carey 1891). Carey sought to impress upon the Christian public its duty to marshal the resources necessary to fulfill "the Commission given by our Lord." He did this, in part, by working out an empirical basis for prosecuting the task and then proposing such practical steps as the founding of missionary societies.

A generation later, in 1837, Rufus Anderson, secretary of the American Board of Commissioners for Foreign Missions (ABCFM), preached a sermon entitled "The Time for the World's Conversion Come" (Beaver 1967, 59-70). Anderson advanced a threefold argument as to why this was now "the fullness of the time" of the Holy Spirit as viewed in the epochs of biblical prophecy. He asserted that only now was the way open for the "universal propagation of the gospel" in terms of three propositions. (1) Although Christians in previous epochs were faithful in their witness, they lacked the necessary knowledge and means to evan-

---

[5] Richard V. Pierard has analyzed how contemporary evangelical mission strategy draws freely on military metaphors (1990).

gelize all nations. (2) Only now, insisted Anderson, were the "evangelical churches of Christendom" organized "with a view to the conversion of the world." (3) Not until the nineteenth century, he argued, did the churches have "a commanding system of missions abroad, designed expressly for the conversion of the world." Lurking behind Anderson's argument are important cultural assumptions.

Between the publication of Carey's *Enquiry* in 1792 and Anderson's sermon in 1837, several proposals had already been made for comprehensive world evangelization, including two schemes by missionaries of Anderson's own ABCFM in 1818 and 1836. Missionaries Gordon Hall and Samuel Newell, working in India's Bombay area, proposed in 1818 that the world be evangelized by the sending of thirty thousand Protestant missionaries from the West to the rest of the world within the next twenty-one years. These missionaries were to be supported with gifts averaging four dollars per Protestant and Anglican communicant. In 1837 the ABCFM passed a resolution at its annual meeting—echoing the 1836 appeal from its Sandwich Islands missionaries—proposing a worldwide evangelization effort.

The Role of Missionary Conferences

During the first several decades of the modern missions movement, strategy was formulated largely by missionary societies within their own sphere of work. The main vehicle for sharing with other agencies and their missionaries was the missions magazines most societies published.

In 1854 an important new instrument for developing mission strategy was introduced. That year the famed Scottish missionary to India, Alexander Duff, visited North America and made a triumphal procession through several regions of the United States and Canada. His visit culminated in the convening of the Union Missionary Convention in New York City, November 4-5, 1854. Duff dominated the proceedings, which were organized around eight topics (*Union Missionary Convention* 1854; *Ecumenical Missionary Conference* 1900, 1:19-23). This first effort was modest compared to later efforts, but it was a model for future gatherings. The first question was: To what extent are we authorized by the Word of God to expect the conversion of the world to Christ? A second group of questions dealt with strategy. The third set centered on issues of cultivating support for missions in the congregations.

In the following years missionary conferences became a standard part of the missions system. These consisted of several kinds: (1) national gatherings, such as the Union Missionary Convention, of mission boards, their staffs, pastors, and missions supporters; (2) major field conferences convened by a board with its missionary staff (as Rufus Anderson and A. C. Thompson did in India and Ceylon, 1854-56); (3) ecumenical and international conferences, such as that held in London in 1888 and, recently, Lausanne II in Manila in 1989; and (4) a conference of all missions working in a particular country, such as those held in China in 1877, 1906, and 1926.

Comparing the proceedings of these early conferences with those of a century later, one notes the similarity in pattern. To be sure, preparation for conferences has become more elaborate, and the use of statistical surveys and data has increased in sophistication. The 1974 Lausanne Congress gave high priority to strategizing world evangelization. Probably the most significant conceptual contribution to missionary strategy in the twentieth century is the notion of "hidden" or "unreached" people groups introduced at the Lausanne Congress and since promoted worldwide (Winter 1984, 17-60). But not all observers have been comfortable with the Lausanne emphasis and ethos. In evaluating the congress Charles E. Van Engen noted that "the mood seemed to be one of pragmatism: 'anything goes—if it works.' The fact that World Vision's highly technological MARC Center was a major consultant to the congress was a signal that the evangelicals were all moving into hi-tech culture" (Van Engen 1990, 222). To be sure, not all conferences throughout these years have had the same balance, but strategy has been a central concern.

As was true a century ago, the approaching end of the twentieth century, which also coincides with the end of another millennium since Jesus Christ, has given rise to an outpouring of proposals for world evangelization at the rate of one new plan per week. Some of these plans draw their inspiration from special views of biblical prophecy, while others trumpet the triumphalist spirit of the High Imperial period of a century ago. Still other plans are based on the traditional concern of missionary agencies to continue evangelizing the world.

According to David Barrett and James Reapsome, however, the effort is "in a mess" (1988, 65). Surveying the whole of Christian history Barrett and Reapsome identify 788 separate plans that have been produced since the time of Jesus. They insist: "We have not obeyed the Commission in the past; we are not obeying it in the present; we are not, on present trends, likely to obey it in the future; we are nowhere near target for fulfilling it by A.D. 2000" (65). In spite of such strictures, plans and proposals continue to be spawned. Two themes predominate: (1) we are in a "countdown," and (2) the world can be evangelized by the end of the twentieth century. Neither notion can be supported from scripture. Barrett and Reapsome react ambivalently toward what they call "a global evangelization movement." On the one hand, they are critical of many of these plans, both past and present; still, they believe it is possible to produce a global strategy, including a centrally monitored "master global plan," which would enable "fulfilling the Great Commission by the year 2000" (64).

COUNTERVAILING CURRENTS

There have long been countervailing views with regard to strategy of mission. One of the most vigorous critics of the missions system during the past century was Roland Allen. Allen was the gadfly of missions, and his criticisms were not welcomed by the mainstream. But his influence has been felt widely because of the way the fledgling Pentecostal missions movement adopted key Allen ideas. Allen took aim at modern missions for being overly institutionalized. He jibed at missions for being preoccupied with "activities" while lacking "manifestations of the Spirit." Always at the heart of Allen's concern was the inevitable (negative) impact of the system on the new church. "The spiritual force, the Holy Ghost," argued Allen, "will be manifested to the people of any country to which we go when they see that spirit ministered by us manifested in the spontaneous activity of their own countrymen" (Allen 1960, 112). He judged the modern missions system to be a blunt instrument.

The father of German missiology, Gustav Warneck, was also widely known for his criticism of what he considered the misguided Anglo-American preoccupation with closely calculated plans and slogans. He called the SVM slogan— The Evangelization of the World in This Generation—dangerous. "The mission command bids us 'go' into all the world, not 'fly,'" declared Warneck to the Ecumenical Missionary Conference in 1900. He referred sarcastically to the watchword as the "catchword" and rejected all attempts to "specify a time within which the evangelization of the world is to be completed" (*Ecumenical Missionary Conference* 1900, 1:290).

A particularly interesting critic of conventional views of mission strategy was J. H. Oldham. He occupied a central role in the World Missionary Conference at Edinburgh in 1910; was founding editor in 1912 of the *International Review of Missions;* and a close associate of figures like John R. Mott, a leading mission strategist in the modern period. Although he does not acknowledge any indebtedness to Roland Allen, Oldham makes some of the same points. In *The World and the Gospel* Oldham argues: "It has often been taken for granted that the aim of foreign missions is to preach the Gospel to the whole world. The bringing of the Gospel within the reach of all mankind is the goal towards which the Church must continually strive with all its might. But it is not the immediate aim of foreign missions, because it is something which foreign missions can never accomplish" (1916, 139). In words that combine elements of Warneck and Allen, Oldham said, "The life of the spirit cannot be measured or described in terms of arithmetic." He emphasized the importance of both the Spirit and the local church in furthering world evangelization without devaluing the role of the missionary. "The aim, then, of foreign missionary work is to plant the Church of Christ in every part of the non-Christian world as a means to its evangelization" (ibid., 141).

In a wide-ranging analysis of how North American Protestants have created mission strategy in the twentieth century, Robert T. Coote faults the present generation of strategists for being guided more by "management by objectives" than by the Holy Spirit and devising grandiose plans that are bound to fail. He objects to those who presume to know precisely the mind and timetable of God. Coote's counsels of caution and humility are timely (Coote 1986).

THE STRATEGIC CHALLENGE

Joseph T. Bayly's *The Gospel Blimp* (1960) is a satire on overweening confidence in technology as a means of evangelization. The church in the West is tempted by technique—the ultimate manifestation of modernity. The temptation is to view technique itself as gospel. Strategy-as-technique is thus confused with the message. It is of urgent necessity that mission strategy and method be subjected to theological critique.

First, more than we may realize, our culture is dominated by the "rationality" of the scientific method. This is powerful, but it is also a source of alienation. The missionary who is surrounded with sophisticated technological apparatus can be formidable vis-à-vis people who live in poverty. Mission strategy becomes an extension of that powerful system in a way that is contrary to the vulnerability of the cross. Second, the final years of the 1980s were full of surprises. The breakdown of totalitarian systems caught many off guard. There is growing evidence that the Christian faith is most vital, both in quantity and quality, in those countries and regions where martyrdom has been visited on the church. Conversely, the faith has been coopted by culture and has become flaccid in those parts of the world where there has been maximum freedom and affluence.

Strategic thinking that is theologically informed and critiqued will take its cues from the fivefold framework presented above: God's redemptive mission as the source; Jesus Christ, who embodied fully God's intention in mission; the Holy Spirit, who is the source of power; the church as God's instrument in mission; and human culture as the medium through which all communication of the gospel must be made. Two pitfalls must be avoided if our strategizing is to be faithful to the gospel. First, we are urged to make one or another emphasis the key to strategy: option for the poor, dialogue, pluralism, evangelism, development. Each one contains an important dimension but is itself only partial. Only when these dimensions are placed within the messianic strategy outlined above can they be saved from distortion. Second, when we uncritically appropriate strategies from sociopolitical models around us, we risk denaturing the gospel by choosing means inconsistent with the goal of mission. The Christ-event holds before us constantly the cross as the fundamental strategy by which all other strategies must be judged.

WHAT THEN SHALL WE SAY ABOUT MISSION STRATEGY?

In the world the Christian mission is subject both to the divine imperative and the sociohistorical forces that give it context. As we approach the end of the twentieth century, that context is again undergoing fundamental shifts. The bipolar world of the past forty-five years has disintegrated with the collapse of the old structures of much of the Soviet bloc. At the same time, new centers of economic and political influence have emerged, with still others in the making. In terms of the Christian church, for more than a decade we have been reflecting on the fact that its center of gravity—measured in membership—has shifted from the West to the rest of the world. However, the church in the West continues to control the bulk of financial and institutional resources.

We do not yet clearly discern the direction Christian mission will go in the next generation. We can, however, make several observations as to the terms and conditions with which we will be working. (1) The ideal relationship for the world Christian community is one of interdependence with a recognized system for shared decision-making and resource allocation. Until that is resolved there will continue to be tensions and resource imbalances. (2) The churches in Africa, Asia, and Latin America presently demonstrate greater vitality and growing missionary commitment, but they tend to be resource poor. This suggests that the ecclesial—rather than the cross-cultural—strategy will predominate over the next couple of decades. (3) The experience of the suffering church since World War I holds important insights concerning the role of the Holy Spirit in the mission of the church and a missionary ecclesiology. Gleaning such insights will be foundational to a theologically informed missiology.

PART THREE

THE FRONTIER OF
CONTEMPORARY CULTURE

If *frontier* means "a place where critical engagement is being staged," then contemporary culture is a frontier. Modern Western culture developed in Europe, whose culture had been influenced by the Judeo-Christian tradition. Important scientific discoveries had been made long before in other cultures. But these discoveries had not been the basis for wider cultural and intellectual development. What has happened in the West in terms of scientific and technological development has no precedent. Some historians have said that the Judeo-Christian tradition provided the oxygen that fed the flame of modernity.

The coming of the Enlightenment in the seventeenth century put church and religion on the defensive. Religion was increasingly excluded from public life, except for ceremonial blessing of the civil order, and consigned to the private sphere. The church was treated as irrelevant to the culture.

Some three hundred years after the rise of the Enlightenment, it is possible to take stock of its major contributions and fundamental flaws. Clearly, the confidence Enlightenment philosophers had in the self-sufficiency of human rationality has proved to be misplaced. Human nature is demonstrably as perverse in "enlightened" culture as in any other.

Contemporary culture challenges the church with a new set of questions. This is a culture that has had a long and intimate relationship with Christianity, but today large numbers of Western peoples are several generations removed from any vital contact with the Christian heritage and indeed many feel hostile to religion. Among contemporary people are many who are anti-religion and anti-church. Their lives are controlled by the culture of consumerism, which draws its inspiration from hedonism.

The church is being called to rid itself of timeworn habits of thought and engage in the demanding work of rethinking its relationship to contemporary culture through the lens of mission.

9

The Church and Contemporary Culture

No question is more urgent for the church in the West as it faces the twenty-first century than how it conceives its relationship to the world. The question is not new. It has been the subject of ongoing debate. The urgency arises from the fact that the message of the church has increasingly lost credibility in that part of the world that has been its "homeland" for some fifteen hundred years. Today it finds itself in an increasingly marginal position.

The church in the West is the church of Christendom, a church without a clear sense of mission in relation to its culture. But a church without mission is an anomaly, a caricature of what it was intended to be. Both scripture and the cross-cultural missionary movement of the past several centuries offer clear guidance concerning the relationship the church ought to have to culture.

In 1909 the Rev. Walter Hobhouse, honorary canon and chancellor of Birmingham Cathedral, former fellow of Hertford College and tutor of Christ Church, Oxford delivered the Bampton Lectures. Hobhouse's theme was *The Church and the World in Idea and History.* In the preface to the published lectures he disclosed his motive for selecting this topic in full knowledge that his treatment of it would be "distasteful" to many in the Church of England while appealing chiefly to "Presbyterians or Free Churchmen":

> Long ago I came to believe that the great change in the relations between the Church and the World which began with the conversion of Constantine is not only a decisive turning point in Church history, but is also the key to many of the practical difficulties of the present day, and that the Church of the future is destined more and more to return to a condition of things somewhat like that which prevailed in the Ante-Nicene Church; that is to say, that instead of pretending to be co-extensive with the World, it will confess itself the Church of a minority, will accept a position involving a more conscious antagonism with the World, and will, in return, regain in some measure its former coherence (Hobhouse 1911, xix).

First published in the *International Bulletin of Missionary Research* 15:3 (July 1991). Revised for publication in this volume.

Hobhouse identified several substantive themes with which he would grapple. The main lines of Hobhouse's argument are as follows:

1. The character of the church was fundamentally altered as a result of the emergence of Constantinianism.[1] The church was now based on coercion rather than a voluntary response to God's grace. This was in conflict with what Hobhouse called the "Divine Method" with regard to humankind: "God always respects human freedom, both in the sphere of moral action and in the sphere of intellectual belief. There is no coercion of human will; there is freedom to sin. There is no coercion of human belief; there is freedom to deny God" (Hobhouse 1911, 13). This entailed the following consequences.

2. The Constantinian era signaled a redefinition of the church-world relationship. Christ founded a visible and clearly defined group to be his body in the world. "This Divine Society He represented as being separate from, and in some sense antagonistic to, the World" (ibid., 15). Thus the clear distinction between church and world was erased by the Constantinian process, and the primal tension between the two was lost. The Christian's primary allegiance to Jesus Christ was compromised and made relative to Caesar.

3. The church lost its sense of mission to the world. Essentially initiative passed to the state, and the church became the religious institution of society. Christendom led to the domestication—the taming—of the church. Christendom resulted in the eclipse of mission as understood by the primitive church.

4. The church forfeited its integrity as the body of Christ. It now functioned as an arm of the state in contributing to the maintenance of the sociopolitical order. Surveying the successive periods of church history, Hobhouse sought to demonstrate that the logical outcome of Christendom was a church that cannot command the deep loyalty of the membership, because membership was no longer a matter of voluntary commitment. He saw the church in 1909 as essentially deformed, afflicted by nominality, and fated to suffer continued decline.

5. Hobhouse argued that now "the Church should recognize more and more that she is in reality a missionary Church, not only in heathen lands and among races which we are pleased to call 'inferior,' but in every country; and that there is much which she might learn from the methods of the Mission Fields" (ibid., 320). He suggested that the most effective Christian work being done in the England of 1909 was that carried on as intentional mission. There were especially urgent needs in the cities where, citing words of Archbishop Lang, people "have not fallen from the Church, for they were never within it" (ibid., 323).

The Hobhouse project is useful in terms of the way he frames certain fundamental issues. His critique was shaped by the established church of which he was a part nearly a century ago. Ecclesiastical arrangements are important, but the issue is deeper than the question of whether or not a church is formally recognized as an "established church." Christendom has cast a long shadow over

---

[1] The reference to Constantine need not detain us. Constantine as such is not under discussion. He is used as a symbol of a period of transition.

all Christians in the West that we have not yet dispelled.[2] All churches in the
West are heirs, to one degree or another, of a Christendom understanding of the
church. This is the basic vision of the church that missionaries from the West
took with them to other parts of the world. And it is precisely the Christendom
spirit and character of the church that have proved to be so difficult to indigenize
in other cultures.[3]

The argument I wish to make here is threefold: (1) that we need to reclaim a
biblically informed metaphor for the church-world relationship; (2) that we consider "missionary encounter" as the normative description of the role of the church
in relation to the world; and (3) that we would do well to appropriate learnings
from the substantial experience in cross-cultural missions of the past two hundred years, for this can furnish clues as to what "missionary encounter" would
mean for the future of the church in the West.

A BIBLICAL METAPHOR

The Church in the West is still captive to the Christendom understanding of
the church. This fact frustrates efforts to visualize what an alternative model for
the church-world relationship should be and what this means for the mission of
the church—not cross-culturally but within the cultural milieu where the church
has been at home for some fifteen hundred years.

The biblical drama is about a cosmic struggle. We describe it in terms of
opposites: holiness/sinfulness; good/evil; life/death; salvation/damnation; kingdom of God/kingdom of Satan; this world/the world to come, and so on. The
Bible leaves us in no doubt: the world is at enmity with God; the powers are
rebellious. But we may not forget that both the world and the church belong to
Jesus Christ because "all things were made through him" (Jn 1:3). Yet only the
church, as the people of God, acknowledges God's sovereignty. The biblical
drama is driven forward by the promise and the vision that "the kingdom of this
world has become the kingdom of our Lord and of his Messiah, and he will reign
forever and ever" (Rv 11:15).

Paul Minear has pointed out it is wrong to distinguish between church and
world in terms of separate headships, for there is only one head, Jesus Christ.
That headship has been disclosed to his body through the death and resurrection
of Jesus Christ, and consequently, the church is mandated to proclaim Christ's
lordship over all. The boundary between the church and the world is marked by
the cross. For the people of God it signals God's victory; for the world it is a sign
of scandal and folly. "But," says Minear, "as boundary the cross is also a bridge

---

[2] See Stephen Neill (1968, 75ff.), for an incisive description of the way sociopolitical
influences shape the church's self-understanding.

[3] The point is that Christendom as a specific religio-cultural phenomenon was ultimately non-indigenizable. This must not be confused with the universal temptation facing the church to accept a position of power and prestige in a society, thereby falling into
a pattern similar to historic Christendom.

for constant two-way traffic. Whatever the distance between church and world, this distance must and can be crossed by the church because it has already been crossed by its head" (Minear 1960, 243). As the first fruit of the resurrection, the church is confident that this same power is available to all. But it always lives and bears witness under the sign of the cross.

Starting with Abraham in the Old Testament and continuing in the New Testament with the apostle Peter, a primary metaphor for describing the status of the people of God in the world is that of "resident alien" or variants of that phrase. When Sarah died at Hebron, Abraham appealed to the Hittites to grant him a burial plot because "I am a stranger and an alien residing among you" (Gn 23:4a). When the aged Jacob met Pharaoh in Egypt he described himself in terms of his "sojourning" (Gn 47:9). Psalm 105:23 remarks that "Jacob lived as an alien in the land of Ham." The book of Hebrews uses the same language in describing the "faithful": "All of these died in faith, without having received the promises, but from a distance they saw and greeted them. They confessed that they were strangers and foreigners on the earth" (11:13). At the end of Hebrews Jesus is linked with this line: "Jesus also suffered outside the city gate in order to sanctify the people by his own blood. Let us go to him outside the camp and bear the abuse he endured. For here we have no lasting city, but we are looking for the city that is to come" (13:12-14). This latter verse resonates strongly with Philippians 3:20: "For our citizenship is in heaven." The apostle Peter, after describing the special vocation and "set apartness" of the people of God, appeals to them "as aliens and exiles" to live a life of holiness and thus commend God to the world (1 Pt 2:9-12). Throughout, the emphasis is not on going but on waiting. The people of God are to wait faithfully for the "fulfillment of the promise" (Heb 6:12, 15; 9:28; 10:23-25; Ps 37:3-9; cf. Phil 3:20). This stance is maintained in the second-century Epistle to Diognetus:

> Christians dwell in their native cities, yet as sojourners; they share in everything as citizens, and endure all things as aliens: every foreign country is to them a fatherland, and every fatherland a foreign soil. . . . They live in the flesh, but not according to the flesh. They pass their time on earth, but exercise their citizenship in heaven. They obey the enacted laws, and by their private lives they overcome the laws. They love all men, and are persecuted of all men. They are unknown, and yet condemned; they are put to death, and yet raised to life. They are beggars, and yet make many rich; they lack all things, and yet abound in all things. . . . In a word, what the soul is in the body, that are Christians in the World (Hobhouse 1911, 80).

This passage compels our attention because of the remarkable self-awareness that characterized the relationship between the Christian and the world. There is no hint here of withdrawal from the world. Rather, the picture is that of critical engagement. The model of the resident alien does not focus on the inward life of the disciple. This is no call to quietism. Instead, it keeps firmly in view the tension between God and the world and the status of the people of God in light of that tension. If the image of resident alien focuses on that tension, there can be neither retreat into a ghetto nor uncritical absorption into the world. Any model predicated on a tension is bound to contain surprises and instabilities. No sociopolitical system can ever adequately and fully embody the new order of God's reign. But the resident alien belongs to a tradition that always views history through the "eyes of faith" while watching and waiting for the full disclosure of the kingdom. In the meanwhile the resident alien is continually pointing to the signs of God's coming and living out concretely God's reign as a counter-demonstration of what the world would be were it, too, submitted to God's will.

MISSIONARY ENCOUNTER

Johannes Blauw asserted that "mission is a summons to the lordship of Christ" (Blauw 1962, 84). Mission is an act of discipleship, and discipleship leads to missionary obedience. In *Christ the Meaning of History*, Hendrikus Berkhof devotes a chapter to "the missionary endeavor as a history-making force" (Berkhof 1966). Mission is integral to God's plan for the salvation of the world, and the election of the people of God has no purpose apart from mission. I want to suggest that the goal of authentic missionary encounter with any culture always must be to bring the life-giving power of God to bear against the power of death.

In the previous section we considered how to visualize the relationship between church and world, especially with respect to the way a Christian understands that relationship and its implications for discipleship. Now we turn to an examination of the process by which that relationship is carried out. We are trying to rethink the role of the church in the world in a way that overcomes the problems created by the long history of Christendom. Christendom insisted that an entire population or society was Christian. No place was given to mission.[4] "Christianization" was a one-time step. Thereafter, the essential task was to maintain this religio-political status quo. To speak of mission would be to question the status quo. This was as much a political matter as it was religious. Religiously, Christendom was maintained through a sacerdotal-sacramental system that was subject to various abuses. From time to time there were appeals for reform and renewal of the church. Important as these reforms were, they largely failed to challenge and overcome Christendom's deeply non-missionary understanding of the church. Consequently, even in Reformation churches individuals who agitated in support of missions—from the sixteenth century onward—typically found themselves on the margins of church life. The solution to this was to encourage the formation of missionary societies, patterned after the trading companies and newly emerging voluntary societies. This provided an outlet for a growing number of people committed to missions to become involved, either as missionaries or as supporters at home.

---

[4] For a discussion of the way evangelism has been understood in Christendom in the modern period, see Shenk 1995, chap. 3.

Two things should be noted, however. First, mission was defined from the beginning as that which took place in lands outside of Christendom. Second, it was an extra-ecclesial activity. This arrangement, in turn, has had two further consequences. First, it helped insulate the churches of Christendom from the challenge that might have come to them out of this involvement in missionary work and that could have stimulated fundamental ecclesial reform. Second, the understanding of church that missionaries took with them overseas inevitably combined Christendom understandings of the church with missionary society structures.

By the beginning of the twentieth century it was evident that the churches in Christendom were in difficulty. Hobhouse was one among many others who read the situation correctly. Christendom for some fourteen centuries had promoted the idea that the church existed as an institution of society. It had lost any awareness of itself as essentially a missionary body.

During the twentieth century we have witnessed massive losses in the numbers of people in Christendom who identify with the church. Conversely, it is precisely in those parts of the world where Christian missions have been active these past two centuries that the church has grown, often under highly adverse circumstances, such as in socialist countries. In such situations to be a Christian is costly. Faith can be maintained only if there is clarity concerning who commands the Christian's ultimate allegiance.

In contradistinction to the Christendom understanding, I propose that we urgently need to recover a vision of the church as being in missionary encounter with the world. Such a stance will mean that the church must confront in the name of Christ those elemental forces in society that are destroying life, for these forces are in opposition to the lordship of Jesus Christ.

Every culture is under the sway of controlling myths that command the loyalties of people—even though these myths are instruments of death. The church is called to unmask these powers and expose them for what they are. Walter Wink has pointed out how the ancient Babylonian creation myth found in the Enuma Elish has continually reappeared in human history in a variety of guises (Wink 1993, 18-21, 35). Wink notes the way this creation myth—based on violence and the doctrine of "might makes right"—is the pervasive message being purveyed through children's cartoons on television today. Wink cites a survey conducted by *U.S. News and World Report* that found that American children will have watched thirty-six thousand hours of television by their mid-teens (ibid., 23 n.33). In response we must ask: How do we expect the church to make a compelling claim on a young person's life based on a few hours of catechism prior to confirmation when he or she has been thoroughly catechized by the TV medium over such a long and formative period?

This mythic structure of violence undergirds many other areas of our culture, including the way governments go about making and interpreting foreign policy. It is within this cultural circumstance that we must define the church's missionary responsibility. "The result of missionary proclamation," says Hendrikus Berkhof, "is the realization throughout the whole earth of the analogy of the cross and resurrection of the Christ event" (1966, 109). It is in the crucified and resurrected Lord that history is made transparent in its depths. In that perspective no human society may be exempted from missionary encounter; we must not succumb to the temptation to think that at some point a culture is "fully evangelized." Scripture gives us no warrant to think in such terms.

This suggests that the church needs to be reformed along two lines. On the one hand, as I have been arguing, we need reform ecclesiologically and ethically. The impact of Christendom, even on so-called free or nonconformist denominations, has been such as to undermine the integrity of the church. The typical congregation is preoccupied with its own welfare and maintenance rather than its mission to the world. Effectively, it has lost its capacity even to discern that it has such a mission.

On the other hand, there is need for missiological reform. By that I mean that we should seek to inculcate the sense that each congregation is a primary arena for missionary encounter in any given community. At first this may sound like a contradiction. I have criticized the widespread preoccupation congregations have with their internal life, and yet I have called the congregation the primary arena for missionary encounter. The contradiction is real, but it is to be found at another point than the one our reflexes have taught us to look for. The contradiction is in the Christendom model of church that has effectively separated the two elements our Lord held together and which the early Christian community understood to be at the heart of the Christian calling. The ecclesiological/ethical must not be separated from the missiological; the one should inform the other.

Surely, the only way any significant reform in a congregation's outlook will come about is if it rediscovers the meaning of the nature of the church. The church is not another form of society or a social subunit. Emil Brunner described the unprecedented character of the church forcefully: "Church is a community which is based on that Word of God which is God's personal deed, and that personal deed of God which is His Word" (Brunner 1931, 108). Communication and action cannot be separated. God's Word creates the community in order that the community might communicate God's Word. "Mission work does not arise from any arrogance in the Christian Church," argued Brunner; "mission is its cause and its life. The church exists by mission, just as fire exists by burning" (ibid.). A properly functioning church is one that is constantly working out its existence through missionary encounter with the world. *Church* without *mission* is a contradiction in terms.

CROSS-CULTURAL LESSONS

In recent years Andrew F. Walls has advanced the thesis that the Christian faith has been saved repeatedly in nearly two thousand years of history by moving from an established heartland to a new environment. The process of cross-cultural transmission has been critical to the survival of the faith (Walls 1990b).

This insight is valuable as we take stock of the remnants of Christendom. The modern mission movement emerged around 1800 and may be viewed as the last grand flourish of Christendom. Indeed, it can be shown that the modern mission movement was both "a powerful last thrust of Christendom and an important instrument in bringing about the dissolution of historical Christendom" (page 142, below). In spite of heroic efforts on the part of many dedicated individuals, Christendom proved to be nonexportable in the modern period. The world was changing; new ideas of democracy and human dignity were in the air. Christendom could only be implanted in other cultures with tactics that violated the integrity of those cultures. As the church began to grow in other soils, Christendom as a religio-political synthesis was increasingly rejected. This act of disencumbering the church of historical contradictions, accretions, and distortions associated with Christendom may be necessary to the recovery of faith in the West itself. Christendom defined mission out of existence in the West. Until the church in the West recovers a full sense of church-as-mission—as an inseparable entity— there will be no genuine missionary encounter.

It is with the promise of discovering new insights that we now turn to the cross-cultural mission of these past two centuries with a view to asking what we can learn that will be useful to the renewal of the church in the West. Four themes are pertinent.

1. The Sense of Frontier

In recent years people become uneasy when one speaks about frontier in relation to mission. *Frontier* conjures up ideas about powerful Western nations carving up the territories and violating the cultures of helpless and weaker peoples of Latin America, Asia, and Africa. It is understandable that we wish to close that chapter. It is true that the idea of a geographical frontier has played an important role in modern mission history. It was the basis of appeal for missionary recruits. Even today it remains an important part of missionary rhetoric in some circles.

Like other terms that have become corrupted through inappropriate use, *frontier* carries some negative connotations. Yet we continue to need it. For one thing, the term conveys other meanings than the geographical one. Many missiologists, for example, have been emphasizing the importance of sociological frontiers such as rural/urban, or groups identified along ethnic lines (associated with the "hidden" or "unreached peoples" groups). Another frontier is the religious one. All peoples of the world can be classified in terms of their religious allegiances, including those who self-consciously declare themselves to be atheists. We know, for example, that the vast majority of all people won to the Christian faith since the time of Christ have come from a primal or traditional religious background, and relatively few from the major world religions. It has long been understood that the training and preparation of a missionary to work in a Muslim society calls for something quite different from what is required to train someone to serve a preliterate, small-scale ethnic group. In either case special attention must be paid to the religious frontier, for religion may well be the single most important fact.

The notion of frontier also applies when we attempt to discern where the Spirit of God is leading the church in witness. Consider, for example, Nepal in the twentieth century. An entire generation of Nepali Christians lived in diaspora, and missionaries waited in faith for the day when the door to the country would be opened. They busied themselves with useful activities in anticipation of the time when they would be allowed to enter the country. Some worked and waited in faith near the border between Nepal and its neighboring countries as long as thirty-five years. Many of this generation did not live to enter Nepal when the door was opened in 1954. But their years of active preparation paved the way for the next generation. Who would doubt that the first generation read correctly the mind of the Spirit and acted faithfully in taking those first steps on a new frontier? The challenge of the frontier is as relevant in the post-Christendom West as anywhere in the world.

2. The Objective Study of Culture

Charles R. Taber (1991) has traced how we have moved from a precritical to a formal and critical understanding of culture. This is a fairly recent development. Until the nineteenth century the vast majority of missionaries—to which there were the heroic exceptions, of course—understood mission as a straightforward process of replicating Christendom in other cultures.

In the West, where there has been a coming together in the twentieth century of peoples from all parts of the world, we are faced with a new degree of cultural pluralism. To take culture seriously for the sake of the gospel will demand a new depth of cultural sensitivity not required in Christendom.

It has long been expected of missionaries working cross-culturally that they would acquire basic training in the human sciences in order to have a grasp of culture as a concept and as a functioning system. It was further assumed that this training would be extended to include in-depth study of the particular culture to which the missionary went in order to understand the worldview and value system. Such specialized training included intensive study of the language.

Finally, the objective study of another culture enables one to be self-critical by heightening awareness of the peculiarities of one's own culture and the relative importance of all cultures. In other words, the study of culture enables the missionary to overcome ethnocentrism through greater self-understanding coupled with appreciation of the other culture. The typical metropolitan area in the West today is a veritable United Nations in microcosm. A church fully alive to the missionary encounter with culture must take seriously the need for thorough and sensitive training in cultural understanding wherever the church is located, but especially when seeking to relate to neighbors who are in physical proximity but culturally distant.

3. Learning to "Read" Culture

The cross-cultural missionary long ago learned to "read" a culture in terms of its felt needs. In other words, it was evident that it is the duty of missionaries to listen deeply and compassionately to the people to whom they wish to relate rather than prejudging them and their situation.

Because of the complexity of cross-cultural communication, it was assumed that a special effort must be made to find the "key" or appropriate cultural analogy by which the gospel can be made understandable. It is becoming increasingly clear that the same requirement is being made of the church in the West. For example, there are large groups of people throughout the West who have had no direct contact with the church or the Christian scriptures for several generations. Contemporary discourse is increasingly bereft of traditional religious—that is, Christian—vocabulary. If the church wishes to communicate with such peoples, it cannot assume that religious language will be understood. Indeed, religious language may form an impenetrable barrier.

Every culture continually expresses its hungers, hurts, aspirations, and sicknesses in a multitude of ways—through song, art, poetry, literature, the myths that control a society, and the way people respond to crises, especially death. What accounts for the escalating violence—both in terms of crimes committed and vicariously experienced through the media, above all television—and the often remarked upon lack of hope in the West? The church that believes that its only raison d'etre is to be in missionary encounter with its culture will not avoid the question.

4. Critical Syncretism

Syncretism has been a long-standing missionary concern. This is understandable, for missionaries were encountering exotic cultures and trying to communicate in strange languages. They learned early that terms important to the Christian faith either had no parallel in the other language or meant something quite different. They had to make many choices in working out a presentation of the gospel that was culturally and linguistically understandable and yet faithful to what they understood it to be. Missionaries continually walked a tightrope between adaptation to culture and rejection of those features that could not be reconciled with the gospel. An uncritical accommodation led to syncretism that diluted or denatured the gospel, while failure to adapt would have meant that the gospel remained foreign and inaccessible.

What is now recognized is that long before missionaries confronted the question of syncretism in non-Western cultures, syncretism was a present reality for the church in the West. The fact that for so long it was not acknowledged that syncretism was a present danger for the Western church is proof positive that the church had lost its missionary consciousness. The church that is aware of being in missionary encounter with its culture is continually wrestling with the issues syncretism poses. There can be no escape. Choices must be made continually. The church enters a danger zone when it is no longer self-consciously critical of its relation to culture and is no longer asking what is the path of faithful discipleship. The church must always adapt to its culture in such a way that it lives and communicates the gospel credibly. That is constructive syncretism. If the church becomes merely the religious reflection of its culture, it has sold its birthright.

That is destructive syncretism. The diverse cross-cultural experience of the past several centuries is an important resource in training missiologists to understand contemporary culture in relation to the gospel.

CONCLUSION

A primary metaphor the Bible uses to describe the relation of church to world is that of the *resident alien,* an image that is used in crucial passages in Old and New Testaments. Some see in this term a license to the church to turn its back on society. Others read it as giving the church too little leverage in society.

To be a resident alien is to exist in missionary encounter with the world. To ask the question most simply and directly: What better position or greater power could the church wish for? The earliest Christians, armed only with the gospel and witnessing in the power of the Holy Spirit, were perceived as people who "turned the world upside down" (Acts 17:6). They succeeded in raising the most fundamental questions and offering liberation from the "powers." Under the thrall of Christendom, modern Christians have come to disbelieve the power of the gospel. They continue to be tempted by the illusion that to be effective in society the church must resort to the conventional exercise of political, social, and economic power. Such doctrine can only sound strange to many Christians who in the twentieth century have kept the faith burning brightly under exceedingly straitened circumstances.

A resident alien lives in an inescapable tension with the sociopolitical order. Rather than focusing inward on individual spiritual and personal concerns, this metaphor turns attention outward, thus maintaining the vital tension between the community of faith and the world. The apostle Paul insisted on his rights as a Roman citizen. But he worked out his vocation as a citizen through missionary encounter with his society (cf. 2 Cor 6:3-10). He amply demonstrated his concern for the welfare of all people. He believed that he was called to confront and overcome those elemental forces that are life-destroying in the powerful name of Jesus Christ. The great apostle modeled life lived as a resident alien. There is no hint that he understood his own vocation to be qualitatively different from that of any other disciple of Jesus. The witness of the church that has emerged beyond the boundaries of historical Christendom over the past two centuries confirms the abiding relevance of this apostolic ideal.

10

Training Missiologists for Western Culture

In 1990-91 I conducted a reconnaissance of mission training in several Western countries to determine (1) if there were programs dedicated to the training of missionaries to the peoples of modern Western culture; and, if so, (2) what the curriculum comprised. I never got beyond the first question.[1]

Frequently my interlocutor would assure me that within that institution a course or unit in evangelism was offered. But when pressed to clarify whether people were being prepared for missionary service in the West analogous to training for cross-cultural ministry, the answer was consistently in the negative. It is evident that if such training was not offered, a supporting missiology has not been a priority concern.[2] All the evidence at hand suggests that mission training pro-

---

This chapter was originally published in J. Dudley Woodberry, Charles E. Van Engen, and Edgar J. Elliston, *Missiological Education for the Twenty-first Century* (Maryknoll, N.Y.: Orbis Books, 1996), 120-29.

[1] A few mission departments now designate as *domestic missiology* what formerly was *evangelism* and *church planting*.

[2] Training for evangelism and church development is not at issue; this is essential to the theological curriculum. However, evangelism has generally been conceived to be an activity conducted within the cultural assumptions that govern the life of the church in a particular society or as an extension from the West to other parts of the world. (It is beyond our purpose here to pursue this theme. See such standard works as Autrey [1959], Sweazey [1953], Templeton [1957], and Scharpff [1964]. Orr [1973, 1974, 1975] continually emphasized the linkages between revival movements as they spread round the world.) By contrast, mission takes as its point of departure the kingdom of God with an agenda for challenging the governing plausibility structure of a culture. The sine qua non of mission is formation of communities of the reign of God that live by its plausibility structure. To be sure, certain evangelists—one thinks especially of E. Stanley Jones— have made the kingdom their central theme, and some missionaries have never gone beyond replicating the socioreligious culture from which they originated, but I hold the basic typology to be valid. Orlando Costas was a vigorous exponent of evangelism based on the reign of God (1989), a conviction intensified by his multicultural background and experience as an evangelist-theologian. William J. Abraham (1989) devotes a chapter to evangelism and modernity. One of the most innovative attempts to rethink evangelization of modern culture by drawing on experience and insights from the non-Western world is Alfred C. Krass's *Evanglizing Neopagan North America* (1982).

grams and missiology continue to be defined by the "foreign missions" paradigm of the past two centuries.

I would be the first to speak in defense of the modern mission movement. But poised as we are on the edge of the twenty-first century, not the nineteenth, that paradigm is untenable for two reasons. First, neither biblical nor theological justifications can be adduced for the dichotomy that stands behind this historical pattern.[3] Second, the church in the West has long been marginalized and on the defensive in relation to the culture of modernity because it is confused about mission to its own culture.

The Protestant Reformation in the sixteenth century breached the wall of sacramentalism-sacerdotalism and reclaimed for the church the liberating reality of justification by faith (Shaull 1991, chap. 1). Through the modern mission movement the church rediscovered its responsibility to the regions beyond. I submit that nothing less than a reformation on that scale will deliver the church in the West from its captivity to its mission-less identity relative to its own culture.

My argument may be outlined as follows: The church's recovery of mission is deeply indebted to the modern mission movement of the past two centuries, but that movement was understood to be directed beyond the culture of the sending church. Mission to modern culture will have to reckon with the history of Christendom in the West, for the ancient cathedral spires continue to cast long shadows. The training of missiologists and missionaries for this culture must be conducted in full view of that history, but it must be based on a renewed understanding of the apostolic character of the church as embedded in the Great Commission.

MISSION CONSCIOUSNESS: WELLSPRING OF MISSION

The church always lives out of the consciousness of its fundamental reality. The self-consciousness inculcated by Christendom was non-missionary (cf. Neill 1968, 71-77). We may posit that there is a direct link between this historical fact and the present lassitude of the church in Western culture. What is required is a fundamental reorientation of the church in modern culture to its mission to its culture. This means missional ecclesiology must be at the top of our agenda.

Some theologians began to address ecclesiology with new earnestness in the twentieth century, but it has been at most a partial recovery (Berkhof 1979, 344; Van Engen 1992, 35ff.). The idea that mission is constitutive of the identity of

---

[3] See Robert Wilder's (1936) history of the Student Volunteer Movement, in which he quotes extensively the reflections of Nellie Dunn Clark, who wrote: "One reason for the great impression created by the Movement was that it made a clear, definite appeal for one cause only, and . . . a great mistake would be made if [it] were now to be made to cover both foreign and home missions, or the enlistment of young people for anything other than definite missionary work" (48). This is a purely pragmatic and tactical argument, but one that has long held sway. Samuel Zwemer (1943) based his interpretation of the Great Commission firmly on this dichotomy.

the church has been acknowledged by some theologians (for example, Brunner 1931, 108). Less clear is what impact this has had on the theological curriculum and particularly on the concept of pastoral formation. If we measure the effects of theological education by what happens in the congregation, then we have to say that little has changed by way of self-understanding. For the majority of congregations in modern culture ecclesial consciousness is shaped by the agenda of self-maintenance as a community of worship and pastoral services, a perspective pandered to and reinforced by the emphasis on "marketing the church."

The Great Commission

In our reading of the Great Commission—the charter of the modern mission movement for the past two hundred years—we have been captive to the hoary Christendom tradition. The result has been an emphasis on territory, that is, the territory of heathendom versus the territory of Christendom[4]; on going as the imperative rather than making disciples; on mission defined as what happens "out there." Apart from being faulty exegesis, this reading has reinforced the traditional view that mission has no place within Christendom. The church in the West must be freed of this distorted understanding of the Great Commission, a notion shaped by the powerful Christendom reality and reinforced by the way it was interpreted during the colonial era.[5] Indeed, the Great Commission judges this deformation and points the church to missionary faithfulness. Missiologists of the West must reclaim the call to mission starting at Jerusalem.

Reading the Great Commission in its biblical context holds the potential to radicalize the church's vision of itself in relation to the world, the environment in which the church exists.[6] The Great Commission is a powerful ecclesiological statement, for it is addressed to the disciple community, not autonomous individuals. It conjoins ecclesiality and apostolicity. The Great Commission thus sets the permanent agenda of the church: making men and women disciples of

---

[4] The genius of Christian faith is that it is not tied to a particular geography—holy city, holy land, holy language. When then comes the recurrent quest for total conquest of a particular country of people for Christ? Another such campaign to "capture America for Christ" is being reported in the new media as I am writing [1992]. Both Old and New Testaments are based on the conviction that the faith is preserved and transmitted through God's faithful remnant, a theme sadly ignored in contemporary theology. Crusades and conquests comport well with Christendom but not with the biblical tradition.

[5] It is not our purpose here to evaluate the modern mission movement. Indeed, much work remains to be done on the relationship between the modern mission movement and the religio-historical conditions in the West that defined it, as well as the influences that came to the West from the missions in Asia, Africa, and Latin America. Some aspects of this reflex action are treated in Walls (1988) and in chapters 11 and 12 of this volume.

[6] Mortimer Arias and Alan Johnson (1992) demonstrate the importance of the Great Commission for full realization of the mission of the church. I wish to press the point further: this can be achieved only by reconceptualizing the nature of the church in terms of the Great Commission.

the reign of God wherever the church is until the end of time. Discipling men and women involves enabling them to embrace the fullness of God's reign in their lives. The training of missiologists of Western culture ought to be based on a biblical understanding rather than historical precedents and theological distortions. The task of the missiologist is to help the disciple community to live out the Great Commission.

We need to rethink the function of the Great Commission biblically and theologically. The modern mission movement did indeed reclaim and restore this portion of scripture to the church's awareness, but this was done without a fundamental rethinking of the nature of the church as it had been redefined from the fourth century within the matrix of the corpus Christianum.[7] Instead, the Great Commission was understood primarily in terms of motivating individual Christians to go or to support missions (in the same way appeal has been made countless times to a text like Isaiah 6:1-8). This inspirational and motivational dimension has been indispensable to the modern mission movement, but it does not begin to exhaust the meaning and function of the text in the canon of scripture (cf. Michel 1983, 35; Bosch 1991, 56f.; Legrand 1986, 302ff.).

The Great Commission structures or institutionalizes the church's relation to the world. In sociological terms, institutions mediate relations between an individual or group and others. These include such matters as conventions that regulate social relationships and extend to all realms where interaction is occurring (Bellah 1991, 287-93). The Great Commission institutionalizes mission as the raison d'etre, the controlling norm, of the church. To be a disciple of Jesus Christ and a member of his body is to live a missionary existence in the world. There is no doubt that this was how the earliest Christians understood their calling.

Training for mission in the region of "Jerusalem, Judea, and Samaria" that makes up our Western culture will require that we approach this frontier in missionary rather than pastoral terms.[8] We must come to grips with a culture that is in crisis and in transition. At the same time, we should become more self-aware of the assumptions that have controlled mission studies and missionary action up to the present. The cross-cultural model(s) of mission cannot be appropriated in toto as the basis for the training of missiologists and missionaries to Western culture, though there is important overlap.

The Model of Mission

Luke's account of the Acts of the Apostles describes the working out of this missionary existence from the beginning: at his ascension Jesus gives the still disconsolate and disoriented disciples their defining purpose (1:8); forty days

[7] A viewpoint that was important in the missiology of Gustav Warneck, from whose pioneering work—forged during the High Imperial period—much of modern missiology descends.

[8] Sacerdotalism is irreconcilable with the prophetic office. While the distinction between apostolic and prophetic vocations must be maintained, neither fits easily with the role of the priest, whose role is to modulate conflict between church and society.

later, at Pentecost, the church is constituted on the basis of that mission (2:41-47); and the remainder of Acts records the unfolding of that mission.[9] In two descriptive passages Luke provides what we may regard as the normative two-fold model by which the church works out its missionary existence in the world.

Acts 11:19-26 depicts what may be called the organic mode. Under the impact of fierce persecution in the environs of Jerusalem (6:8–8:4), the disciple community was scattered, with a contingent going to Antioch, at that time the third largest city in the Roman Empire. Far from being intimidated by the persecution they had endured, the disciples continued their evangelizing activity—the very thing that got them into trouble in Jerusalem—and were indiscriminate as to whether they witnessed to Jews or Gentiles. The result was "the hand of the Lord was with them, and a great number that believed turned to the Lord" (11:21). Luke presents no honor role of outstanding evangelists. Reading this account in the context of the varied encounters the young community was having, it is evident the scattered disciple communities challenged the regnant plausibility structure of their culture on the basis of the claims of the reign of God (cf. Acts 17:6f.). Witness to God's reign, present and coming, was at the heart of the disciple community's life. The church grew organically. This mode has been the main vehicle of the expansion of the church historically and is an authentic outworking of the Great Commission.

Acts 13:1-3 describes a contrasting but complementary mode. The Holy Spirit leads the church at Antioch to an innovation. Certain individuals are set apart for an itinerant ministry that will enable the faith to spread to key cities and regions throughout the Roman world. This creates the precedent for the sending mode and, by extension, cross-cultural mission that has played a crucial role in the expansion of the church precisely because it guards against the parochialism—the entropic syndrome—which is the slow death of the faith. The Great Commission continually holds this dimension before the church.

Luke's account of the development of the early church may be seen as proceeding from the thesis statement in Acts 1:8. The model for mission is the missionary church actualizing its true existence through these two modes (11:19-26 and 13:1-3). From Acts we understand that the Holy Spirit leads the church in working out its obedience to the Great Commission. There is no place here for dichotomous thinking—no home versus foreign missions. The Antioch church is the base from which both expressions of missionary obedience emanate. The authenticity and vitality of the church in its local environment is validated by the fact that the Holy Spirit calls out of it select individuals, with confirming response by the church, as witnesses to the gospel among Jews and Gentiles farther away and where cultural and linguistic barriers may be greater. But those

---

[9] Modern commentators help to perpetuate a Christendom reading of the Acts account by the way they divide up the material and insert editorial heads and commentary that draw on modern practice and assumptions. Taking a random selection of commentaries, one notes that the majority introduce the term *mission* only at 9:32, with the beginning of the Gentile mission, or at 13:1-3 (Barclay [1953], Bruce [1954], Marshall [1980]), in contrast, Munck (1967) entitles 1:6-14, "The Mission to the World and the Ascension."

individuals also feel themselves accountable to the church through which they receive their commission.

Reign of God as Criterion

The phrase "kingdom of God" occurs only eight times in Acts (1:3, 6; 8:12; 14:22; 19:8; 20:25; 28:23, 31). This does not mean it is of little importance. Luke reports that Jesus in his final forty days with the disciples was occupied with expounding to them the meaning of the reign of God (1:3). And the last thing we hear of Paul is that he is prisoner in Rome where he "welcomed all who came to him, preaching the kingdom of God and teaching about the Lord Jesus Christ" (28:31). The emerging Messianic movement is based on the reign of God as criterion, that is, what marks this movement as being different from all others is its loyalty to God's rule. The Great Commission calls the church to keep the kingdom of God as its central focus. The model of mission identified by Luke guides the church in witnessing to and living out the reality of God's reign in the world. Whenever the church lives out of that dynamic there will be a strong mission consciousness. Conversely, when awareness of the kingdom of God is weak, there will be a corresponding feeble sense of mission, or else the church will rely on missionary approaches motivated by sources other than the reign of God.

MISSION CONSCIOUSNESS: THE WORLD

In the first part I have emphasized the importance of the church renewed in mission consciousness in response to the reign of God. Discussion of mission, and the role of training, would be incomplete without a consideration of the world that is the object of this extraordinary undertaking. This means the world of Western culture. More particularly, it requires that we become self-critically aware of the "kingdom of the Western world," which presents itself as an alternative to the reign of God.[10] All cultures are human constructs. None, including the culture of Christendom, approximates the kingdom of God. Consequently, wherever this "gospel of the kingdom" is proclaimed, deep tensions with the world appear.

Those who are indigenous to modern Western culture easily accept the dubious assumption that they know it in its depths. But many Western Christians have considerable difficulty distinguishing between God and Caesar in their loyalties. That we must subject the fundamental presuppositions on which our culture rests to rigorous missiological scrutiny and criticism is a foreign notion. They accept that the individual needs to be saved from personal sin, but this has to do with one's personal status before God rather than social relations and the wider culture.

---

[10] This does not mean all cultures are of the same moral caliber. Cultures may be deeply influenced by values that move them closer to the kingdom-of-God ideal. But at their best, such cultures remain marred by human fallibility.

To train missiologists concerned with Western culture who can lead in this kind of critical analysis will require the acquisition of a countercultural stance in the sense that we must overcome the undertow of resistance, especially by fellow Christians, to raising these fundamental questions concerning our culture. Any profile of modern culture would need to include such basic themes as how the human being is understood, the importance of technique, and the role of power and violence.

The Modern Self

The crowning achievement of the Enlightenment was the emergence of "the autonomous self." Traditional society had no place for such autonomy. The individual's place was assured by virtue of conformity to the role or station defined by society. The Enlightenment proclaimed a radical freedom for the individual from such arbitrary constraints (Brown 1968, 90-106). It was argued that the human being can achieve fullest potential only if set free. The corollary conviction was that problems can be solved through the rational application of knowledge. The ideals of freedom and rationality soon entered political discourse and were enshrined in both the United States Declaration of Independence (1776), with its "self-evident truths," and the French Statement of Human and Civil Rights (1789). "Life, liberty, and the pursuit of happiness" became hallmarks of modern culture.

Since the eighteenth century the West has idealized and pursued the autonomous individual. Positively, this has encouraged people the world over to resist and reject all forms of tyranny and inhumane conditions. A new appreciation of the dignity of the human being, and consequent "human rights," are the fruits of this movement. But certain other facts are inescapable. Two hundred years after Immanuel Kant defined enlightenment as the "coming of age" of humankind through the throwing off of external constraints and after vast sociopolitical changes have greatly enlarged individual freedoms, we are a culture driven by the quest for self-esteem, a totally elusive goal.

The temptation to "be as God" in modern culture has taken the form of making the self the goal. Ironically, the Enlightenment has fostered alienation (Gunton 1985). Modern culture's love affair with "expressive individualism" is "corrosive of both true love for the self as well as love of others. Conceiving of persons as unrelated and finally unrelatable social 'atoms' allows one to recognize self-seeking and self-expression, but not self-love" (Pope 1991, 397). This has produced far-reaching consequences for inhabitants of modern culture.[11] We can identify several issues here. First, it may well be asked whether we now have a sound understanding of personhood at all. Second, our long preoccupation with

---

[11] Space limits disallow pursuing this important point. Rollo May (1969) has argued that the rise of psychiatric science is a direct consequence of modern culture but criticizes psychotherapy for being itself a part of the problem. See further, Rieff (1966) and Menninger (1973).

the "self" has resulted in the atrophying of our sense of what makes for a viable society (Bellah 1985, 1991). And, third, we urgently need to reconsider the meaning of Christian conversion in light of the impact of modern culture on Christian thought and practice.[12]

Technique

Modernity is the culture of scientific technique, a point made with great force forty years ago by Jacques Ellul. This means not only that we have developed more and more machines to do our work; it points to the fact that technique has become pervasive in our lives. Technique shapes the ways we communicate and relate to others. Studying the impact of the modern system on the human being, social scientists have discovered that technological culture results in anomie and alienation. The rise of the counterculture movement in North America and Europe of the 1960s was, in part, a reaction to this feature of modern culture.

Modern technology is displayed at its most brilliant, perhaps, in the appliances of modern warfare. The United States government force-fed the military-industrial complex over the past fifty years with huge infusions of capital to enable continual technological innovation in order to build the most sophisticated weapons ever devised. It is salutary to recall, therefore, the failure of the United States military campaign in Southeast Asia, in which technological warfare was defeated by a poor peasant army fighting for its political, not simply its military, life (Baritz 1985).

There are important questions begging to be considered in terms of Christian witness in modern culture. On the one hand, we must reflect on the extent to which the church has understood the nature of modern culture and its impact on the human—individually and collectively. On the other hand, the church can ill afford to appropriate uncritically from culture as it works out its witness. For example, technology seems to offer many opportunities for expanded and au courant means of witness. But all technology is based on technique. Scholars have demonstrated that technique results in alienation. If the church relies on technique to carry out its witness, what is to guarantee that it will not result in alienation? To ask the question is not to presume to have the answer. But if we wish to engage modern culture with the gospel, it is a question we cannot evade.

Power and Violence

Power is essential to human existence. Life can be lived only because of the power—the means—to set goals and work them out. More than we recognize,

---

[12] One might start with an examination of the classical evangelical expression of conversion: "I have decided to accept Jesus as my personal savior." Revivalist culture arose concurrently with the Enlightenment, and its preoccupation with the self bears its imprint. This reduces to an instrumental understanding of religion, hardly to be reconciled with the call of Jesus to discipleship.

we are preoccupied with power. The consciousness of power in modern culture has been heightened by the confidence that we possess the means through scientific technology actually to bend the forces of nature to our purposes, to control our environment, to conquer disease, and to be in control of our destiny. These achievements have been real but remain relative and ambiguous at best. More sobering still is the extent to which modern culture is a culture of violence, that is, power turned to destructive ends.

In his Nobel Lecture on Literature, Aleksandr Solzhenitsyn characterized modern culture thusly: "Violence, continually less restrained by the confines of a legality established over the course of many generations, strides brazenly and victoriously through the whole world . . . [which] is being flooded with the crude conviction that force can do everything and righteousness and innocence nothing" (1972, 25). This should not surprise us when we examine the myth of violence, which can be traced to primal creation myths and continues to give legitimacy to so much in modern culture, from children's cartoons to foreign policy (Wink 1993, 13-31).[13]

In spite of the pretenses and illusions of mastery of life forces that are purveyed in our society, modern culture is incapable of delivering itself from the forces of death. These pretenses and illusions are offset by the extraordinary measures modern people take to extend youthfulness and deny the reality of death. The gospel confronts all such pretense with the realism of truth and good news about God's alternative in the message of the reign of God; in that message redemptive power, as defined by the cross, holds out hope to men and women in modern culture. It is through *metanoia,* a turning toward God's new heaven and new earth, that we have the promise of salvation.

THE TASK OF MISSION TRAINING IN MODERN CULTURE

I have presented only a rough sketch of the type of work that needs to be done if we are to develop a responsive missiological approach to modern culture. The task is threefold: (1) We must have a clear conceptual framework. This may not be quickly accomplished. One of the reactions I often get is that of puzzlement: "What is it you think you are doing that we are not already doing through our well-honed evangelism training program?" This implies that the interrogator is not thinking in self-critical terms regarding modern culture. At that point one must appeal to the cross-cultural example and indicate some of the learnings that might apply in modern culture. (2) We must seek to reorient the whole of theological education so that theology is informed by mission and mission is strengthened by theology (Kirk 1990). The proper anchor of all theology is the

---

[13] One area of modern culture where the role of violence is rising steadily is sports. On the one hand, sports dominates our culture to an extent frequently not acknowledged. On the other, it is becoming clear that exploitation and violence are essential to the sports system. The relation of sport and religion deserves close scrutiny (cf. Deford 1976; Hoffman 1992).

missio Dei, God's redemptive mission, and this needs to be worked out in relation to modern culture. (3) Training programs are needed that equip people for
mission to modern and postmodern culture. Specialized training will be required
to meet needs that the usual theological education program cannot offer. Above
all, we need to take the long view and lay a solid foundation for what promises
to be as demanding a mission frontier as the church has yet faced (Newbigin
1983, 1986, and 1989).

PART FOUR

DISCERNING
CHANGING FRONTIERS

The period since 1700 has been tumultuous. These three centuries have coincided with the scientific and technological revolutions that gave rise to industrialization, urbanization, and Western expansion round the world. It was in this environment that the modern mission movement was conducted.

Modern culture has moved at an accelerating pace, and the missionary movement has been carried along by this comprehensive and expansive sociocultural development. At each stage missionary thought and approach have been shaped by the dominant cultural motifs and models. In this regard we must take account of the emergence of such key ideas as *culture*.

As the result of growing intercultural contact, especially through the mission movement and the founding of the social sciences in the nineteenth century, the tools and resources for empirically based critical reflection and comparative studies became possible. The traditional static view of culture that had dominated mission thought in the seventeenth and eighteenth centuries gradually gave way to more dynamic understandings. The earlier view of civilization as a fixed deposit to be transferred from the so-called civilized West to other peoples of other continents gave way to a more flexible and dynamic understanding of indigenous cultures. Ultimately, in an effort to break completely with the idea that the standards for evaluating any culture originate with another cultural tradition, indigeneity was superseded by the notion of *context*.

Not surprisingly, this conceptual change has coincided with the growth of the church in Africa, Asia, and Latin America to the point where the majority of Christians are now to be found in these continents. The particular institutionalization of mission that is called the modern mission movement has increasingly come under strain. Agencies unable to adapt to the changing geopolitical and economic realities are disappearing from the scene. Others are being modified.

The future of mission does not, in the end, depend on particular agencies or certain institutional forms. Organizations, including mission agencies, must be responsive to the historical context. The changing mission frontier includes the challenge of discovering the new forms and patterns that will be the sine qua non of missionary faithfulness in the twenty-first century.

11

The "Great Century" Reconsidered

In a 1965 essay entitled "The New Ethical Possibility: The Task of Post-Christendom Ethics," Paul Peachey surveyed the course of world history, including the impact of the West on other cultures since the sixteenth century. He concluded: "In sum, thus, history has disowned the expectation that world society would be made in the image of Christendom" (Peachey 1965, 31). A scholar standing within the Free Church/Believers Church tradition might be expected to arrive at such a conclusion, but Peachey adduced his evidence from wide-ranging sources. None of those he called to the witness stand were representative of Peachey's own tradition.

In this chapter I argue that the "Great Century" in missions was both a powerful last thrust of Christendom and an important instrument in bringing about the dissolution of Christendom. When we speak of the Great Century, we refer to that initiative in missionary action beginning roughly around 1800 and climaxing at the start of World War I in 1914.[1]

This movement, on the Protestant side, had its roots in Pietism and in the eighteenth-century Evangelical Revival. Although the formation of missionary societies occurred on a broad front—in Europe, the British Isles, and North America—Great Britain quickly became the leader. The British dominated missions until around 1900. Coincidentally with the World Missionary Conference at Edinburgh in 1910, the British relinquished the premier place they had held for a century. American Protestant missionaries now outnumbered the British.

The Great Century meant less in terms of the actual numbers of new adherents won to the Christian faith on the fields of Asia, Africa, and Latin America than in the formative impact the movement had on the Christian world. Far greater numbers of new believers have joined the Christian family in the non-Western world in the twentieth century than during the Great Century, but the nineteenth century remains crucial because of the way it shaped the twentieth.

This chapter was orignally published in *Missiology* 12:2 (April 1, 1984):133-46. Revised for publication in this volume.

[1] Kenneth Scott Latourette coined the phrase "the great century" as a title for three volumes of his seven-volume *History of the Expansion of Christianity* (1970).

When we speak of Christendom we refer to that understanding of the Christian church which prevailed following the Treaty of Milan between Constantine and Licinius in A.D. 313. That treaty called for toleration for all religions, but Christianity soon became the religion of the emperor and thus of the empire. This marriage between church and state altered the character of the church. Rather than being the faith of those who voluntarily responded to the call to follow Jesus Christ as Lord, Christianity was now identified with the political power structures and struggles of the world.[2] While the Treaty of Milan initially promised religious toleration, Constantinianism soon came to signify religious intolerance. Europe would be Christianized through state-supported missionary action, often by force.

Despite the vicissitudes of fifteen centuries, the Christendom mentality remained largely intact in the nineteenth century. "In the sphere of mission to lands where the Gospel had not been preached," observes Ronald K. Orchard, "the task was conceived in a fashion which seems to owe a good deal to the medieval concept of Christendom" (1958, 174). "Christian nations" stood in contrast to "the heathen." "Christendom" connoted geography, cultural forms and tastes, political structures, and legal systems.

Western culture made a fundamental shift during the nineteenth century. London's 1851 Crystal Palace Exhibition is a symbol of this transition into modernity. Religion had lost its authority by mid-century, and modernity took over (Bell 1976, 55-54; 1980, 334-37). Although British evangelicals exerted a salutary influence on social policy through the leadership of the Wilberforces and Shaftesburys, this movement was largely a spent force by mid-century. The church became increasingly preoccupied with defending itself against the assaults from science.

THE GREAT CENTURY: DISCONTINUITY AND CONTINUITY

New Voluntary Structures

Participants in the nineteenth-century missionary movement had a clear sense of its novelty. The first response to this fresh religious impulse was to create new structures. The formation of missionary societies, beginning in Britain with the Methodists in 1787 and the Baptists in 1792, rose to a crescendo during the next three decades in Europe and the United States of America. The final quarter of the century saw an even greater organizing effort with many new missionary societies formed (Beaver 1968, 113-15).

Protestant societies tapped the reservoir of voluntarism among the laity, which enabled unprecedented growth in financial support and workers. The "faith mission" epitomized this development, drawing support from individuals in various denominations. Whether church-related or independent, a missionary society was sustained by individuals committed to world mission.

---

[2] A critical minority has borne witness against this compromise from early times—a testimony which has continued into the modern period (cf. Durnbaugh 1968).

In *The Missionary Enterprise* Edwin Munsell Bliss repeatedly made the point that missions meant voluntarism: "The keynote of modern missionary activity is the personal responsibility of the individual for the individual salvation of non-Christians." Then he added, "To develop this individual responsibility and activity required first that men should learn to think for themselves; then act for themselves; then act together without losing the individual consciousness" (1908, 52). He insisted that all initiatives originate with the individual. Bliss hailed "this sense of mutual, individual responsibility" as the birthmark of the modern missionary movement, in contrast to earlier periods (ibid., 67). He did not relate this action to the church theologically or ecclesiastically. In fact, he seemed to view the church as a liability—an impediment to action.

Regardless of ecclesiastical tradition, missionary societies found themselves in tension with the church. For an established church like the Church of England, the existence of missionary societies, which were not constitutionally linked to the hierarchy, was a source of particular frustration. Yet the hierarchy was not at all prepared to sponsor and administer a missionary program.

The sheer scale of the missionary movement in the nineteenth century finds no precedent in history. Although the Christian church was self-consciously missionary in its first decades, it was largely a spontaneous and organic movement outward. In the nineteenth century formal organization and conscious strategizing became hallmarks of this movement to reach the ends of the earth with the message of Jesus Christ. The vision that spurred mission supporters to action was firmly grounded in the Old Testament prayer, "that thy way be known upon earth, thy saving power among the nations" (Ps 67:2). It was a vision reinforced by Isaiah's promise that "the earth shall be full of the knowledge of the Lord as the waters cover the sea" (Is 11:9b).

Even the most culturally isolated churches in the North Atlantic basin eventually responded to the missionary impulse. The churches that made up the sending base underwent profound change in their self-understanding as well as in their sense of responsibility for the world beyond their own national boundaries.

Although the movement began with all the assumptions about Christendom intact—effectively captured in the regnant slogan of the period, "Christianity, Civilization, and Commerce"—the movement outward into diverse cultures and climes soon taxed the old synthesis to the breaking point. The movement was fashioning a new empirical reality that stubbornly resisted being fitted into the old mold.

Tensions with the State

Until the nineteenth century it had been assumed that the state was a legitimate sponsor of missions. The roles of the Spanish and Portuguese crowns in missions in the fifteenth and sixteenth centuries were emulated by the other European powers through charters granted to trading companies. By the nineteenth century the companies were increasingly wary of ties to the religious establishment, especially where this involved evangelizing activity among the indigenous peoples. Motivated by profit rather than altruism, these companies saw clearly that missionary work was not greeted enthusiastically by the local peoples. Their task of imposing rule from the outside and managing an economy for profit was immeasurably complicated by the presence of religious interlopers. It had become patently clear to these quasi-state trading companies, in contrast to Constantine, that their interests were not going to be served by coopting the church.

The history of the nineteenth century is replete with episodes where mission clashed with state. The East India Trading Company long withstood pressures to allow missionaries to enter India. When by an act of the British Parliament in 1813, the Company charter was amended to open India to missionaries, it was a hard-won victory for mission supporters (Stock 1899: 1:92-104). Pro-missionary forces within the East India Company itself were aided by William Wilberforce, who repeatedly used his powerful oratory in Parliament in behalf of the missionary cause. No one questioned the propriety of exerting political pressure to get a Christian nation to do what Christian governments ought to be concerned with—the Christianizing of the nations.

Even though no clear theory of church-state relations guided missionary leaders during the nineteenth century, they were increasingly mindful of past abuses and misuses of political power in the service of evangelization. Missions did not always follow a consistent course where government was concerned, but the trend was toward independence of the church from the state (Latourette 1965, 330-49).

As a corollary to the growing separation of church/mission and state, missions became increasingly involved in the quest for religious liberty and human rights. Despite the witness of the Radical Reformers of the sixteenth century, which laid the foundation for the Free Church tradition, the notion of religious liberty had remained only a faint hope (Bender 1970). Indeed, the Reformation inspired renewed persecution (Bates 1945, 148-86). Far from being an experiment in religious liberty, the first two centuries of American history were of a piece with Europe's (Littell 1962, 1-29). The nineteenth century marks progress on this front.

Developing a Strategy of Mission

Mission leaders in the nineteenth century saw themselves as pioneers in missionary principles and action. The foremost American missions leader in the nineteenth century was Rufus Anderson of the American Board of Commissioners for Foreign Missions (Congregationalist). In his book *Foreign Missions: Their Relations and Claims*, Anderson treated what he labeled "principles and methods of modern missions." After summarizing the main features of St. Paul's missionary approach, which Anderson held to be normative for all subsequent efforts, he called attention to "a discovery of recent date" (1869, 111). This discovery was that an indigenous church must be led by an indigenous pastor. Anderson's insight, for which he did not take credit, became the chief cornerstone for the foundation of indigenous churches wherever missions went. The emergence of this principle assured the end of Christendom, for it freed the church politically and culturally to find suitable forms in particular contexts.

Anderson's fellow pioneer on the other side of the Atlantic, Henry Venn, shared in the search for principles. In a letter to Anderson in 1854 Venn wryly observed that "while the present era is one for the development of Missionary principles in action, it is also one of incompetent theorizing and with a tinge of Missionary romance." Both felt the urgency of learning from the example of the first apostles as well as from contemporary missionary practice.

Venn encouraged his missionary colleagues to apply these principles in their work. He instructed missionaries to work inductively by starting with the local culture, searching for bridges between the missionary and local peoples, respecting the people enough to learn from them (Venn 1868, 316-20). He urged the missionary to organize the local church as early as possible and adapt to its culture.

During the Great Century missions set high standards for the admission of converts. Not since the days of the early church had the demands been so strict. Both Pietism and the Evangelical Revival had drawn attention to the problem of nominal church membership. Evangelicals kept up their guard against nominal adherents. Henry Venn is representative of this concern. Although he could appreciate the broad impact of Christianity on a culture, he feared that people would stop short and settle for a diluted form. He pressed for a full commitment to the church as a visible body of believers, founded upon "the conversion of the sinner to Christ, the radical renewal of the individual" (Venn 1861, 183-88).

But mission leaders such as Venn were vulnerable to the charge that the church set higher standards of personal piety and moral conduct overseas than were maintained at home. They wanted a disciplined believers' church in Asia and Africa while the church at home was co-extensive with the citizenry. This was not simply a problem of the double standard. The missionary became arbiter of right and wrong in ethical matters in a foreign culture, the very thing Venn had cautioned against in his 1868 statement. Christendom patterns and styles were treated as normative for other peoples in other lands, with little awareness of the fact that Christendom itself was an admixture of European culture and Christian belief.

The Christendom Vision

The missionary movement during the Great Century was more than a religious movement, though this was its driving force. Missionaries pioneered in creating educational, medical, and other social service systems in many countries. The idea of development that came into vogue following World War II had its precedent in missionary practice in the nineteenth century. For example, as a part of the effort to combat the slave trade in Africa, missionaries and their collaborators introduced numerous schemes to provide legitimate economic opportunities that would make the illicit trade in slaves economically unattractive. Their slogan was, "The Bible and the Plow." The goal was to drive out bad trade with good.

Some missionary leaders concerned themselves with an overall strategy for the development of Africa. Taking their cue from Great Britain's experience in the Industrial Revolution, they gave priority to preparing a middle class that would provide leadership in Africa's own eventual Industrial Revolution. Such steps had impact far beyond the immediate goals of a mission. In the judgment of Nigerian historian E. A. Ayandele, "If any individual is to be credited with originating Nigerian nationalism, ideologically, then that individual is unquestionably the Rev. Henry Venn. . . . Single-handed and deliberately, he urged Africans to be prepared to assume the leadership of their countries" (1966, 180). Venn gave some of his most dedicated and creative energy to this task. The same story can be told through other biographies in other parts of the world.

Each of these innovations contributed to the transformation of Christendom by realigning relationships between church and world and by driving Christian leaders back to first principles of Christian discipleship. But the impulse to maintain and even strengthen Christendom was strong and continued to influence missionary action. The appeal to extend the Christian commonwealth throughout the world by the conquest of "heathen" lands remained strong until well into the twentieth century.

In the popular mind, missions in the Great Century sailed under the flag of "Christianity, Commerce, and Civilization." But in the nineteenth century voices began to be raised against the popular formulation that made civilization the precursor to conversion. Leaders such as Rufus Anderson and Henry Venn from time to time protested against the old formula, calling for conversion as the priority. Anderson lamented that modern missions labored under a burden the early apostles did not face. He took the position that "the higher civilization of the Christian Church" is not what we are to propagate even though that is what many Christians assume (Anderson 1869, 95f.). He urged that attention be focused rather on the "simple form of the gospel as a converting agency" (105). Anderson could not rid himself of his ambivalence. He wished to concentrate missionary resources on evangelization but acknowledged that other services were required to sustain the growing church. Anderson and Venn took refuge in conversion as the priority. They argued that the individual, once converted, would be motivated to make cultural, economic, and social advances.

Venn died in 1873 and Anderson in 1880. However, even before these missionary statesmen passed from the scene, the mood in Christendom began changing. The age of the "humanitarians," who felt a responsibility to be guardians of the "weaker" peoples of the world, had suffered eclipse by 1850, and the winds of the new imperialism began to pick up force. John Robert Seeley, professor of history at Cambridge, was the chosen vessel to give voice to these incipient longings for empire. His book *The Expansion of England*, published in 1883, offered "a dream of empire without conflict or coercion" (Seeley 1971, xxvi).[3]

---

[3] Seeley was the product of a staunch Anglican evangelical family. His father, a publisher, was a close friend of Lord Shaftesbury and Henry Venn. Like many other second- and third-generation evangelicals, he had increasing intellectual difficulties with evangelicalism and ultimately moved to the broad church position.

Seeley's phrase quickly entered common parlance. Bishop Alfred Barry reflected this heightened sense of identity between national mission and church mission in the title of his Hulsean Lectures, *The Ecclesiastical Expansion of England in the Growth of the Anglican Communion* (Barry 1895).

On the western side of the Atlantic, Josiah Strong, secretary of the American Home Missionary Society, published a tract in 1885: *Our Country: Its Possible Future and Its Present Crisis* (Strong 1891). Strong appealed for the United States, as a part of the Anglo-Saxon world, to take seriously its larger mission. The book met with immediate success. Unfortunately, Strong's liberal and compassionate vision, in the hands of others, soon provided reinforcement for a spirit of manifest destiny that ran counter to Strong's own intention. United States Senator Albert J. Beveridge was in the vanguard of those urging the expansion of the United States into the Caribbean and the Philippines. "The dominant notes in American history thus far have been self-government and internal improvement," said Beveridge. "The dominant notes in American life henceforth will be not only self-government and internal improvement, but also administration and world improvement. . . . It is ours to govern in the name of civilized liberty. It is ours to administer order and law in the name of human progress" (Beveridge 1970, 118). Within this historical and political context mission leaders did their strategizing.

A. T. Pierson was a leading missions strategist who thought globally. In the January 1889 *Missionary Review of the World*, Pierson challenged the churches to take as their resolution, "The whole world to be evangelized in the present generation" (Pierson 1889, 5-14). He sketched out a scheme whereby the world's thirty million Protestants would reach the one billion non-Christian inhabitants of the world by the turn of the century.

Robert E. Speer served for forty-six years as a missions executive and leading proponent of missions. He ably articulated the Christendom position to his generation. In his book *Missionary Principles and Practice* he devotes a chapter to "the civilizing influence of missions." Speer offered a sturdy defense of missions based on their social and political impact. He claimed that "the missionaries are the greatest pioneer agencies opening the world and bringing the knowledge of it to the civilized nations" (Speer 1902, 415). He pointed to the ways in which missions have aided governments in establishing order and improving the common weal.

In the Duff Lectures for 1910 in Scotland, Speer discussed at length the relationship of politics to missions. He spoke approvingly of the responsibility the powerful nations carry for the weaker ones and described the necessarily close cooperation between the Western nations and missions. So intimate is this relationship that "just as the missionary inevitably has a political message wrapped up in his mission and his Gospel, so the statesman or the merchant has a religious message, which he delivers in spite of himself, for or against Christ and the aim which the missionary serves" (Speer 1910, 233). Yet he did admit that the image of "missions and governments" remained ambiguous in the eyes of the peoples of other nations. He appealed for more fully Christianized governments to ensure they would act in a manner compatible with missionary aims and Christian ideals.

Following World War I, the Committee on the War and the Religious Outlook prepared a report that was published as *The Missionary Outlook in the Light of the War* (1920). What is striking about the report as a whole is the absence of any serious ethical reflection on the fact of war itself. In his introduction to the report Robert E. Speer congratulated the missionary movement because its goals and ideals were adopted by the United States government "as its moral aims in the conflict" (xv). These aims were fivefold: (1) establish permanent peace, (2) safeguard democracy and human freedom, (3) assure the application of the law of righteousness to both nations and individuals, (4) offer service to humanity, and (5) secure a social order based on brotherhood. For Speer this was merely a political statement of the goals of the missionary enterprise. He suggested that missions had "been doing peacefully, constructively, unselfishly, quietly, for a hundred years the things that, in a great outburst of titanic and necessarily destructive struggle, we tried to do by war" (xviii). The missionary movement was thus inextricably linked to national purpose.

The report interpreted the missionary contribution as creation of a new internationalism. Shades of President Woodrow Wilson's hopes for the League of Nations lingered in the background. The report asserted, "The missionary has held before the nations—is holding before them today—the ideal of a Christian national life, insisting that it must be built on righteousness and presenting Christianity as the power without which the highest nationhood cannot be realized" (7). A new international order would assure peace and prosperity.

Despite the gathering momentum of nationalist movements in Asia and Africa, beginning in India and Indonesia, toward the end of the nineteenth century, the Christendom vision remained a force in missionary thought until after World War II. Walter Marshall Horton averred, "In an age when world peace, world citizenship, world fellowship, are the goals after which popular imagination reaches out, the only objective big enough to define the comprehensive aims of the Christian world mission is the creation of a world Christian civilization" (Horton 1946, 177). Horton suggested that the first part of the Great Commission had been fulfilled. The next stage should be devoted to the second half—"teaching them to observe all things." The church could now offer a religious center around which nations and peoples might unite.

Christendom depended on a close integration of the political, religious, and cultural. But the tide of "rising expectations" of the peoples of the non-Western world, especially from the late 1880s onward, was to obtain the freedom to restore their *corpus Islamianum* or *corpus Hinduianum*, rather than domination by a hated foreign *corpus Christianum*. Furthermore, the vision of freedom for the individual, learned at the hands of missionary teachers in mission schools or in European universities, was set within a framework of a democratic political system that guaranteed the right of private conscience. The Western colonial powers were caught in an untenable contradiction: in the end, an expansionist Christendom could be maintained only by coercion. Even the peoples of the

West had tired of the constraints of the old order; the other peoples of the world were simply unwilling to submit.

Indonesia declared its independence from the Netherlands in 1945; Great Britain peacefully—but only after long opposition to the indigenous independence movement—transferred sovereignty to India and Pakistan in 1947. China closed its door to Christian influence in 1949, decisively rejecting what the missionary had tried to bring. These were harbingers of the movement toward political independence in Asia and Africa in the 1950s and 1960s.

Observers have only recently recognized that the mission-founded churches of Asia and Africa spawned their own independence movement. Religious independency was a complex combination of political, religious, and social drives that issued in a new genre of church, combining indigenous elements of ethos, form, and symbol with what had been learned from the Western church, but independent of all Western control or support (Turner 1981, 45-55; Walls 1979, 48-51).

That part of the missionary movement most closely identified with the Christendom thrust of the Great Century rapidly lost momentum after 1945, while independent and Free Church groups surged forward. The latter often acted as if they were still living in the nineteenth century. They treated sociopolitical issues simplistically and interpreted the missionary call as the simple and unambiguous action of saving souls.

The Church

In the previous section we have described the Great Century in terms of the dialectic between continuity and discontinuity. The drive to extend Christendom worldwide and maintain Western hegemony carried the seeds of its own destruction. And the discontinuities unleashed their own disintegrating impact. In the process the church was being freed from the burden of a compromise made one and a half millennia earlier. Indeed, it now had the possibility of rediscovering its true identity. However, this transformation came at a time when the church as a whole was ill-prepared to accept it.

The missionary movement in the nineteenth century found its theological dynamic in soteriology. Ecclesiology played no significant role in the development of mission theology, except for marginal Tractarian influence in Great Britain. Only in the twentieth century, under the stimulus of missiologists such as Hendrik Kraemer and theologians such as Karl Barth, has the challenge of reconstructing ecclesiology from the standpoint of the apostolate begun to be taken seriously (Berkhof 1979, 410-22). To put the matter in overly simple terms, in the nineteenth century the doctrine of the church functioned primarily in defense of the church as institution. Earlier renewal movements, such as Pietism and the Evangelical Revival, had skirted the issue by concentrating on the salvation of the individual, and this mentality continued to dominate evangelical thought. Mainstream Protestantism also lacked a dynamic ecclesiology.

The situation was no better in terms of pastoral theology. One of the outstanding British pastoral figures of the Great Century was Charles Simeon (1759-1836), for fifty-four years vicar of Holy Trinity Church, Cambridge. Simeon, who played a major role in founding the Church Missionary Society in 1799, was more self-conscious about the church than most evangelicals in his generation. Yet in his voluminous writings the church emerges as little more than a collection of individuals, and discipleship is construed as the individual's duties before God without reference to the community. Evangelicals moved even more strongly toward individualism after Simeon's time (Webster 1959, 128f.).

A classic formulation appears in the basis for membership in the Evangelical Alliance, adopted at its formation in 1846. Although the Alliance understandably tried to chart a course that avoided conflict with the organized churches, and consequently made no explicit reference to the church as such, its leaders were equally intent on ensuring doctrinal correctness on the part of its members. The second of the statement's nine points affirms "the right and duty of private judgment in the interpretation of the Holy Scriptures" (Rouse and Neill 1967, 320). The thrust of the statement emphasizes the individual.

In his history of the Second Evangelical Awakening in Great Britain in 1859, J. Edwin Orr devotes a chapter of a scant four pages to "revival theology" (Orr 1949, 51-54). He concludes that the Revival contributed nothing new theologically or doctrinally. It made its impact in the awakening to life of nominal church members and those outside the pale of the church.

This was the theological womb of the modern missionary movement: missionary theory based on soteriology as personal experience. Stephen Neill concluded that "Protestant missionaries have gone out with the earnest desire to win souls for Christ, but with very little idea of what is to happen to the souls when they have been won" (Neill 1970a, 109). As a result, the emphasis in missionary practice fell largely on the ecclesiastical and sociological aspects of the church—its organization, growth toward independence of foreign sponsorship, numerical expansion, and affiliations with other church bodies, rather than its ecclesiological dimension.

All of the newly planted churches in non-Western lands had to begin, by definition, as believers' churches. They are products of primary evangelization, whereby men and women have voluntarily declared their allegiance to Jesus Christ and his body. They have existed from the beginning independent of political control. Many of these churches have been able to survive only by continued evangelization. Even after several generations they have retained some of this character. But this is largely the result of circumstance, not of conscious design by the parent missions. The possibility of developing *in loco* an ecclesiology at once biblically and theologically responsive was passed by.

Such a development should have proceeded along two lines: (1) the church local, and (2) the church universal. The church is more than a collection of saved individuals. The body of Christ is a corporate expression of the living Christ; it becomes concrete in particular cultures and among particular peoples. It is a worshiping, serving fellowship that manifests to the world God's righteousness now in its midst as a witness to the reign of God. But no local fellowship, no association of churches, no national church is complete in itself. The church universal embraces each local fellowship, bringing it to the completeness it cannot achieve alone. The church universal is both empirical reality and eschatological hope. It stands in a tension with the sociopolitical order. One strand of the missionary dynamic is that the body of Christ is not yet complete. Christ as head of the church impels his body to continue working to complete the body. This clearly calls for the witness to be carried to the four corners of the world.

Such an ecclesiology has immediate implications for the church as a disciplined community living under the lordship of Christ, a community of ethical discernment. The church as a missionary community is always aware of its pilgrim character, and its first loyalty in both its universal and local manifestation is to Christ and his body, rather than to the kingdoms of this world. Anything that might compromise its missionary task must be rejected. It witnesses to a kingdom of a different order than this world. And yet in this century, when two world wars and numerous lesser ones threatened human life on a scale without precedent in human experience, the church universal had no prophetic word for a divided world (Beaver 1964, chaps. 3-4; Iglehart 1948, 118-51).

12

The Modern Missionary Movement: 1792–1992

INTRODUCTION

The year 1992 marked the bicentennial of the publication of William Carey's tract *An Enquiry into the Obligation of Christians to Use Means for the Conversion of the Heathen* at Leicester, England, and the founding that autumn of The Particular Baptist Society for the Propagation of the Gospel amongst the Heathen (later known as the Baptist Missionary Society) at Kettering.[1] As a publishing event the appearance of Carey's little book was unremarkable. One of the problems Carey faced when he offered for India the following year was the disposal of unsold copies. Nonetheless, Carey's *Enquiry* soon gained symbolic significance and furnished a convenient starting point for a movement and an era.[2] By 1825 Protestants had organized some thirty missionary societies in the

---

This chapter was originally published in *Mission Studies* 9:1, 17 (1992):62-78. Revised for publication in this volume.

[1] It is not our purpose here to consider William Carey (1761-1834) himself. A critical missiological study of Carey and his associates at Serampore, Joshua Marshman and William Ward, is forthcoming from A. Christopher Smith, *The Mission Enterprise of Carey and His Colleagues* (to be published by Mercer University Press). Meanwhile, see A. Christopher Smith 1992.

[2] A good case can be made for other starting dates, for example, 1786. Eugene Stock (1899, 1:57) characterizes 1786 as "Annus Mirabilis" and lists the following influential events of that year: William Wilberforce dedicated his life to the overthrow of slavery, Thomas Clarkson published his essay on the slave trade, William Carey made his first effort to promote missions, Charles Grant proposed a plan for a mission to India, David Brown landed in Bengal, Bishop Thurlow pled India's needs in the annual sermon before the Society for the Propagation of the Gospel in Foreign Parts, the British Parliament passed the Colonial and Missionary Bishoprics Act, and the Eclectic Society— which would have much to do with the founding of several missionary societies a decade later—discussed foreign missions for the first time. He could have added that this was also the year in which the Wesleyan Methodist Society established missionary work in the West Indies.

British Isles, Europe, and the United States, while Roman Catholics had seen a revival of missionary passion among them.

During the past two centuries the world has had to negotiate change on a scale and at a pace that, even in retrospect, is difficult to comprehend.[3] Two dimensions of that change are growth in population and church membership. In these two centuries world population has grown from some 902 million people to 4.3 billion in 1980, while the number of Christians has risen from an estimated 208 million in 1800 to 1.4 billion in 1980. Stated in percentages, the number of Christians increased from 23 percent in 1800 to 32.8 percent in 1980 (Barrett 1982, 796). Especially telling is the contrast in geographical distribution of the Christian population in 1800 with that of 1980. More than 86 percent of all Christians in 1800 could be classified European. By 1980 half of all Christians were to be found outside the North Atlantic heartland of historical Christendom. Given the rates of growth among the newer churches and the static or declining membership of the North Atlantic churches, it is projected that, by the year 2000, 60 percent of all Christians will be in Asia, Africa, and Latin America. Such a shift occurs but rarely; the modern missionary movement, however it may otherwise be evaluated, has been an instrument of momentous change. And yet a mere recital of the facts does not begin to lay bare the meaning of such a development.

Here we wish to reflect on what the modern mission movement has meant for world and church. I propose to do that by exploring the following thesis: *The modern mission project has been a special locus of the larger confrontation among modernity, the Christian faith, and world cultures.* This requires that we take account of the secular context in which this movement has taken place and the ecclesiastical soil in which the movement took root.

BACKGROUND TO MODERN MISSIONS

The whole of the modern period is overshadowed by the Enlightenment, the powerful philosophical movement that emerged toward the end of the seventeenth century in Europe and set the terms for intellectual discourse for the next centuries. The historian Peter Gay has characterized the impact of the Enlightenment in these terms:

In the century of the Enlightenment, educated Europeans awoke to a new sense of life. They experienced an expansive sense of power over nature

---

[3] There was widespread awareness in the nineteenth century of the threat of expanding world population. In 1798 Thomas Malthus published his influential *An Essay on the Principle of Population*, republished in several editions, which held that population growth, if unchecked, will always tend to outrun growth of production. See also, James Johnston (1886): "Thoughtful men are staggered by this rapid increase of populations in view of the limit to the increase of food supply. Scarcity is already felt in India. Millions do not know what it is to have more than one meal a day and millions more are never free from the feeling of hunger" (19).

and themselves: the pitiless cycles of epidemics, famines, risky life and early death, devastating war and uneasy peace—the treadmill of human existence—seemed to be yielding at last to the application of critical intelligence (1969, 3).

This sense of mastery issued in a mission to bring the world within the orbit of this "enlightened" universal rationality. The universe was conceived to be an orderly machine governed by laws that ensured predictability. These laws could be discovered through experiment and analysis. Matter was increasingly broken down into smaller parts. In contrast to the medieval tradition, where authority resided in tradition, the modern outlook took scientific fact to be the source of authority. The modern intellectual outlook was one of radical skepticism toward all except skepticism itself. Science and technology were indispensable; religion was increasingly consigned to the realm of superstition. Technology and science promised unlimited improvement in human welfare. According to this new view, life was divided between the public and the private. The public sphere was governed by rationality and objective facts. The private sphere was controlled by sentiment and subjective values—and this is where religion belonged.

The Enlightenment was possessed of a strong purpose to make the world over in its own image. It infused the Western worldview with a great sense of buoyancy, self-confidence, and optimism. Not everyone received this missionary cause enthusiastically. Although the Chinese emperor in the seventeenth century was sufficiently intrigued by Western science to allow the Jesuit missionary contingent to remain at court, China firmly resisted further Western incursions until finally forced by the colonial powers in the nineteenth century to admit Westerners. India was slow to accept the Enlightenment project, and the East India Company, fearful of unnecessarily rending the social fabric, resisted attempts to introduce Western civilization until overridden by the British Parliament in 1813. By contrast, the Japanese, who were more successful in controlling access to their country by the Western powers, made a deliberate political decision to appropriate Western science and technology selectively in order to expedite the modernization of their society in the latter part of the nineteenth century. These and other cultures ultimately refused to accept the Enlightenment meta-narrative as their own. It is only as we have come to the end of the modern period that we appreciate the enormity of Enlightenment presumption.

In the wake of the Enlightenment, theology had become rationalistic and religion formal. Deism in Great Britain and North America was a cerebral affair. On the Continent, Enlightenment forces opposed Pietist missions, which had conversion as their goal (van den Berg 1956, 124). The rise of Methodism in Great Britain after 1735 elicited a strong reaction from leading churchmen, who were under the sway of rationalism, because of its "enthusiasm." But it was Pietism on the Continent, the Evangelical Revival led by the Wesleys and Whitefield in the British Isles, and the Great Awakening in America, shaped by individuals such as Jonathan Edwards, that revitalized the church and provided the creative matrix and motive power for the modern missionary movement along with a wide range of philanthropic initiatives by the end of the eighteenth century.

Taken as a whole, the eighteenth century was not a hospitable environment for missions. One of the few bright spots was the Moravian missions launched in 1732, a movement of lay people going largely to unknown corners of the world and there identifying with humble folk. The Moravian example was a source of inspiration to many. The missions founded in the seventeenth century had lost much of their momentum. Organizations such as the Society for Promoting Christian Knowledge (1699) and the Society for the Propagation of the Gospel in Foreign Parts (1701), which at their founding enjoyed the official patronage of the Church of England, during the next hundred years steadily lost strength, victims of the malaise that characterized the church generally (Thompson 1951, 104). Roman Catholic missions were in decline during much of the eighteenth century; and when Pope Clement XIV ordered the disbanding of the Jesuits in 1773, Catholic missionary activity effectively ceased for the next forty years.

MISSIONS AND MODERNITY

The modern missions project sought to hold together, on one hand, fidelity to the command of Jesus Christ to disciple the nations in his name and, on the other, a commitment to modernity. In spite of the constant tension between Christian faith and the modern worldview, Christians, including advocates of mission, did not question the superiority of Western culture or the assumption that the rest of the world needed the benefits of modernization. Indeed, the possibility of taking the benefits of modern culture to other peoples was one of the main motives for mission in this period. William Carey's voice was representative in this regard when he argued in his *Enquiry*: "Can we hear that they are without the gospel, without government, without laws, and without arts and sciences; and not exert ourselves to introduce amongst them the sentiments of men, and of Christians?" (1891, 70). Carey boldly advocated a missionary approach that combined Christianity and civilization as a single offer. No one asked whether mission and modernity might be irreconcilable, either in part or as a whole.

Indeed, this is a postmodern question. The earliest Christians made their witness from a position of marginality—social, economic, and political. From the fourth century onward the church had increasingly enjoyed a position of privileged power. It had come to depend heavily on Western culture in the way it conceived its role vis-à-vis the world, a view that contrasted with first-century missionaries.

Whether or not it is avowedly conversionist in intent, mission is intrusive and disruptive.[4] Sooner or later, either explicitly or implicitly, it questions the status quo, calls for change, and proposes an alternative allegiance. Missions are a

---

[4] See Matthew 10:34, which is set within the first missionary charge and instructions Jesus gave to the disciples.

fundamental threat to accepted values and standards of the cultures into which they are inserted (cf. Acts 17:6f.). Let it be noted that the secular development movement since 1945 has been as disruptive of traditional societies as any religious mission.

The modern missions movement was encumbered from the outset by the fact that the attitude of the churches toward missions remained ambivalent at best.[5] This debate was staged primarily within the church, since that is where the decisions were being made; but it was conducted with full awareness of the unsympathetic, even hostile, attitude of the secular order. Opposition within the church came from two sources. From the seventeenth century, theological liberalism had sought accommodation with the emergent modern culture. Many had grown weary of the ecclesiastical battles that characterized the post-Reformation years, and a liberal outlook that made doctrine more culturally acceptable was welcomed. Liberal theology instinctively reacted against a missionary approach that contained elements critical of the prevailing modern worldview. Liberalism has embraced the Enlightenment mission, which was inherently opposed to competing forms of mission. At the same time, many in the churches were in the thrall of a mission-less traditionalism. The call to mission threatened this homeostasis. It is hardly surprising that advocates of mission in the period leading up to 1800 faced enormous obstacles. This was an initiative promoted by a committed minority willing to question the status quo in light of what they believed to be the will of Jesus for his church.

The struggle to develop support for the missionary cause in Scotland is not atypical, and its roots go back to the sixteenth century. Heading the Scottish Confession of 1560 was the stirring missionary text: "This gospel of the kingdom shall be preached in all the world for a witness unto all nations; and then shall the end come" (Mt 24:14). But the Scottish Church of the sixteenth century manifested no missionary consciousness. The Book of Common Order contained many prayers for protection against the power of the Roman Catholic Church but only a single petition for "the conversion of the heathen" (cf. Mackichan 1927, 64f.). The Scottish Society for Promoting Christian Knowledge, inspired by the English SSPCK, was founded in 1709 largely for the purpose of providing Christian instruction for people in Scotland. Other initiatives, such as Robert Millar's (1723) missionary scheme[6] and support by SSPCK for David Brainerd's missionary work in New England, kept prodding the churches; but many remained unconvinced. In a sermon in 1755 Principal Robertson defended the apathetic response to the appeals of the SSPCK for support of foreign work by arguing that the progress of science in the Christian nations was preparing the world to receive the gospel. He expressed the faint hope that God might raise up

---

[5] For a thorough investigation of the Carey era, see J. van den Berg 1956.

[6] Robert Millar of Paisley, mission promoter, published his two-volume *A History of the Propagation of Christianity* (Edinburgh: n.p., 1723) and urged the sending of missionaries.

those willing to propagate the gospel so that "we might see the knowledge of the Lord filling the earth as the waters cover the sea" (Mackichan 1927, 72f.). This traditional outlook remained strong. Robertson dared to offer neither a rationale for mission nor a call for support for the cause.

Toward the end of the eighteenth century the pace of missionary initiatives was quickening. The nonconformists and supporters of missionary societies were able to take decisions more readily in support of missions than was the Church of Scotland. A crucial debate took place in 1796 when a motion was introduced before the General Assembly. The debate turned on several points. The opposing arguments are summed up in remarks by a Mr. Hamilton: "To spread abroad the knowledge of the Gospel among barbarous and heathen nations seems to me highly preposterous" (Millar 1723, 80), he exclaimed, "in as far as it anticipates, nay, as it even reverses the order of nature. Men must be polished and refined in their manners before they can be properly enlightened in religious truths. Philosophy and learning must in the nature of things take the precedence." He extolled the virtues of "untutored" peoples but warned that simply bringing the Christian message "will not refine his morals nor ensure his happiness." It merely disrupts a tranquil way of life. Hamilton concluded by pointing to the plight of the Scottish masses, saying that all the resources available were needed to meet the needs in Scotland. John Erskine, using an argument that Thomas Chalmers would deploy with effect in the future, countered this by saying that the genius of the gospel was that it was accessible to all peoples regardless of their ability or cultural attainments. Erskine cited the words of St. Paul: "I am debtor both to the Greeks and to the Barbarians" (ibid., 85). He challenged the notion that the church is truly motivated to generous giving by concentrating only on domestic needs. Yet Erskine's viewpoint did not carry the day. The question of mission was sufficiently divisive that a substitute motion to delay decision was adopted by the Assembly. When nearly thirty years later the Church of Scotland returned to the question of mission, a motion in support of organizing for mission passed unanimously.

Missing from this particular strand of the story is the moral passion that played an important part from the 1780s onward in motivating both missionary and humanitarian action: antislavery. The strategic role played by the Clapham Sect has been recounted frequently. This close-knit group of influential English aristocrats of evangelical persuasion made the antislavery cause their own, founding the colony of Sierra Leone in 1787 to be a "Province of Freedom" and participating in the organizing of missionary and philanthropic societies to further their religious and humanitarian interests (Jakobsson 1972, 578-92). The views of William Wilberforce and his friends left their imprint on modern missions with their emphasis on personal conversion, world evangelization, humanitarianism, and affirmation of modernity.[7]

---

[7] See Karl Rennstich (1982) for a brief characterization of the understanding of the mission task of the first inspector of the Basel Mission, Christian G. Blumhardt. It tracks well with that identified with the English evangelicals.

THE TRANSFORMATION OF CATEGORIES

One way of viewing the impact of the modern mission movement is to consider the ways in which certain concepts have been developed or fundamentally challenged as a result of this experience. Three areas will be noted: culture, church, and theology.

1. Culture

The modern mission movement was launched on a great uncharted sea called culture. Although a few individuals had begun to think along new lines about culture from the seventeenth century, by 1800 the human sciences had not been established and there still was no explicit and abstract concept of culture.[8] This meant that a precritical understanding of culture prevailed. A precritical perspective means a people take their own culture to be self-evidently correct and the norm by which the behavior and mores of other people are judged. If we are to draw comparisons between cultural system we must develop theories of culture and systems for classifying cultural phenomena. This conceptual development can be dated from the 1840s.[9] It was stimulated by the general intellectual ferment arising out of the Enlightenment, the rapidly expanding intercultural relations between people of the West with other peoples round the world, and the sustained involvement of missionaries with the peoples to whom they went. The missionary was committed to learning language so as to enable preaching and teaching. Since many of the peoples to whom missionaries went did not have a written language, linguistics had to be developed. All of this required accurate and careful observation of culture and languages. Wherever missionaries went, a priority was to provide the Christian scriptures in the vernacular language of the people.[10]

To be sure, the nineteenth-century story is riddled with contradictions with regard to missionaries and their attitudes toward other peoples and their cultures. Not all were models of sensitivity and insight. William Carey and his associates at Serampore are representative of those who invested heavily in linguistic and cultural studies and won respect from the Bengali community in this regard. On the other hand, Robert Moffat, who displayed many remarkable qualities in his pioneer missionary work in Southern Africa, nonetheless was prepared to believe that "Satan has employed his agency with fatal success, in erasing every vestige of religious impression from the minds of Bechuanas, Hottentots, and Bushmen" (Edwin Smith 1961, 83). One could go on citing examples *ad*

---

[8] This section depends on Taber 1991, chap. 1.

[9] H. P. Thompson (1951) reports that the term *culture* was first used for this emerging concept in German in the 1840s and in English in the 1860s.

[10] Cf. William A. Smalley (1991) for a comprehensive history. Lamin Sanneh (1989) emphasizes the importance of the vernacularization of the Christian message and the role, often unwitting, played by the missionary outsider in the process.

nauseam to reinforce the point already made: this was a period of considerable confusion combined with arrogance with regard to culture, and the missionary was by no means the only culprit. One of the special burdens many missionaries had to bear was the conduct of Western traders, military personnel, settlers, and colonial servants who flagrantly contradicted moral decency and Christian ideals but who were frequently identified, on cultural grounds, as Christians.

One of the remarkable early works on missions and culture was the study produced by the indefatigable Gustav Warneck, *Modern Missions and Culture: Their Mutual Relations*, translated into English by Thomas Smith from the German edition of 1879 and published in Edinburgh in 1883. In the preface Warneck reports that he has had an abundance of mission literature at his disposal and observed that it

> has hitherto, in a remarkable way, devoted only a somewhat step-motherly attention to the subject in hand. It has been its part both in reports, and also in monographs of missionary history—and generally quite properly—to present the peculiarly religious side of the missionary enterprise; and the excursions which it has made, often very effectually, into other territories, and for the benefit of geography, ethnology, the science of religion, and philology, rather than of culture-history.[11]

This is an accurate assessment of the state of play at that time. Warneck was sensitive to the conflict between Enlightenment views and Christianity reflected in the attacks being launched against missions in the press and other publications. He held that a healthy culture held together the material, intellectual, and moral dimensions of healthy existence, but that modern culture took a narrower and more limiting view inasmuch as it emphasized the material and intellectual dimensions while slighting the moral. Warneck depicted the gospel as the "new leaven of culture . . . a culture-force of the first rank" (Warneck 1883, 5). In short, he argued that the gospel must be the leading edge of mission and that culture could not be trusted to safeguard the welfare of the human community on its own.

It would be pleasant to report that this growing knowledge of culture was rapidly applied to mission theory and policy, resulting in guidance that was more sensitive, insightful, and serviceable in the cause of the Christian gospel. But experience was otherwise. From about 1840 to 1870 mission theory was being developed with the indigenous church ideal formulated by Rufus Anderson, Henry Venn, and others as the key concept. The virtue of this formula was that it focused the task of the missionary on a clear goal. It did not address many related

---

[11] In some ways Warneck's work anticipates the three volume sociological survey by James S. Dennis (1897, 1899, 1906), but Warneck's work is more theoretical and analytical than that of Dennis.

questions—for example, the relations between the emerging church and its cultural context—but it did set priorities. Although mission societies continued to swear allegiance to the indigenous church in the period after 1870, the High Imperial period is devoid of a clear theoretical framework. To the extent this theoretical vacuum was filled, it was done by imperialism itself. In this regard several summary points can be made: (1) Few missionaries or administrators of mission societies questioned the role the West was destined to play in relation to other world cultures. (2) However, there were those throughout the period who criticized the imperialist system and pointed out its incompatibility with Christian missions. (3) Missionaries were to be found at all points of the spectrum, from uncritical advocates of collaboration between imperialism and mission to those who argued for careful separation.[12]

Surveying the course of Christian history these past two centuries, Kenneth Cragg warns: "It has to be remembered that the universal is always in the trust of the particular—particular persons, conditions, occasions, and places" (1968, 18). As we have observed, the human sciences were becoming established at the same time the West was entering the High Imperial period. At that particular moment the Enlightenment project seemed more credible than ever. The imperial cause was readily justified inasmuch as new theories of culture and race demonstrated ways of evaluating and grading peoples and their cultures, from lower to higher.[13] From the vantage point of that particular time and location, Western civilization was "self-evidently" the most highly developed of all, and this bestowed a moral duty to furnish tutelage to the "weaker" peoples. Throughout the modern period the Industrial Revolution provided an economic basis for worldwide activity by the Western nations, including missions. The entire period cannot be understood without taking this into account.

By the end of the nineteenth century there were growing signs of fundamental conflict between the universal rationality of the Enlightenment, allied as it was with Western imperialism, and the universal reach of the kingdom of God. This reaction took two forms. One was the emergence of indigenous movements in most of the colonies that ultimately won political independence from the Western powers. The other was a growing movement of religious independence, usually in reaction to Western missions, which eventuated in the formation of thousands of new Christian denominations worldwide.[14]

---

[12] See, among others, the essays by Forman, Webster, Gluer, and Rennstich in Christensen and Hutchison 1982.

[13] Cf. Philip D. Curtin 1960. From the beginning the social sciences displayed no special ethical insight or sensitivity; but many social scientists as heirs of the Enlightenment have exhibited hostility toward religion, especially where missions have been concerned.

[14] The literature on religious independence is immense. A pioneering study of the phenomenon is Bengt Sundkler (1960 [1948]). For the field as a whole, see H. W. Turner 1977.

2. Church

It has long been an acknowledged fact that the modern mission movement was birth mother to the ecumenical movement of the twentieth century. The earliest and strongest impulses for Christian unity came from those places where new churches were being founded and the scandal of Western denominationalism was thrown up in bold relief. Church union schemes such as the one that led to the formation of the Church of South India in 1947 were a direct fruit of this vision. Important as this movement has been, there are other dimensions to be considered.

The faith tradition that we trace to Abraham (Gn 12:1-3) was forged in Diaspora—in Abraham's going out from his ancestral home and security in response to the call of God to mission. This mission was marked from the beginning by the vulnerability of being without the usual securities of a settled existence. This way of life is marked by utter dependence on God, living by faith. Later, in the time of the Judges, the people of Israel demanded kingship in order "to be like the other nations" (1 Sm 8:5). This signaled a settling in and becoming dependent on conventional political and economic power and enmeshed in local loyalties. Biblical faith was renewed from time to time as the representative few were thrust out into exile, where they rediscovered the genius of their calling.

Martin Buber made a compelling characterization of the Christian faith that is consistent with the Abrahamic tradition sketched above. Buber said: "Christianity *begins [sic]* as Diaspora and mission. The mission means in this case not just diffusion; it is the life-breath of the community and accordingly the basis of the new People of God" (1951, 10).

Turning Godward, *metanoia*, involves turning away from every other power and casting oneself wholly on God's mercy; just as for Abraham, so too for the Christian being called and being sent is one and the same. The integrity and vitality of the community depend on the continual renewal of this consciousness.

The Christendom model of church was deformed by its disallowance of Diaspora and all that entails. The Diaspora that went out from Christendom was a catalyst for growth of the church elsewhere. The modern mission movement recovered for the world church the importance of Diaspora.

The dominant understanding of mission these past two centuries has been that of sending specially commissioned people to do specified tasks in the name of the gospel. That is a valid view but too limited. It is important that we learn again "that the central mystery of Christianity can only be fully realized when it informs, and is informed by, the variety of social orders and cultural traditions that exist" (Burridge 1991, 58). The realization of that enlarging meaning of the faith depends on a continuous forward movement in mission. The people of God are called to be in the service of the kingdom of God, the universal that constantly seeks to draw into itself all the particularities—all peoples, the ends of the earth.

As a consequence of the modern mission movement a world church has emerged that cannot be contained or understood based on the old categories. But Western ecclesial reality remains largely the one-dimensional model of Christendom that continues to resist being converted by Diaspora. Like Esau, the Western church risks forfeiting its birthright for a mess of pottage.

3. Theology

Western theology has yet truly to discover the modern mission movement and the ecclesial reality that has issued from it. Conventional theology bears the imprint both of its scholastic heritage and dependence on the "universal rationality" of the Enlightenment. Neither of these sponsors was sympathetic to a missionary theology; neither did they take seriously the pluriform church that came into existence beyond the traditional boundaries of Christendom.

One of the regrettable aspects of the modern mission movement was that it was largely unaccompanied by theologians committed to mission. For mission involves the church in the most fundamental of theological questions, and it is at the point of missionary engagement that critical theological reflection is called for. One has only to turn to the New Testament to find the basic model for theology that is missionary and mission that is theological. But that model was not operative in the church of Christendom. It was only toward the end of the modern mission movement, as it became increasingly evident that the new churches required their own theology, that efforts were made to break with the traditional academic model that was missionally sterile and begin the search for one that recognized the new realities.

Various initiatives have been taken to rethink the task of theology *in loco* and to encourage theologians from churches in Africa, Asia, and Latin America to take the lead in developing theology that is contextually sound. A start has been made; the old category has been shown to be bankrupt. The way forward is still being canvassed.

SUMMING UP

1. Modern Missions a Failure

In his book *Asia and Western Dominance*, Indian historian K. M. Panikkar surveys the Vasco da Gama epoch, 1498-1945. One short chapter is entitled, "Christian Missions." Panikkar drives home the point that in spite of the immense and sustained effort made by the missions, "the attempt to conquer Asia for Christ has definitely failed" (1959, 297). Writing in the aftermath of the communist takeover when China expelled all Westerners, including missionaries, the picture seamed clear. Panikkar could report that for the missions "the collapse has been most complete" in China. Similarly, after India gained independence from Great Britain in 1947, Prime Minister Nehru took the decision to begin the systematic—albeit gradual—elimination of Christian missionaries from that country, a decision that was carefully implemented. Forty years later the failure Panikkar reported may appear less clear-cut. In 1979, thirty years after China closed her doors to the West, she began to reestablish relations and allow various exchanges. It soon became clear that, although the missionaries had been driven from China, the church had not been eliminated. Instead a church that had endured great persecution and suffering in the period after 1949 had grown in these adverse circumstances.

However, Panikkar's fourfold critique of modern missions must be taken seriously. Missionary work had been needlessly weakened by four facts: (1) an attitude of moral and religious superiority; (2) the association of missions with aggressive imperialism; (3) attitude of European/Christian superiority toward other cultures and peoples; and (4) the divisions among Christians, which together with the crisis of Western civilization, left Christianity discredited in the eyes of Asians. Other critics beyond the Christian circle, friendly and otherwise, have expressed similar sentiments. Christians as well have criticized modern missions (cf. Cragg 1968, 19-30). Missions have attracted almost continuous controversy.

In the early years of the modern mission movement the Rev. Sydney Smith was a colorful critic of missions with his cartoon-like caricatures of missionaries and their works. He was the quintessential Enlightenment devotee, who allowed that missions might play a useful role in "civilizing" lesser peoples, but he could never countenance overt "Christianization." By the 1830s Protestants of all varieties had generally embraced the missionary cause pioneered by the evangelicals, albeit with particular modifications in mission theory—for example, the Anglo-Catholic theory that episcopacy is the basis for the apostolate. During the final quarter of the nineteenth century new fissures opened, separating Christians into new groups. These changes reflected both external as well as internal forces. The imperial spirit encouraged a new aggressiveness on the part of the Western nations and fostered proprietary interest in other parts of the world. Within the church diverse renewal currents were being felt—some emphasizing inward piety and individual responsibility, others reflecting growing confidence in evolutionary progress. The lines of division between liberal and fundamentalist were increasingly drawn with liberals embracing the "civilizing" vision of modernity and fundamentalists reacting by emphasizing what they felt the liberals had abandoned of Orthodox faith (Hutchison 1982, 168). Both tendencies were reductionistic. The controversy stirred by the report of the Laymen's Foreign Missions Commission, *Re-Thinking Missions* (Hocking 1932), is best understood as an expression of this polarization.

From within the missionary community itself there have been critics, none more forceful than Roland Allen in the twentieth century who would have agreed with several of the points raised by K. M. Panikkar. Allen advocated reform of missionary attitude toward other peoples and asserted their competence to govern themselves based on the apostolic model of the early church. Coming as they did during the age of empire and the rising demand for independence on the part of both colony and mission-founded church, Allen's strictures were like salt on an open wound.

2. Modern Missions a Success

One cannot study the record of modern missions since the 1920s without gaining the impression that it is an aging movement, increasingly unable to adapt to the times. At the Ghana Assembly of the International Missionary Council, Walter Freytag compared the situations at the time of the 1928 Jerusalem Assembly and thirty years later. With penetrating insight Freytag said: "Then missions had problems, but they were not a problem themselves. There was no question that the initiative in witness and action was with Western missions as they stood. Today we do not speak of the initiative of Western missions but only of their contribution" (1958, 138-50). Such a change represents a shaking of the foundations. The basic pattern that guided missions for more than 150 years has crumbled. The great concern of leaders like Freytag was to preserve the churches' commitment to mission while negotiating this thoroughgoing change. The old structures have continued to be dismantled in the three decades since Freytag spoke. Every sign points to the fact that with the end of the modern period in world history has also come the end of modern missions.

Although there is much that is ambiguous about the record of the modern missions movement, it is not being presumptuous to speak of success. In the nineteenth century, missions were described as the scaffolding of the new church under construction. In too many cases the scaffolding seemed oppressively heavy or was allowed to stay in place far longer than necessary. As the scaffolding has been dismantled—at times forcibly, especially in the years since 1945—we are continually impressed that viable churches were constructed in which the Spirit of God dwells. The treasure was indeed entrusted to earthen vessels, but it was God's treasure. And God never sends laborers into the harvest field without supervision (Mt 28:20b).

13

Mission in Transition:
1970–1994

Following World War II the entire world system entered a time of rapid development and crisis. The stresses of that period were centered in two facts: this was the final phase of the dismantling of the apparatus of European dominance in world affairs, and these were the years of the formalized and protracted Cold War between the United States and the Soviet Union. Crisis is the mother of change. The strains within the sociopolitical systems exerted their influences directly, at times forcibly, on the Christian movement. Inevitably, Christian missions changed during these decades.

Hendrik Kraemer (1938, 24) asserted that "one ought to say that the Church is always in a state of crisis and that its greatest shortcoming is that it is only occasionally aware of it." My aim in this chapter is to examine how geopolitical and socioeconomic features have shaped the Christian mission and to explore how the most recent period has thrust mission into a state of flux and transition. I attempt to throw light on what has been happening to the Christian mission in the period since 1970. My argument is that the much discussed crisis of the 1950s and the 1960s was pivotal for what has developed since; hence, we need to concentrate our attention on that period. For the Christian movement, the crisis stemmed from both internal and external forces.

EUROCENTRIC HISTORY

The formal dismantling in the decades of the 1950s and 1960s of the remnants of the several European empires signified far more than the transfer of political power from colonizer to colonized. It coincided with the end of several centuries of European dominance in the world. We may sketch briefly the main features of this history.

This chapter was first published in *Missiology* 15:4 (1987):419-30. Revised for publication in this volume.

The seeds of what was to become Europe were sown in the fifth and sixth centuries of the Christian Era. But Europe actually began when the rising forces of Islam established their sphere of influence, which reached as far west as Spain and shut off Europe from contacts to the south and east. Even then, no one thought in terms of *Europe*, as such. The continent was populated by disparate tribes parochial in outlook and loyalty. It took the march of the Ottoman Turks into Europe during the fourteenth century to implant the idea of Europe as an entity. Various emperors, starting with the Frankish Charles the Great in the ninth century, had ambitions to unite the tribes of Europe under their rule, but none had succeeded.

Historian Geoffrey Barraclough suggests that the first "turning point"—that is, a crisis producing a fundamental new direction—in the development of Europe occurred during the period 1076-1122 (Barraclough 1977, 22). These fifty years were a time of prolonged struggle between the papacy and the crown. The presenting issue was who should control the appointment of bishops. The underlying issue was conflicting views of society and the place of the church in it. In the end the pope successfully blocked efforts that might have led to the creation of a single European empire. Instead, there emerged a series of regional states. The conflict had fostered an attitude of critical inquiry that came to characterize the European mind. It is arguable that had an emperor won, thus forming a monolithic empire, Europeans would in the long run have had far less intellectual freedom. And it was this freedom that became foundational to European development.

At the end of the fifteenth century Europe was still only one of five major civilizations. Each was essentially regional and self-sufficient. Europe was neither as powerful nor as wealthy as some of the others. Compared to the Chinese, Indian, and Islamic civilizations, Europe showed up a distant fourth. But this was one of those fateful moments in history. Whereas Europeans were beginning their first voyages of exploration, a step that was to alter permanently the nature of the world system, the emperors of China and India were moving toward greater isolation from the rest of the world.

By the end of the eighteenth century the world situation had changed dramatically. Europeans now controlled the ocean trade routes and were engaged in commerce worldwide. They had taken control of great areas of territory outside of Europe. What made all this possible? The second turning point in European history was the Scientific Revolution, which may symbolically be dated from the founding of the Royal Society in London in 1662. Earlier that century Francis Bacon wrote *The New Atlantis* (1626) in which he characterized the spirit of inquiry that was to become the hallmark of science. It would search out "the knowledge of causes and secret motions of things, and the enlarging of the bounds of human empire, to the effecting of all things possible" (Barraclough 1977, 25). What is important to bear in mind is that, contrary to our usual way of reading the history of this time, European expansion worldwide had been rather negligible prior to this time. It was the application of scientific technology that enabled Europe to rise to a position of preeminence in the world. This large-scale expansion took place only in the late eighteenth and nineteenth centuries.

The Scientific Revolution, the fruit of a thousand years of development, was uniquely European. It had no parallel elsewhere in the world of the seventeenth century. It was the last great pivotal development until the present.

Ethnocentrism is not necessarily a dangerous commodity. No one gets greatly concerned over the dietary habits or exotic folkways of a particular group. They may even be exploited for commercial purposes by the more enterprising outsider. But let that group set out to impose its peculiarities of religious belief, economic practice, or worldview on other peoples, and reaction will be swift and certain. This is what happened as Europeans extended their domination worldwide. On the one hand, with their growing sense of power arising out of scientific discoveries and the harnessing of science for industry, Europeans became imbued with the idea of a *manifest destiny* that called them to be directors and protectors of the weaker peoples of the world. This included not only serving as guardians of other peoples but schooling them in the ways of true "civilization." On the other hand, the recipients of European beneficence began reacting with growing intensity to this unwelcome imposition. Already in the nineteenth century revolts and mutinies occurred in the colonies. Both the American and French revolutions had raised important questions. The successful American revolt against the British served as a warning that the colonized would sooner or later sue for independence. The French Revolution embodied new ideals against which the old political order would in the future be measured.

In spite of these influences, the European powers grew more self-assured about their role as colonizers. After 1860 there was a hardening of attitude on both sides. The colonized asked with increasing insistence why they could not be governed according to the same democratic ideals and political system as the colonizer. In the end, the force of this moral argument could not be ignored. It fueled both the determination of the nationalist movements to win freedom and eroded whatever justification had been contrived earlier to sanction colonialism.

It was in this milieu that the modern missionary movement was birthed and its theoretical and practical underpinnings were worked out. As Max Warren demonstrated in two highly suggestive series of lectures, we cannot begin to understand this movement without placing it within its sociopolitical context (Warren 1965 and 1967). For example, there can be little doubt that what became the basis of the theory of mission in the nineteenth century—the indigenous church—is heavily indebted to the British colonial experience. The basic assumptions and approach were already taking shape by the 1820s. What is generally not remembered is that Henry Venn's brother-in-law, Sir James Stephen, was the outstanding and influential under-secretary for the colonies, making him the top civil servant in that ministry. Stephen helped shape colonial policies through his own theoretical writings and policy proposals. His view of the colonies was that this was a *temporary* responsibility, which Great Britain should discharge as humanely as possible and only so long as required. The British should share their experience and organize appropriate political structures but always with a view toward turning leadership back to the indigenes as early as possible. At the same time, Stephen was an active member of the Church

Missionary Society's executive committee for a number of years. It thus remained for Henry Venn and his counterpart, Rufus Anderson, across the Atlantic, to take these somewhat unorganized ideas and reduce them to a formula and program policies to be applied to missions.

It is unthinkable that anything like the theory of the indigenous church would have emerged, say, in 1875 or 1890. By that time the winds had shifted. This was now the High Imperial period. In the Colonial Office Sir James's ideas were deemed to be quite out of step with the times. In missionary circles the Venn-Anderson formulation remained on the books, but it was actively disregarded by the vast majority of missionary societies and their field staffs right up to World War I. The tragedy was that this new colonial mindset was generating plenty of reaction. For the missions the reaction took two forms. Within the mission-founded churches there was growing restlessness and criticism of missionary attitudes and practices. But there were others who chose to make their exit from these churches in order to found churches free of missionary patronage or control. With the emergence of aggressive nationalist movements in many of the colonies in the twentieth century, missions could no longer ignore efforts to make the indigenous church the goal of their work.

BIPOLAR GEOPOLITICS

A World Dominated by Ideological Conflict

The Eurocentric geopolitics we have been surveying were supplanted in the twentieth century by bipolar geopolitics. The United States emerged from World War I as a dominant power but was reluctant to assume the mantle of leadership. Instead, the USA lapsed into isolation. It took World War II to thrust the USA into world leadership. The Union of Soviet Socialist Republics resulted from the Bolshevik victory in 1917. In the years following the revolution, Russia weathered a number of internal crises. World War II set the stage for Russia to seize world leadership of the socialist cause.

The decade following the end of the Second World War was critical. The USSR and the USA quickly adopted antagonistic positions toward each other. Each was driven by a desire to defeat the other on ideological grounds. Each sought to line up other nations on its side, for the whole world was the theater for this conflict. Out of this came the Soviet-led bloc and the USA-led bloc, with the two sides engaged in what was soon called the Cold War. The USSR successfully brought all of Eastern Europe, China, and North Korea within its orbit, while the USA sought to develop alliances with the nations of the free world. This placed the world system under unprecedented strain. Every part of the globe was affected. Tensions were high as the world lived with the prospect of a third world war between the superpowers.

By 1955 cracks began appearing in the respective blocs. Russia's allies grew restive, and revolts broke out from time to time. John Foster Dulles anathematized those countries that preferred neutrality. The Bandung Conference in 1955, where Jawaharlal Nehru of India and Gamal Abdel Nasser of Egypt led in the formation of a bloc of Nonaligned Nations, marked the beginning of the end of USSR-USA domination of the world through the two blocs. The Nonaligned Nations never were able to act in concert, but symbolically they served as a counterbalance to the superpowers. Still, the two superpowers were set on a course from which neither could pull back. The conflict was to prove a costly venture for both. It spawned a proliferating defense buildup and the development of terrifying new weapons that threatened the entire world. The rift put a serious drag on the economies of both the USA and USSR.

This period of bipolar geopolitics offers a valuable comparative missiological perspective. The USA, while officially neutral in religious matters, is positively disposed toward religion. Few eyebrows were raised in 1945 when General Douglas MacArthur, as military governor of Japan, called for the sending of a thousand missionaries to that country. The USSR, consistent with its guiding Marxist ideology, was officially atheist and antagonistic toward religion. Wherever communist governments have come to power, attempts have been made either to eradicate or strictly regulate religious activity. This was brought home to the Western world when the communists came to power in China in 1949 and proceeded to expel all foreign missionaries.

Following the Bolshevik victory in 1917 the Christian movement in Russia did indeed undergo a period of adjustment under the impact of sustained government efforts to eliminate religion. But by 1980 there were as many practicing Christians in the USSR as in 1900, and the number was growing steadily (Barrett 1987, 85). Although we do not have a fully satisfactory picture of the church in China, there is mounting evidence of how Christians survived the long years of persecution between 1949 and 1979, and there are continued reports of substantial growth in the number of adherents.

Measured by its ability to survive and even grow, the Christian movement has managed to adapt to all kinds of political systems. What has not changed is the negligible penetration of the Christian message in communities loyal to one of the great world religions. Political ideologies and systems have proved unable to command either the depth of loyalty or to have the staying power of religion.

In contrast to the Eurocentric period, the bipolar period has been of short duration. In terms of its impact on the Christian movement, it has perhaps been too brief to have allowed for the formation of a missiological vision especially suited to the period. The bipolar period has, in fact, overlapped substantially with the final phase of the Eurocentric period. Nonetheless, this bipolar period has been more than the antechamber to the future. It has been the catalyst for a new era and a new paradigm.

The Impact of American Culture

The American experience is one particular strand within the ambit of Western civilization. In its development the American nation has drawn freely on its

European inheritance. But it has nonetheless pursued its own course, based on abundant natural resources, ample land mass, and variegated ethnic traditions that form the American people. American culture was pervaded by a sense of crisis in the 1960s. John F. Kennedy was elected president in 1960 by skillfully exploiting the growing sense of uneasiness the American people felt. He promised to get the country moving again and challenged the nation with a vision of the New Frontier. But Charles R. Morris has argued that the Kennedy-Johnson administrations represent not the beginning of a new era but the end of a tradition. In Morris's words, Kennedy offered "an *attitude* toward American government, a sense of omnicompetence that had been missing during the Eisenhower years, a style of problem-solving—cool, pragmatic, nonideological, to be sure, but brimming with confidence that the world could be made a much better place than it was" (Morris 1984, 3). Speaking in 1962, Kennedy said there were no great ideological issues left. What the country faced were "technical problems, administrative problems" (ibid., 5). Yet the decade of the 1960s was to be one of the most troubled and ideologically divisive decades in American history.

President Kennedy was the quintessential pragmatist, a product of the dominant philosophical tradition in twentieth-century America. William James and John Dewey, founders of pragmatist philosophy, insisted that truth was determined by an idea's usefulness. As James put it in *Pragmatism*: "Either a concept is useful because it is true or it is true because it is useful" (Morris 1984, 6). Pragmatist thought proved to be highly congenial to the American mind and came to permeate all areas of life—legal, educational, social, economic, political. John Dewey advocated vast social engineering schemes in the 1920s that presaged the Great Society of Lyndon Johnson's administration in the mid-1960s. But it was the war in Vietnam that proved to be the severest test of American culture.

An insightful study of American culture is Loren Baritz's book *Backfire*, an investigation of how the United States conducted the war in Vietnam. He observed that each culture has its own way of waging war and "there is an American way of war that is congruent with the American way of life, with American culture. . . . We cannot understand war without understanding culture" (Baritz 1985, viii). The American approach to war was thoroughly technological, and the entire system was brought to heel by Robert McNamara, who introduced the Program Planning and Budget System (PPBS). In the end it resulted in a massive defeat. In the preoccupation with statistics, results, and technological capabilities, the United States largely ignored the South Vietnamese—despising their culture, refusing to learn their language, and failing to take them seriously as allies. The American military seemed mesmerized by its technological apparatus and oblivious to the people on whose behalf, supposedly, it was fighting the war. Indeed, in the end the American public refused to lend support for the war because people could see no sense in it; it lacked a clear goal.

The thrust of the Baritz argument is that technology has had a wide-ranging impact on American culture. It goes well beyond the application of science to the production of goods and services. It has come to define reality. Baritz reports having dinner with some top-ranking engineers who insisted that "if it doesn't have a solution it isn't a problem" (Baritz 1985, 32). This was the mentality of the pragmatic technocrats who presided over the American defeat in Vietnam.

The Baritz study is a mirror—undoubtedly with some distortions—that we may use to understand better this particular culture and the way it has made its impact on the world since 1945. Europe led the way in technology in the eighteenth and nineteenth centuries. But on American soil technology was carried to new heights in the service of a pragmatic vision. All of this has contributed to the shaping of the American character, which played a key role in the ideological conflict that dominated the bipolar period.

The Indigenous Church Revisited

The years following World War II were a time of frustration for missions and the churches they had founded. In spite of sustained rhetoric about the indigenous church in the post–Rufus Anderson/Henry Venn era, mission-church relationships remained troubled and unsatisfactory. At least three streams of discourse intermingled in the debate about the indigenous church. The first of these streams was carried by books that were published with regularity, starting with John L. Nevius and running right up to T. S. Soltau, that reiterated what might be called the classical indigenous church theory. H. H. Rowland's *Native Churches in Foreign Fields* (1925) is representative of this stream in its attention to correct formulae, methods and strategies.

The second stream emerged in the 1930s through the historical studies of Kenneth Scott Latourette and the missiological studies of Hendrik Kraemer. Stephen Neill, Max Warren, Walter Freytag, and others contributed to these studies as well. Today Kraemer's landmark book, *The Christian Message in a Non-Christian World,* which appeared in 1938, is remembered chiefly for the position he took with regard to other religions. However, a major theme of the book is how the church is to relate to its culture; the last chapter is entitled "Christian Mission in Relation to Its Environment." Kraemer occupied an unusual place in the mission world. He had spent fifteen years in Indonesia on the staff of the Bible society rather than as a missionary. He had been called on to investigate and study the mission situation throughout the islands. (Extracts from these reports were published in English in 1958 as *From Missionfield to Independent Church*.) Along with J. H. Bavinck, he had urged a reform of theological training through a curriculum geared to the study of theology *in loco*.

In *The Christian Message in a Non-Christian World* Kraemer conducted a profound and searching investigation of the nature of the church and the critical importance of the church being vitally related to its socio-historico-cultural milieu. He returned frequently to the point that the essential calling of the church is to be apostolic and prophetic in its world. Clearly, Kraemer was disturbed over the impasse he observed in the development from mission to church. He saw the solution as lying in a more theologically informed understanding of both church and culture.

One of Kraemer's sub-themes was the importance of worship in the life of a church. A decade later Stephen Neill took up this theme in an essay entitled "The Worship of God" (Neill 1948). He described perceptively the way missionaries introduced the form of worship familiar to them. This form was frequently gratefully accepted by the new converts. Of course they were not in the best position to evaluate critically whether the form was suitable or not. But it was an unfortunate decision, said Neill, because "the element of discontinuity is too marked. Spiritual health is not easily maintained unless the new retains its connection with the old and transforms it from within" (ibid., 124). Neill rejected the criticism that missions had a denationalizing effect. "The most Europeanized among the younger Churches is not the least like a Church of Europeans, since deep racial inheritances have a way of asserting themselves and disturbing merely superficial assimilations" (ibid., 124). The real problem is that the convert is caught between two worlds and feels uncomfortable with both. Ultimately, this tension must be resolved. Although Kraemer was aware of churches that had arisen in countries like China and Japan and were fully autonomous and indigenous—having never been under mission control—he paid no attention to them as a possible source of insight into the processes of indigenous church development.

The third stream of influence may be traced to the pioneering work of anthropologists and linguists such as Eugene A. Nida and Kenneth L. Pike. Nida developed the concept of dynamic equivalence in translation, and this informed the missionary anthropology that began to flourish in the 1950s, especially after the founding of *Practical Anthropology* in 1953. Using the tools of anthropology, this generation raised new questions about culture and the nature of the church. William A. Smalley subjected the time-honored indigenous church to fresh scrutiny. He found "the 'three selfs' are really projections of our American value system into the idealization of the church" (Smalley 1958, 51-65). This was an important straw in the wind.

Thus from the side of the sending churches voices continued to be raised out of concern for observable problems that had resulted from the classical missionary approach. From the side of the mission-founded churches, the pleadings that had been voiced for a long time—among others, V. S. Azariah at Edinburgh in 1910 and the Chinese church leaders at the Missionary Conference at Shanghai in 1922—were becoming more insistent. In a series of broadcast talks in 1961, "The Problem of the Indigenization of the Church in Nigeria," E. Bolaji Idowu put the issue forcefully: "The Church in Nigeria is on trial: she is being called upon to justify her existence in the country; to answer in precise terms the question as to whether her purpose in Nigeria is not to serve as an effective tool of imperialism" (Idowu 1965, 1). He drew a portrait of a church in, but not believably of, Nigeria. He lamented its secondhand theology, liturgy, and art. He compared unfavorably the mission-founded churches to the indigenous movements, with their freshness in worship, fully indigenous leadership, and the fact that they spoke deeply to the felt needs of Nigerians in relation to spiritual realities. A generation later Idowu's words—and he represents a host of concerned church leaders of his time—sound reasonable and moderate. In the early 1960s such an appeal was an astringent many Westerners refused to receive. The clamor for change finally climaxed around 1970 in the call for moratorium. This call stirred deep emotions. In practical terms it achieved few results. Symbolically, it marked a watershed, a turning point. The "plausibility structure" that had given life to the indigenous church had collapsed. Concurrent with the call for moratorium came a basic shift in mission theory. The bipolar period had ended.

POLYCENTRIC HISTORY

The theory of mission based on the indigenous church was a product of a particular historical period and culture. Out of the crisis of the bipolar period a new theoretical construct had to emerge. In 1972 the term *contextualization* entered missiological vocabulary through the report of the director of the Theological Education Fund, Shoki Coe.[1] Reading the definition and defense of the new term that Coe offered at that time in the light of later developments, one gets the impression that the concept was still inchoate. It was more an intuition than a clear concept. The need to defend the new as an extension of the old tended to inhibit. Coe said:

> Indigenization is a missiological necessity when the Gospel moves from one cultural soil to another and has to be retranslated, reinterpreted, and expressed afresh in the new cultural soil. Why, then, do we now use a new word, contextualization, in preference to indigenization? (Coe 1976, 20).

Coe went on to explain that indigenization was too static a concept and was oriented to the past. Furthermore, it had become identified exclusively with Asia and Africa. A new concept was needed that would serve the needs of all churches everywhere:

> So in using the word contextualization we try to convey all that is implied in the familiar term indigenization, yet seek to press beyond for a more dynamic concept which is open to change and which is also future-oriented (ibid.).

---

[1] The suddenness of the shift is illustrated by the fact that the term does not appear in the literature prior to 1972. *The Concise Dictionary of the Christian World Mission* (Neill, Anderson, and Goodwin 1970) does not note it. The festschrift in honor of R. Pierce Beaver (Danker and Kang 1971) makes no reference to it. The symposium *Mission in the '70s* (Boberg and Scherer 1972) does not discuss it.

Coe was speaking, of course, from the perspective of theological education. But contextualization itself was the fruit of much wider historical developments: the movement leading to political independence of colonized peoples; the coming into their own of more and more mission churches, along with the anguish over the lingering "Westernness" of these churches; and the changing evaluation of indigenous churches that had sprung to life in the wake of the modern missionary movement. All this and more documented the inadequacy of the old paradigm and the urgent need for a new one.

In 1979 Karl Rahner gave a lecture in the United States, "Towards a Fundamental Theological Interpretation of Vatican II" (Rahner 1979). He began by suggesting that Christian history in the Catholic tradition can be divided into three periods: (1) the Jewish period—up to A.D. 70; (2) the European period—up to A.D. 1962; and (3) the universal period—since Vatican II. I find this helpful. I agree with part of Rahner's schematization but wish to modify it as well.

A basic feature of the new period is the collapse of the system of blocs. Instead, we are witnessing a resurgence of ethnic groups, the emergence of new regional spheres of influence such as that of East Asia, and reinforcement of nation-states. The centers of power will likely be increasingly dispersed in this era of polycentric history. This poses important questions for missiological theory.

The theory of the indigenous church emerged to explain and make more efficient a unidirectional movement from West to non-West. Shifting the emphasis to context requires a complete revisioning of how mission is to be carried forward.

It appears to me that in the years since 1970 we have made the transition from the old era to the new to the extent of having identified the key theme. But we have not yet worked out a full-blown theoretical framework. Literature on contextualization burgeoned after 1972. Yet we "see through a glass darkly." Do we still view contextualization as Coe explained it originally, primarily as a linear extension—albeit a refinement—of indigenization? Or does it represent discontinuity with the previous era? What may prove decisive is that the locus of power has shifted irreversibly away from its longtime Western base to multiple centers on all continents.

There are numerous signs of initiatives being taken in these new centers across the world in working out local theologies, reforming church structures, and launching missionary action programs. Eventually this will bring into focus in a new way the age-old tension with which the church has always had to reckon: preserving both the universality and the locality of the church. A universality defined by Eurocentric dominance left little room for a genuine locality on the part of the non-Western churches. Indigenous churches that have emerged wherever missions have gone typically are characterized by a profound sense of locality without much awareness of the universal. Viewing the world as consisting of multiple centers of resource and initiative will force us to think in new ways about the shape of Christian mission in the twenty-first century.

As we anticipate the development of mission in this changing world, what are the critical points to hold before us? Three themes come to mind. First, the coming of God in Jesus Christ, God incarnate in human form, is normative for all missionary insertion into the human situation. The incarnation led to crucifixion and out of crucifixion came resurrection. Missionary witness that is genuine always unites full identification with unlimited service. Second, the developing church is the body of Christ. But as Kraemer pointed out forty years ago, missionaries have often worked with too limited an understanding of the church. An adequate ecclesiology will take into account the role of the church in the world, a role that embraces both its prophetic and its apostolic calling. Third, this movement toward contextualization calls for a new openness to the work of the Holy Spirit. The Spirit both converts and reforms in order that the church might be a co-participant in God's saving mission.

14

Missions in Search of Mission:
The Changing Fortunes
of the Mission Agency

INTRODUCTION

Theologically, mission is focused on the future, for mission is God's means of carrying forward the work of redemption until it is completed in the eschaton. The scriptures show the human drama coming to a grand climax in God's purpose and time. The people of God are called to bear witness before all the nations to God's gracious provision for all peoples in the light of that summing up in Christ Jesus. Adapting the phrase of Hendrikus Berkhof (1966, 81), "mission is a history-making endeavor." The eschaton draws mission towards its end point. But God has committed this mission to human agency in its implementation. In reflecting on the course of mission down through the years, we see the interplay between God's mission and human participation in it.

The human response to this theological impulse has been to create an agency or institution in the light of a vision of what the mission of God is calling us to do in a particular place and time. Inescapably agencies and institutions are the products of the particular historical and sociopolitical context in which they are created. Every organization bears the full marks of its human creators and reflects the qualities of imagination and leadership of its board and staff. We expect to find in the first stage of development a keen sense of vision. The way the program is carried out reflects that clarity of purpose. As the program evolves new stages appear in response to the changing environment. Indeed, institutions that fail to adapt to a changing world become obsolete. But adaptation can go in various directions. What is crucial is whether, in the course of making adjustments, an agency maintains fidelity to its founding purpose as its organizing principle or allows itself to be coopted by other matters. This chapter considers

This chapter was first published in *Mission Focus: Annual Review* 1 (1993):83-91. Revised for publication in this volume.

the crisis of identity that many long-established Western missionary societies are facing today. The thesis is that this crisis arises out of the disjunction between the era for which these organizations were designed and the emerging new phase. Three important facets of the present crisis are: (1) the origins of the society as an agency of mission, (2) the changed historical situation, and (3) the process of institutionalization.

THE ORIGINS OF THE MISSIONARY SOCIETY

What we know as the missionary society had its origins in the period around 1800 when the modern missionary movement came to birth. At that time churches had no structures for mission, and regardless of the ecclesiastical tradition, there was little sympathy for the cause among church leaders. But it was a time of growing awareness of the world combined with great cultural self-confidence on the part of the West.

What Peter Gay has described as the "recovery of nerve" among Europeans as a result of the Enlightenment easily and quickly translated into a sense of cultural superiority and proprietary responsibility for the rest of the world (Gay 1969, 3). The church was not immune to the spirit of the age. It was in the very air that early missions enthusiasts breathed. Although William Carey's first attempt to get Baptist backing for the sending of a mission overseas was brusquely rejected, it was an idea whose time had come. His 1792 appeal for Christians to "use means for the conversion of the heathens" soon gained a wide hearing.

The modern missionary movement would have been inconceivable apart from the missionary society. It was an innovation that led, in Andrew Walls's phrase, to "the fortunate subversion of the church" (Walls 1988, 141). That is, the church in the West began shedding its provincialism and became more effectively involved in society at home as well as abroad in the following years. The missionary society became the potent symbol of the church reaching out to the world in response to the call of God. Every such innovation reflects both the sociopolitical and historical context and the theological vision of particular people. For example, three institutional precedents stand behind the missionary society: the monastic movement, the trading company, and the voluntary principle. These remained three discrete developments from different historical periods until the modern missions paradigm emerged around 1800. Drawing on a fresh theological imperative, that paradigm gave coherence and power to this new thrust in world mission. The missionary society provided an effective and efficient means whereby interested individuals could become subscribing members and support the sending of missionaries to "earth's remotest bounds." In the sociopolitical climate of 1800 this had become a credible thing to do, and in the changing ecclesiastical climate it increasingly became a matter of Christian duty.

In spite of wide-ranging changes over the next two centuries touching all aspects of church and society, the missionary society as the primary instrument of mission has remained essentially unchanged, and it has left its imprint on all missionary activity—whether conducted as a voluntary society or as a church board. But its historical character must be emphasized. It was developed as a means for missionary action beyond Christendom, following the trading company pattern of establishing entrepôts, as it were, and on the basis of the voluntary principle, creating a support base among the Christian public in the homeland. It has neither direct sanction nor precedent in scripture. It was a strategic expedient. One can argue that the perennial debate between advocates of the voluntary society, on the one hand, and defenders of the church-as-mission, on the other, misses an important point. Regardless of the particular organizational arrangement adopted, conceptually, theologically, and ecclesiastically the mission of the church has remained a specialized activity of a minority of Christians. The question we need to ask now is whether the missionary society still has the symbolic power to continue calling forth missionary commitment. Certainly today there are many competing causes, some clearly patterned after aspects of the Christian mission but completely secular in purpose and ethos.

CHANGED HISTORICAL AND CULTURAL SITUATION

When the International Missionary Council met at Whitby in 1947, there was a strong sense that a historical watershed had been crossed. The meaning of this became clearer during the following decade. In 1960 Hendrik Kraemer argued with characteristic incisiveness that we were at the end of a specific period of history (Kraemer 1960). Consequently, we had reached the end of a particular era in mission, but not the end of mission.

The world had indeed entered a new stage in terms of political and economic relations. This changed sociopolitical reality subtly but powerfully fostered the sense of disorientation and crisis. World War II had ended with the world divided into two power blocs. For the next fifteen years international relations were shaped by this bipolar reality. But the bipolar pattern began to come apart in the early 1970s with a more complex multi-polar international system emerging in its place (see chapter 13 above). Economic and political power shapes, in important ways, our perception of the world and what it is possible—indeed what it is appropriate—to do in the way of Christian ministry. As the church in the West has come under the sway of the widespread perception of decline and even decay, rank-and-file Christians have been asking what business we have going to other parts of the world when we face mounting problems at home.

Culturally and politically the West went through a time of testing in the 1960s and 1970s marked by rising racial tensions, the Vietnam war, and student uprisings in many countries. In contrast to the self-assurance that the Enlightenment inculcated in eighteenth century Western society, the West was now in a quite different mood. Daniel Bell caught some of the themes in this passage:

We stand, I believe, with a clearing ahead of us. The exhaustion of Modernism, the aridity of Communist life, the tedium of the unrestrained self, and the meaninglessness of the monolithic political chants, all indicate that a long era is coming to a slow close. The impulse of Modernism was to leap beyond: beyond nature, beyond culture, beyond tragedy—to explore the *apeiron*, the boundless, driven by the self-infinitizing spirit of the radical self (Bell 1980, 353).

Bell goes on to say that the keyword in the new vocabulary seems to be "limits." There is a widespread feeling that Western culture must once again learn to set limits on conduct, appetites, and expectations. What the West has to rediscover is that moral vision and ethical standards require an anchor in the Transcendent. The resurgent religiosity of these past three decades, contrary to the predictions of the 1960s, has offered an important clue. The quest for experience of the Sacred or the Transcendent is as intense as ever. The fact that traditional religious structures and patterns no longer attract the masses should not be construed as rejection of the religious dimension.

INSTITUTIONALIZATION

As already noted, the modern missionary movement has been well served by the institutional innovation, the missionary society. But the laws of bureaucracy and the processes of institutionalization eventually overtake all organizations. This condition develops in stages. In the early 1960s it was observed that the number of missionaries supported by the old, established missionary agencies was rapidly declining while conservative evangelical societies were growing steadily in numbers. It was a trend that continued, though at a perhaps slower rate, into the 1970s and the 1980s. Several reasons were given for this loss on the part of the mainline societies. The first cited was a failure of "nerve" (read: loss of theological conviction). Whether this failure of nerve can be fully explained in terms of a changed theological outlook, it was certainly intensified by the mounting criticism of missions coming from the mission-established churches, which reached a climax in the call in 1971, first issued from Africa and then echoed by other continents, for a moratorium on the sending of missionaries from the West. Second, the mission system was increasingly preoccupied with being a channel for inter-church aid. The time-honored ideal for the missionary society was that of a temporary apparatus—a scaffolding—that would in time be removed and put to use elsewhere. In practice this seldom happened. Instead, an increasingly elaborate set of institutional and administrative relations bound together the missionary society and the churches it had founded.

In contrast to many of the conservative evangelical agencies that were entering the field late in the day and consequently had not yet built up such encumbering obligations, the old societies found themselves burdened with maintaining the system. It was a system that was now preoccupied with something quite different from what it had been organized to do. By the 1990s the evangelical agencies appeared to be facing the same forces.[1]

The situation was further complicated by the worsening world economy after the OPEC crisis of 1973.[2] At the same time the cost of maintaining a missionary in the field has risen markedly over the past two decades, the result of inflationary pressures together with increased mandated benefits. These forces combined to create a situation in which any program innovation became increasingly difficult. Instead, an agency found itself drawn into this downward spiral—shrinking program and an increasing percentage of resources committed by policy or contract to meeting fixed obligations. It was a straitjacket difficult to escape.

As institutionalization overtook the older missionary societies, a vacuum was created. The leadership the churches had come to expect from the missionary societies in terms of world ministry seemed to atrophy after 1960. Increasingly, this vacuum has been filled by parachurch multinational agencies devoted to emergency relief, development, and various specialized evangelistic programs. Virtually all of these newer agencies have been founded with a specialized or narrowly focused object. Among those that have grown most rapidly have been several devoted to providing programs for youth. These newcomers are unencumbered by commitments to local churches in places where they conduct projects. They have unhesitatingly employed the latest technology and have adopted the most advanced advertising and marketing techniques to get their appeals across to the public. The older missionary societies, by contrast, have continued to follow their time-honored approaches in cultivating support. The result has been a diminishing of support, both financial and moral, for the long-established agencies.

Jocelyn Murray's history of the Church Missionary Society, *Proclaim the Good News* (1985), is valuable as a study of a society, established in 1799 at the beginning of the modern missionary movement, responding to the vicissitudes of a long and dynamic history. The book's final chapter, depicting CMS's struggle to redefine its mission in light of the changed situation, can be read as the present struggle of the missionary agency writ large.

---

[1] See Siewert and Kenyon, *Mission Handbook: USA/Canada Christian Ministries Overseas* (1993), which reports that the total number of missionaries from Canada and the United States has declined from a 1988 all-time high of 55,469 to 44,713 as of 1992 (59, 68). This is the first time since publication of the *Handbook* began that a decline has been reported.

[2] One can only get a realistic picture of the impact of changing economic conditions by comparing an agency's income at regular intervals, say annually or biennially, restated in constant monetary value, over a period of fifteen or twenty years. When income is restated on this basis it is possible to determine whether an agency is commanding less, equal, or more financial support over a period of years. In terms of the United States economy of the late 1980s, it was necessary to raise five times as much support—stated in current dollars—than in 1967 in order to achieve equivalent buying power.

THE USES OF AN IDENTITY CRISIS

It must be insisted that there is nothing exceptional about the fact that missions are facing a crisis. It is a term that crops up frequently in mission history. It would be a rare mission agency, indeed, that has not had to face crisis at one time or another. Some of these crises in the past were brought on by severe financial changes, controversy within a society, or political upheaval. Furthermore, it can be said that some of the most decisive developments in mission history arose out of a crisis experience. The financial crisis that beset the Church Missionary Society in 1841 became the motor driving Henry Venn and the Society to clarify goals and set in place what became known as the indigenous church policy, an innovation that was to exert influence on the practice of Protestant missions generally.

A crisis in identity may signal one of several conditions: (1) The context in which an agency is mandated to work has changed substantially, but the agency has not adjusted to meet the new demands. Yet the continued existence of any agency depends on its ability to fulfill its purpose. This identity crisis may serve as a wake-up call to rescue an agency that has been performing in a dysfunctional manner. (2) The purpose for which an organization was founded has been fulfilled. The organization has no further usefulness and should be terminated. (3) A crisis may occur as a result of a rite of passage from one stage of service to another. It is a moment of risk but also of hope. It indicates that growth and adjustment are taking place in response to a changing environment.

The prolonged period of crisis for many missionary societies has involved a number of factors mentioned above: a changed environment, inability to terminate commitments that belonged to an era now past, difficulty in creating a program consistent with its founding charter, and lack of response to its environment. As a result some agencies are simply marking time by keeping up the appearance of performing important work. For example, a growing number of mission societies have been reduced to the role of placement agencies for short-term workers serving in stopgap assignments. The churches making the requests for workers feel they must play this game in order to get aid; the mission society keeps alive the illusion of still being in business; and it gives a certain number of people an international experience. But it is not sound programming. Agencies feel they cannot justify investment in language study and cultural preparation for workers who will serve only three years or less. Short-term assignments do not allow for the development of deep and lasting relationships with a church and community, and the church justifiably cannot grant the same level of confidence to a temporary worker as to someone who will remain over a long period. What this means is that the modern missionary movement is facing increasing difficulty in defining its object because we continue to think in terms laid down in the past while the present palliative misses the mark.

At the heart of the situation described above is the matter of the locus of decision-making with regard to programs: Whose prerogative is it to take the initiative and arrive at the final decision? The missionary society represented in its home board and staff or missionaries on location? How is the local church related to the decision-making process? To what extent is the program approach couched in terms that will appeal to the interests of, say, Western youth, and to what extent does the group being served have a voice in program decisions that will affect it directly? Questions such as these were not a part of the calculus of program development a generation ago. They become genuine and inescapable matters only where there exists a deep and strong ecclesial relationship between local church and mission agency. Agencies not facing these questions either do not have close relationships with local churches or are not listening to the wishes of the churches. It has become a universal expectation and demand.

This calls for inspired discernment. If the Carey generation can be charged with having too uncritically imbibed of the spirit of cultural self-confidence that marked that era, is it unreasonable to expect that our generation will in the future be judged for having taken our cues more from a culture in decline than from the gospel? This is not a plea for an easy optimism but rather a plea that we take our cues from God's redemptive mission. God does not abandon the world, regardless of the historical moment; and the church is called to respond through faith in God to a world alienated from God and itself. At the outset we noted that, theologically, mission is propelled forward by a vision of the future. When the human response is closely attuned to God's mission it will be facing toward the future.

ON TO THE FUTURE

Hendrik Kraemer insisted that we distinguish between *missions* as expressions of human response and the *mission* of God. The former, said Kraemer, will bear the mark of a particular era—in this case the modern period now hastening to its end. The latter transcends historical epochs.

We have emphasized that mission is future-driven, while missions are time-bound and subject to becoming entrapped in institutionalism. Missions cannot be faithful servants and instruments of God's mission when they are taken captive by the status quo. It is in the nature of mission always to seek the frontier where the struggle between faith and unfaith is most clearly and urgently drawn. The first essential of leadership, the one above all others with regard to mission, is to see the vision of the reign of God being established in these frontier situations and then to hold that before the church. All else is secondary.

One of the most decisive developments in the late twentieth century is the changed center of gravity for the Christian church worldwide. This shift is intimately connected to the nearly two centuries of dedicated and focused effort.[3] No clearer evidence of the success of the modern missionary movement can be

---

[3] In making this point, we are not saying that this achievement is to be attributed to the efforts of the Western missionary alone. From the outset the missionary worked collaboratively with local counterparts. We are speaking rather about the total process engendered by the modern mission movement.

adduced than this fact. To put it differently: the center of Christian vitality today
is precisely where the missionary energies of the church have been focused over
the past two hundred years. Conversely, losses to the faith have been occurring
in those places where it has long been assumed that the missionary task was
completed and where there has been a subsequent sustained attack on Christian
faith. This attack takes a variety of forms: intellectual, ideological, or political.
Often it has come from people who themselves are disaffected heirs to the Christian tradition.

Two facts face Christians in the West. On the one hand, we need to acknowledge that Western culture is one of the major mission frontiers of the next century and take steps to respond with the same sense of purpose and dedication as
did those who led the way during the modern missionary movement. On the
other hand, the crisis in identity facing many of the long-established missionary
agencies should not be trivialized by treating it simply as a matter of outmoded
policies. I believe these two challenges are intimately related. And yet more is at
stake than changing the focus from *foreign* to *home* mission.

The present danger is that in the West the church is succumbing to the rising
tide of isolationism and chauvinism. To capitulate to these forces is to accept a
reduced and therefore impoverished understanding of the church. To be fully the
church, we must maintain commitment to world mission—and that in its two-
fold definition: (1) A key theological meaning of *world* is "the realm that does
not yet acknowledge the rule of God." (2) The geopolitical meaning of *world,*
which has dominated the vocabulary of missions for the past two centuries, is
"that which lies beyond our national and cultural boundaries." If we join these
two meanings, we get a comprehensive definition of world mission that encom-
passes the whole of the globe, including one's own country, and every sphere of
human existence. Only such an inclusive definition will enable us to hold together the full dimensions of the missionary task. And it is this task that is the
raison d'être of the church. The mission of the missionary agency must, regardless of the form it takes in a given period, arise from a clear discernment of the
particular frontier on which the church is being called to bear witness to the
redeeming love of God revealed in Jesus Christ.

As one reflects on the spiritual situation in Western culture today, a range of
descriptors comes to mind: the erosion of moral values; the idols of materialism,
hedonism, nationalism, militarism, racism, sexism; the collapse of ideologies by
which millions of people have ordered their lives; new religions that vie for the
allegiance of the masses; uncertain truth; the loss of hope and joy; the growing
injustices of society based on the pursuit of self-interest; the despoliation of the
environment; and the aggressive attack on the Transcendent by secularists. The
list can be extended, but this is sufficient to demonstrate that we do indeed face
a situation of profound spiritual need. Because the church in the West is so much
a part of the culture, there is a tendency not to see the situation for what it is.
Those who understand the nature of the present challenge most acutely are those
who view the situation comparatively, who have learned to think in missionary

terms in other cultures, and who bring to bear a compelling sense of compassion joined with commitment to this mission frontier.

Such a careful and full assessment must precede any attempt to (re)organize structures for mission. Structures cannot lead the way. They must be devised in response to a vision.

CONCLUSION

We have argued that the mission society (agency, or board) which has been the organizational mainstay of the modern missionary movement is in institutional crisis. This crisis can be explained in historical and sociological terms. Many mission agencies are no longer certain of their mission because they have been increasingly overtaken by institutionalism and a vastly altered sociopolitical context. Two things should be avoided at this juncture. (1) We must be vigilant against a loss of the sense of mission, which is the life purpose of the church. (2) Further, we will not find the way forward by concentrating on salvaging or reviving old structures. Indeed, we ought to be prepared to evaluate them honestly and take necessary decisions to terminate those that no longer serve a valid purpose. We should turn our energies to discerning what the shape of mission is to be in the changed world situation and find the wineskins that can hold the new wine of God's Spirit. This will allow us to celebrate the remarkable accomplishments of the modern missionary society while remaining poised to follow the new paths called for as the Holy Spirit leads us toward the future of God's mission.

15

Christians living elsewhere

The Future of Mission

Christian mission is future-driven. The eschaton establishes the goal—the consummation of all things in Jesus Christ—and impels the church to compassionate witness and work in the world now. Although the future always remains uncharted, the church can move toward it with confident hope because it discerns a providential pattern in the past. Efforts to anticipate the future ought to follow a twofold approach: reflection on God's action in history, and reading with discrimination the signs of the times. Surely one of the most important lessons from history is that Christian faithfulness and hopefulness do not depend on external circumstances.

Missionary obedience arises from faith response to the triune God. From our contemporary vantage point what reflections and clues seem important as we look to the future?

1. The modern missionary movement, an epoch beginning around 1800 and extending well into the twentieth century, has ended, and a new epoch in Christian mission is unfolding.

Not everyone of course will accept such an assertion. Some voices continue to call the church to the "classical" missionary task, which suggests maintaining the system associated with the modern missionary movement. If one were indeed able to confine it strictly to the biblical call to mission, such an appeal might have validity. For the biblical mandate ever confronts the church with its missionary obligation. But an appeal that prescribes for today that which served yesterday is ahistorical. Missionary leaders in the early nineteenth century were duly impressed with the novelty of their situation and the challenge of fashioning an effective response. They had an acute sense of their historic opportunity.

At the other pole are those who have written the obituary for the modern missionary movement, as if that were the end of mission. Such a perspective is trapped within history.

This chapter was first published in *International Review of Mission* 76:301 (1987): 59-63. Revised for publication in this volume.

The modern missionary movement is one of the truly creative and revolutionary episodes in Christian history. Far from enjoying wide popularity, it had to persevere against great odds—appalling apathy in the church, less than united support among church leaders, ridicule and opprobrium from the public. Despite such odds, and operating out of a multitude of centers of initiative, a dedicated minority managed to motivate and mobilize resources for the spread of the gospel of Jesus Christ to the ends of the earth. Today we can speak only nostalgically about the geographical frontiers. We now require new metaphors to describe the missiological frontier in this space age.

The evidence that the modern missionary movement succeeded is the emergence of new churches in those parts of the world to which missionary energies were directed. These churches, in turn, are now wrestling with their missionary responsibility.

We stand at the junction between two eras. Indeed, we are moving ineluctably into the postmodern period without knowing quite what to name it. The era just past was marked by modernity and the "Westernity" of the sending base. The new era will be shaped by the vitality of the faith in the newly established centers in the non-Western world and sociopolitical forces quite different from the period dominated by Pax Britannica and Pax Americana.

2. Christian faith is inherently expansionist; this expansionist impulse is linked to the goal of history.

Central to the Johannine-Pauline understanding of mission is God's boundless love for the world, expressed Christologically in the goal to "unite all things in him" (Eph 1:10; Jn 3:16). The Holy Spirit is bringing this to completion by constantly energizing God's people for witness (Eph 3:14-21).

Today many Western Christians feel guilty about some aspects of modern missions. In spite of having troubled consciences and being divided over what they should do, missionaries at times did allow themselves to be coopted by imperialism—as in China—or other forces inimical to the gospel. Thus we have to admit that the history of the church includes occasions when this expansionist dynamic was distorted or turned against the movement of Jesus. But nothing is gained by now trying to denature and domesticate the faith in order to find respectability and atone for past wrongs. The gospel demands to be shared; the church that does not move out toward the world soon becomes an archaism.

Every generation risks turning what is "good news" into "bad news" by trying to make the gospel serve the gods and ideologies of the time. Missionary obedience demands that God's people themselves live by the power of the gospel as the first step in the witness to the world. At the heart of such obedience is vulnerability—first to the gospel and then to the world. This is the model Jesus gave.

3. Renewal of faith will be linked to the recovery of a vision of Jesus Christ as God incarnate who became savior and lord; genuine renewal will issue in fresh missionary witness.

Ezekiel's message to Israel becomes normative for renewal of faith in every generation. Through Ezekiel, God declared that renewal is not directed at restoring the fortunes of the people in the first instance. Rather, God rekindles faith by a fresh revelation of God. The people had "profaned among the nations to which you came" the very name of God (Ez 36:22c). By their apostasy God's people denied to the nations knowledge of the God who saves. The people's unfaithfulness obscured God's holiness and saving power.

The history of the church demonstrates the intimate link between a renewed vision of God through the work of Jesus Christ and the church's response to the world. A cold church is not a compassionate one. A compromised church no longer speaks "good news" in situations of injustice and corporate corruption. A defensive church finds it difficult to be the means of liberating grace to a world in bondage. But a renewed church will witness to what it has "seen and heard" in encounter with God, who has come in renewing grace.

In the postmodern period missionary obedience will be found where God's people have been gripped afresh by a vision of Jesus Christ.

4. Faithful mission is always in vital relationship with the sociopolitical realm.

In 1824, with tensions over slavery rising in the West Indies, R. W. Hamilton rose to the defense of missionaries who had thrown their weight against the system by declaring: "We cannot conceal the fact that Christianity may affect political systems." Christians have often been perplexed and divided over how to relate faith to life in the world. Some flatly reject the Hamilton statement. Others take an essentially opposite tack.

The emphasis on context, which has come to the fore in missiological discussions since 1972, has made it increasingly difficult to sustain the old dualism. If it is important to pay attention to the context in which people live in order to understand what is "good news" to them, then we must be open to listening to them as they define their reality.

We must expect any future discussion of this theme to be marked by tension from two angles. First, it is never easy to know exactly what strategy is most appropriate, and Christians can honestly disagree on what alternative to adopt. Second, the relations between church and world are *normally* marked by tension. There is no political system that represents the kingdom of God. Every human system partakes of human folly and sin and contains elements that are anti-Christ. Indeed, when that tension disappears it is a sign that the church has been coopted by the system.

5. The church of the future will be a minority church in most parts of the world.

One of the traumas Christianity has suffered in recent history has been the breakup of Christendom. A combination of both external and internal forces brought this about, but Christendom as a historical reality is finished. The conditions that made it possible in the past no longer exist.

Although the church in Africa has grown dramatically during this century, it remains a minority in most countries. It is even more of a minority in most of

Asia. While we cannot describe the church in Latin America in the same terms, an important ferment is evident, in which old churches are being renewed and evangelization is being carried out based on the fullness of the gospel. The traditional Latin Christendom is being dismantled in many areas. The new times demand the dethronement of triumphalism. Only a servant church can be a true instrument of God's mission.

The prospect of a church stripped of the accoutrements of privilege and power and committed to servanthood "in the power of the Spirit" promises a real gain. One hopes that a reinvigorated ecclesiology from Asia, Africa, and Latin America can minister hope and fresh vision to an increasingly dispirited Western church.

6. In every age the church must struggle to remain open to the fullness of the gospel.

The history of the church is filled with examples of how it has, over time, found ways to qualify and reduce the gospel to fit the expediencies of the times, to line up with the particularities of an ideology or worldview. Consequently, in each situation, we have ended up with a theology of the status quo rather than sailing against the winds of the age.

One of the debates that plagued the modern missionary movement was how to relate witness and service. Throughout its history the two have tended to coexist uneasily at best. This is yet another example of the difficulty Christians have had in serving and witnessing to the whole gospel. The reason for the "reduction" of the gospel often derived from theological debate or ecclesiastical struggle within the sending church, whereas the challenge to this "reduction" arose from the missionary context.

We can only pray that the church everywhere increasingly will develop an identity that consists of two things. First, the church exists for mission to the world, and its identity is authentic only when it is worked out in genuine missionary encounter. Second, the church always stands under the judgment and mandate of the gospel. It is the church's privilege to be the bearer of the life and love of Jesus in the world, to be the instrument of good news. But it is always incumbent on the church to allow the fullness of that life to be expressed rather than seeking to reduce it to fit a formula convenient to the times and context.

7. The Word is the singular seminal force.

Today there are many important elements with which we must reckon, including the resurgence of religion in general, as well as living traditions, religio-cultural pluralism, the quest for justice by the poor and oppressed peoples, and rising ethnic consciousness.

Each of these is significant and accounts for much of the turmoil in our world today. Octavio Paz has written: "The history of the twentieth century has confirmed something well known to all historians of the past, something our ideologies have stubbornly ignored: the strongest, fiercest, most enduring political passions are nationalism and religion" (1985, 9). At times nationalism and religion become allies; often they are antagonists.

What is significant as we think of the future in light of these forces is to recognize that none of them—revitalized religion, pluralism, the quest for justice, ethnic pride—can produce life. Each one is subservient to the powers of this world. Each arises out of human initiative. Only the Word can infuse vitality into the human situation. It is through encounter with the Word, which leads to transformation and redirection of the human project, that life overcomes death.

8. The greatest integrity and vitality of faith today appears to be found in those churches that have suffered and known martyrdom firsthand.

The Christian movement worldwide is comprised essentially of two classes. On the one hand, we find the churches located in lands governed by liberal democracies. For many generations the churches in this group have lived without much contact with religious persecution. It is these churches that have a monopoly on academic theology, with a specially trained guild of theologians and biblical scholars. On the other hand, we note the churches that live under various forms of totalitarian or authoritarian government. They generally endure numerous restrictions. Some have survived several generations of persecution and must endure continuing harassment. These churches seldom have the luxury of adequate training, Bibles and other literature, or freedom to practice their faith without restrictions.

The scale of martyrdom in the twentieth century has not been fully established. Preliminary estimates indicate this to be perhaps the bloodiest and most costly century in all of Christian history. The testimony of the martyr church, as it becomes more articulate, is going to pose a fundamental challenge to how we interpret the faith in practical witness as well as how we do theology.

As one listens to the witness of Christians who have suffered for their faith, one is impressed by the depth, simplicity, and authenticity of what they have to say. They have not had opportunities to partake in ongoing theological debate or to develop intricate formulations. Given the intensity of their existential situation, intellectual abstractions or theoretical approaches to theology seem singularly irrelevant. Surely one of the reasons for the power of Dietrich Bonhoeffer's theological witness since 1945 stems from the context in which he wrote and thought—amid a life-and-death struggle.

We can expect a fresh missiology to emerge—indeed it is already well on the way—that deepens and extends the witness to liberation through the gospel. But it will draw directly on the witness of the martyrs of this century. Some scholars have argued that a touchstone in the formation of the New Testament canon was whether a document helped prepare the disciple community for suffering, even unto death. A corollary for a missionary church in the twenty-first century may well be that only that theology which prepares the church to bear witness to Jesus Christ, even at the price of death, will be accredited.

Bibliography

Abraham, William J. 1989. *The Logic of Evangelism*. London: Hodder and Stoughton.

Allen, Roland. 1960. *The Ministry of the Spirit: Selected Writings of Roland Allen*. Grand Rapids, Mich.: William B. Eerdmans Publishing Co.

——————. 1962. *Missionary Methods: St Paul's or Ours?* Grand Rapids, Mich.: William B. Eerdmans Publishing Co. First published in 1912.

American Board of Commissioners for Foreign Missions. 1856 "Outline of Missionary Policy." Boston: ABCFM.

Anderson, Gerald H., and Thomas F. Stransky, eds. 1976. *Mission Trends No. 3: Third World Theologies*. New York: Paulist Press; Grand Rapids, Mich.: William B. Eerdmans Publishing Co.

Anderson, Rufus. 1869. *Foreign Missions: Their Relations and Claims*. New York: Charles Scribner and Co.

Arias, Mortimer, and Alan Johnson. 1992. *The Great Commission: Biblical Models of Evangelism*. Nashville, Tenn.: Abingdon Press.

Autrey, C. E. 1959. *Basic Evangelism*. Grand Rapids, Mich.: Zondervan.

Ayandele, E. A. 1966. *The Missionary Impact on Modern Nigeria, 1842-1914*. London: Longmans.

Baeta, Christian. 1971. "Some Aspects of Religious Change in Africa," *Ghana Bulletin of Theology* 3:10.

Baldwin, S. L. 1878. "Self-Support of the Native Church," *Records of the General Conference of the Protestant Missionaries of China*. Shanghai: Presbyterian Mission Press.

Barclay, William. 1953. *The Acts of the Apostles*. Philadelphia: Westminster Press.

Baritz, Loren. 1985. *Backfire: Vietnam—The Myths That Made Us Fight, the Illusions That Helped Us Lose, the Legacy That Haunts Us Today*. New York: Ballantine Books.

Barker, Eileen. 1985. "New Religious Movements: Yet Another Great Awakening?" in Hammond 1985.

Barraclough, Geoffrey. 1977. *Turning Points in World History*. New York and London: Thames and Hudson.

Barrett, David B. 1968. *Schism and Renewal in Africa*. Nairobi: Oxford University Press.

——————. 1987. "Annual Statistical Table on Global Mission: 1987," *International Bulletin of Missionary Research* 11:1 (January):24-25.

Barrett, David B., ed. 1982. *World Christian Encyclopedia*. Nairobi: Oxford University Press.

Barrett, David B., and James W. Reapsome. 1988. *Seven Hundred Plans to Evangelize the World: The Rise of a Global Evangelization Movement*. Birmingham, Ala.: New Hope.

Barry, Alfred. 1895. *The Ecclesiastical Expansion of England in the Growth of the Anglican Communion*. London: Macmillan and Co.

Barth, Karl. 1962. *Church Dogmatics: The Doctrine of Reconciliation.* Edinburgh: T. and T. Clark.

Bates, M. Searle. 1945. *Religious Liberty: An Inquiry.* New York: International Missionary Council.

Bayly, Joseph T. 1960. *The Gospel Blimp.* Grand Rapids, Mich.: Zondervan.

Beaver, R. Pierce. 1952. "North American Thought on the Fundamental Principles of Missions during the Twentieth Century (A Survey Article)," *Church History* 21:4:3-22.

—————. 1957. *The Christian World Mission.* Calcutta: Baptist Mission Press.

—————. 1958. *The Christian World Mission: A Reconsideration.* Calcutta: Baptist Mission Press.

—————. 1964. *Envoys of Peace: The Peace Witness in Christian World Mission.* Grand Rapids, Mich.: William B. Eerdmans Publishing Co.

—————. 1968. "Missionary Motivation through Three Centuries," in *Reinterpretation in American Church History*, edited by Jerald C. Brauer. Chicago: University of Chicago Press, 113-51.

Beaver, R. Pierce, ed. 1966. *Pioneers in Mission.* Grand Rapids, Mich.: William B. Eerdmans Publishing Co.

—————. 1967. *To Advance the Gospel: Selections from the Writings of Rufus Anderson.* Grand Rapids, Mich.: William B. Eerdmans Publishing Co.

—————. 1977. *American Missions in Cicentennial Perspective.* South Pasadena, Calif.: William Carey Library.

Bediako, Kwame. 1983. "Biblical Christologies in the Context of African Traditional Religions," in *Sharing Jesus in the Two-Thirds World*, edited by Vinay Samuel and Chris Sugden. Grand Rapids, Mich.: William B. Eerdmans Publishing Co.

Bell, Daniel. 1976. *The Cultural Contradictions of Capitalism.* New York: Basic Books.

—————. 1980. *The Winding Passage.* New York: Basic Books.

Bellah, Robert N., et al. 1985. *Habits of the Heart: Individualism and Commitment in American Life.* Berkeley and Los Angeles: University of California Press.

—————. 1991. *The Good Society.* New York: Alfred A. Knopf.

Bender, Harold S. 1970. *The Anabaptists and Religious Liberty in the Sixteenth Century.* Philadelphia: Fortress Press. Reprinted from *Archiv fur Reformationsgeschichte* 44 (1953):32-50.

Berkhof, Hendrikus. 1964. *The Doctrine of the Holy Spirit.* Richmond, Va.: John Knox Press.

—————. 1966. *Christ the Meaning of History.* Richmond, Va.: John Knox Press.

—————. 1979. *The Christian Faith: An Introduction to the Study of the Faith.* Grand Rapids, Mich.: William B. Eerdmans Publishing Co.

Beveridge, Albert J. 1970. "For the Greater Republic, Not for Imperialism," in *Nationalism and Religion in America*, edited by Winthrop S. Hudson. New York: Harper & Row.

Blauw, Johannes. 1962. *The Missionary Nature of the Church.* New York: McGraw-Hill Co.

Bliss, Edwin Munsell. 1908. *The Missionary Enterprise.* New York: Fleming H. Revell and Co.

Blough, Neal. 1993. "Messianic Mission and Ethics: Discipleship and the Good News," in Shenk 1993, 178-98.

Boberg, John T., and James A. Scherer, eds. 1972. *Mission in the '70s.* Chicago: Chicago Cluster of Theological Schools.

Boer, Harry R. 1961. *Pentecost and Missions.* Grand Rapids, Mich.: William B. Eerdmans Publishing Co.

Bond, George, Walton Johnson, and Sheila Walker. 1979. *African Christianity: Patterns of Religious Continuity.* New York: Academic Press.

Bosch, David. 1972. "Systematic Theology and Missions: The Voice of an Early Pioneer," *Theologica Evangelica* 5:3:165-89.

——————. 1980. *Witness to the World.* Atlanta: John Knox Press.

——————. 1982. "Theological Education in Missionary Perspective," *Missiology* 10:1 (January):13-34.

——————. 1983. "An Emerging Paradigm for Mission," *Missiology* 11:4 (October):485-510.

——————. 1991. *Transforming Mission: Paradigm Shifts in Theology of Mission.* Maryknoll, N.Y.: Orbis Books.

Bright, John. 1953. *The Kingdom of God.* Nashville: Abingdon.

Brown, Colin. 1968. *Philosophy and Christian Faith.* Downers Grove, Ill.: Inter-Varsity Press.

Bruce, F. F. 1954. *The Book of Acts.* Grand Rapids, Mich.: William B. Eerdmans Publishing Co.

Brunner, Emil. 1931. *The Word and the World.* London: SCM Press.

Buber, Martin. 1951. *Two Types of Faith.* London: Routledge and Kegan Paul.

Buhlmann, Walbert. 1976. *The Coming of the Third Church.* Maryknoll, N.Y.: Orbis Books.

Burridge, Kenelm. 1991. *In the Way: A Study of Christian Missionary Endeavours.* Vancouver: University of British Columbia Press.

Capps, Walter H. 1978. "The Interpenetration of New Religion and Religious Studies," in Needleman and Baker 1978, 101-5.

Carey, William. 1891. *An Enquiry into the Obligation of Christians to Use Means for the Conversion of the Heathen.* London: Baptist Missionary Society. Facsimile of 1792 edition.

Carpenter, Joel A., and Wilbert R. Shenk, eds., 1990. *Earthen Vessels: American Evangelicals and Foreign Mission, 1880-1980.* Grand Rapids, Mich.: William B. Eerdmans Publishing Co.

Chaney, Charles L. 1976. *The Birth of Missions in America.* South Pasadena, Calif.: William Carey Library.

Chao, Samuel. 1991. *John Livingston Nevius (1829-1893): A Historical Study of His Life and Mission Methods.* Ph.D. dissertation. Pasadena, Calif.: Fuller Theological Seminary.

Christensen, Torben, and William R. Hutchison, eds. 1982. *Missionary Ideologies in the Imperialist Era: 1880-1920.* Aarhus, Denmark: Forlaget Aros.

Clark, Sidney J. W. 1913. *The Indigenous Church.* World Dominion.

Coe, Shoki. 1976. "Contextualizing Theology," in Anderson and Stransky 1976, 19-24.

Coleman, John, and Gregory Baum, eds. 1983. *New Religious Movements.* New York: Seabury Press.

Coleman, Richard J. 1980. *Issues in Theological Conflict.* Grand Rapids, Mich.: William B. Eerdmans Publishing Co.

Comblin, José. 1979. *Sent from the Father.* Maryknoll, N.Y.: Orbis Books.

Committee on the War and the Religious Outlook. 1920. *The Missionary Outlook in the Light of the War.* New York: Association Press.

Conference on Missions. 1860. London: James Nisbet.

Conn, Harvey. 1984. *Eternal Word and Changing Worlds*. Grand Rapids, Mich.: Zondervan.

Coote, Robert T. 1986. "Taking Aim on 2000 A.D.," in *Mission Handbook*, edited by Samuel Wilson and John Siewart. Monrovia, Calif.: MARC, 35-50.

Costas, Orlando E. 1989. *Liberating News: A Theology of Contextual Evangelization*. Grand Rapids, Mich.: William B. Eerdmans Publishing Co.

Cragg, Kenneth. 1968. *Christianity in World Perspective*. London: Lutterworth Press.

Cullmann, Oscar. 1963. *The Christology of the New Testament*. Philadelphia: Westminster Press.

Curtin, Philip D. 1960. "'Scientific' Racism and the British Theory of Empire," *Journal of the Historical Society of Nigeria* 2.

Daneel, M. L. 1980. "The Missionary Outreach of African Independent Churches," *Missionalia* 8:3.

————. 1984. "Towards a Theologia Africana? The Contribution of Independent Churches to African Theology," *Missionalia* 12:2.

Danker, William J., and Wi Jo Kang, eds. 1971. *The Future of the Christian World Mission*. Grand Rapids, Mich.: William B. Eerdmans Publishing Co.

Dayton, Donald W. 1976. *Discovering an Evangelical Heritage*. New York: Harper & Row.

De Ridder, Richard R. 1983. "The Old Testament Roots of Mission," in Shenk 1983b, 171-80.

Deford, Frank. 1976. "Religion in Sports," *Sports Illustrated* April 19, April 26, May 3.

Dennis, James S. 1897, 1899, 1906. *Christian Missions and Social Progress: A Sociological Study of Foreign Missions*. Three volumes. New York: Revell.

Desroche, Henri. 1979. *The Sociology of Hope*. London: Routledge and Kegan Paul.

Donovan, Vincent J. 1978. *Christianity Rediscovered: An Epistle from the Masai*. Notre Dame, Ind.: Fides/Claretian.

Douglas, J. D., ed. 1975. *Let the Earth Hear His Voice*. Minneapolis, Minn.: Worldwide Publications.

Driver, John. 1983. "Mission: Salt, Light, and Covenant Law," *Mission Focus* 11:3 (September): 33-36.

————. 1993. "The Kingdom of God: Goal of Messianic Mission," in Shenk 1993, 83-105.

Drummond, Richard H. 1971. *A History of Christianity in Japan*. Grand Rapids, Mich.: William B. Eerdmans Publishing Co.

Duff, Alexander. 1868. *Evangelistic Theology. An Inaugural Address*. Edinburgh: Andrew Elliot.

Durnbaugh, Donald F. 1968. *The Believers' Church: The History and Character of Radical Protestantism*. New York: The Macmillan Company.

Ecumenical Missionary Conference. 1900. New York: Religious Tract Society. 2 vols.

Eliade, Mircea. 1970. "'Cargo Cults' and Cosmic Regeneration," in Thrupp 1970.

Ellwood, Robert S., Jr. 1978. "Emergent Religion in America: An Historical Perspective," in Needleman and Baker 1978, 267-84.

Elsbree, Oliver Wendell. 1928. *The Rise of the Missionary Spirit in America, 1790-1815*. Williamsport: Williamsport Printing and Binding Co.

Fasholé-Luke, E. W. 1976. "The Quest for African Christian Theologies," in Anderson and Stransky 1976.

Forman, Charles W. 1977. "A History of Foreign Mission Theory," in Beaver 1977, 69-140.

Freytag, Walter. 1958. "Changes in the Patterns of Western Mission," in Orchard 1958, 138-50.

Gager, John G. 1975. *Kingdom and Community: The Social World of Early Christianity.* Englewood Cliffs, N.J.: Prentice-Hall.

Gay, Peter. 1969. *The Enlightenment—An Interpretation: 2. The Science of Freedom.* New York: Alfred A. Knopf.

Geertz, Clifford. 1973. *The Interpretation of Cultures.* New York: Basic Books.

Gilliland, Dean S., ed. 1989. *The Word among Us.* Dallas, Tex.: Word Publishing Co.

Green, Michael. 1975. "Methods and Strategy in the Evangelism of the Early Church," in Douglas 1975, 159-72.

Guiart, Jean. 1970. "Conversion to Christianity in the South Pacific," in Thrupp 1970.

Gunton, Colin. 1985. *Enlightenment and Alienation.* Grand Rapids, Mich.: William B. Eerdmans Publishing Co.

Hammond, Phillip E., ed. 1985. *The Sacred in a Secular Age: Toward Revision in the Scientific Study of Religion.* Berkeley and Los Angeles: University of California Press.

Hardman, Keith J. 1990. *Charles Grandison Finney—Revivalist and Reformer.* Grand Rapids, Mich.: Baker Book House.

Hargrove, Barbara. 1978. "Integrative and Transformative Religions," in Needleman and Baker 1978, 257-66.

Henry, Carl F. H. 1947. *The Uneasy Conscience of Modern Fundamentalism.* Grand Rapids, Mich.: William B. Eerdmans Publishing Co.

—————. 1971. *A Plea for Evangelical Demonstration.* Grand Rapids, Mich.: Baker Book House.

—————. 1976. "The Purpose of God," in Padilla 1976, 17-32.

Hermelink, Jan, and Hans Jochen Margull, eds. 1959. *Basileia.* Stuttgart: Evangelische Missionsverlag GMBH.

Hesselgrave, David J., ed. 1978. *Dynamic Religious Movements.* Grand Rapids, Mich.: Baker Book House.

Hobhouse, Walter. 1911. *The Church and the World in Idea and History.* Second edition. London: Macmillan and Co.

Hocking, William Ernest. 1932. *Re-Thinking Missions.* Report of the Laymen's Foreign Missions Commission. New York: Harper and Brothers.

Hodges, Melvin L. 1953. *The Indigenous Church.* Springfield, Mo.: Gospel Publishing House.

Hodgson, Janet. 1984. "Ntsikana—Precursor of Independency," *Missionalia* 12:1.

Hoffman, Ronan. 1968. "Conversion and the Mission of the Church," *Journal of Ecumenical Studies* 5 (January):1-20.

Hoffman, Shirl, J. 1992. *Sport and Religion.* Champaign, Ill.: Human Kinetics Books.

Hollenweger, Walter J. 1980. "Charismatic Renewal in the Third World: Implications for Mission," *Occasional Bulletin for Missionary Research* 4:2.

Hood, George A. 1986. *Mission Accomplished? The English Presbyterian Mission in Lintung, South China* (republished in several editions). Frankfurt am Main: Verlag Peter Lang.

Horton, Walter Marshall. 1946. "Mission Strategy Yesterday and Tomorrow," in *Christian World Mission*, edited by William K. Anderson. Nashville, Tenn.: Commission on Ministerial Training.

Howard, David. 1983. *From Wheaton 66 to Wheaton 83.* Manuscript.

196 *Bibliography*

Hutchison, William. 1982. "A Moral Equivalent for Imperialism: Americans and the Promotion of 'Christian Civilization,' 1880-1910," in Christensen and Hutchison 1982, 167-78.

Idowu, E. Bolaji. 1965. *Towards an Indigenous Church*. London/Ibadan: Oxford University Press.

―――――. 1968. "The Predicament of the Church in Africa," in *Christianity in Tropical Africa*, edited by C. G. Baeta. London: Oxford University Press, 417-37.

Iglehart, Charles W. 1948. "Modern War and the Christian Mission," in *The Church, the Gospel, and the War*, edited by Rufus M. Jones. New York: Harper and Brothers.

Isichei, Elizabeth. 1970. "Seven Varieties of Ambiguity," *Journal of Religion in Africa* 3:3.

―――――. 1973. *The Ibo People and the Europeans*. New York: St. Martins Press.

Jakobsson, Stiv. 1972. *Am I Not a Man and a Brother? British Mission and the Abolition of the Slave Trade and Slavery in West Africa and the West Indies, 1786-1838.* Uppsala: Almquist and Wiksells.

Johnston, Arthur. 1978. *The Battle for World Evangelism*. Wheaton, Ill.: Tyndale House.

Johnston, James. 1886. *A Century of Protestant Missions*. London: James Nisbet; Edinburgh: Oliver and Boyd.

Kane, J. Herbert. 1976. *Christian Missions in Biblical Perspective*. Grand Rapids, Mich.: Baker Book House, 73-85.

Kirby, Jon P. 1985. "The Non-Conversion of the Anufo of Northern Ghana," *Mission Studies* 2:2:15-25.

Kirk, Andrew. 1990. "Theology for the Sake of Mission," *Anvil* 7:1:23-36.

Koyama, Kosuke. 1984. *Mount Fuji and Mount Sinai: A Critique of Idols*. Maryknoll, N.Y.: Orbis Books.

Krabill, James R. 1990. "Dida Harrist Hymnology (1913-1990)," *Journal of Religion in Africa* 20:2 (June):118-52.

Kraemer, Hendrik. 1938. *The Christian Message in a Non-Christian World*. Grand Rapids, Mich.: Kregel.

―――――. 1958. *From Missionfield to Independent Church*. London: SCM Press.

―――――. 1960. "In World's Student Christian Federation," *History Lessons for Tomorrow's Mission*. London: SCM Press.

Kraft, Charles H. 1979. *Christianity and Culture*. Maryknoll, N.Y.: Orbis Books.

Krass, Alfred C. 1982. *Evangelizing Neopagan North America*. Scottdale, Pa.: Herald Press.

―――――. 1983. "Church Growth among the Chokosi of Northern Ghana," in Shenk 1983a, 49-59.

Kraus, C. Norman. 1993. *The Community of the Spirit*. Scottdale, Pa.: Herald Press.

Kreider, Alan. 1990. "The Growth of the Early Church: Reflections on Recent Literature," *Mission Focus* 18:3 (September):33-36.

Kselman, Thomas A. 1983. *Miracles and Prophecies in Nineteenth-Century France*. New Brunswick, N.J.: Rutgers University Press.

Kuitse, Roelf S. 1993. "Holy Spirit: Source of Messianic Mission," in Shenk 1993, 106-29.

Küng, Hans. 1967. *The Church*. New York: Sheed and Ward.

Ladd, George Eldon. 1964. *Jesus and the Kingdom*. New York: Harper & Row.

Lane Fox, Robin. 1986. *Pagans and Christians*. New York: Alfred A. Knopf.

Latourette, Kenneth Scott. 1953. *A History of Christianity*. New York: Harper and Brothers.

——————. 1965. "Colonialism and Missions: Progressive Separation," *Journal of Church and State* 7:3.

——————. 1970. *A History of the Expansion of Christianity: Three Centuries of Advance, 1500 A.D. to 1800 A.D*. Seven volumes. Grand Rapids, Mich.: Zondervan Corporation. Reprint of 1939-45 edition.

Lausanne Committee for World Evangelization/World Evangelical Fellowship. 1982. *Evangelicalism and Social Responsibility*. Wheaton, Ill.: LCWE.

Lawrence, Edward A. 1895. *Modern Missions in the East: Their Methods, Successes, and Limitations*. New York: Harper and Brothers Publishers. First edition 1894.

Lee, Robert. 1989. "From Ancient Jerusalem to Modern Tokyo: Contextualization in Japanese Culture and Society," *Mission Focus* 17:2 (June):24-30.

Legrand, Lucien. 1986. "The Missionary Command of the Risen Christ," *Indian Theological Studies* 23:3:290-309.

Littell, Franklin Hamlin. 1962. *From State Church to Pluralism*. New York: Anchor Books.

Lofland, John, and Rodney Stark. 1965. "Becoming a World-Saver: A Theory of Conversion to a Deviant Perspective," *American Sociological Review* 30:6 (December):862-75.

Lohfink, Gerhard. 1984. *Jesus and Community*. Philadelphia: Fortress Press; New York: Paulist Press.

Luzbetak, Louis. J., SVD. 1988. *The Church and Cultures*. Maryknoll, N.Y.: Orbis Books.

McClendon, James Wm., Jr. 1994. *Doctrine: Systematic Theology*. Volume 2. Nashville, Tenn.: Abingdon Press.

Mcgavran, Donald A. 1955. *The Bridges of God*. London: World Dominion Press.

Mackichan, D. 1927. *The Missionary Ideal in the Scottish Churches*. London: Hodder and Stoughton.

Magnuson, Norris. 1990. *Salvation in the Slums: Evangelical Social Work*. Grand Rapids, Mich.: Baker Book House.

Marsden, George M. 1972. "Evangelical Social Concern—Dusting Off the Heritage," *Christianity Today* 16:16:8-11.

——————. 1980. *Fundamentalism and American Culture*. New York: Oxford University Press.

Marshall, I. Howard. 1980. *The Acts of the Apostles*. Grand Rapids, Mich.: William B. Eerdmans Publishing Co.

May, Rollo. 1969. *Love and Will*. New York: Norton.

Mbiti, John S. 1976. "Theological Impotence and the Universality of the Church," in Anderson and Stransky 1976, 6-18.

Menninger, Karl. 1973/1978. *Whatever Became of Sin?* New York: Hawthorne/Bantam.

Michel, Otto. 1983. "The Conclusion of Matthew's Gospel: A Contribution to the History of the Easter Message," in Stanton 1983, 30-41.

Míguez Bonino, José. 1975. *Doing Theology in a Revolutionary Situation*. Philadelphia: Fortress.

Millar, Robert. 1723. *A History of the Propagation of Christianity*. Edinburgh: n.p. 2 vols.

Miller, Elmer S. 1967. *Pentecostalism among the Argentine Toba*. Doctoral dissertation, University of Pittsburgh.

Bibliography

Miller, Larry. 1993. "The Church as Messianic Society: Creation and Instrument of Transfigured Mission," in Shenk 1993, 130-52.

Minear, Paul S. 1960. *Images of the Church in the New Testament*. Philadelphia: Westminster Press.

Moberg, David O. 1972. *The Great Reversal—Evangelism versus Social Concern*. Philadelphia, Pa.: J. B. Lippincott.

Moffat, Robert. 1969. *Missionary Labours and Scenes in Southern Africa*. New York and London: Johnson Reprint Co. (from 1842 edition).

Moltmann, Jürgen. 1967. *Theology of Hope*. London: SCM Press.

——————. 1974. *The Crucified God*. New York: Harper & Row.

Morris, Charles R. 1984. *The Time of Passion—America 1960-1980*. New York: Harper & Row.

Munck, Johannes. 1967. *The Acts of the Apostles. The Anchor Bible*. Garden City, N.Y.: Doubleday and Co.

Murray, Jocelyn. 1985. *Proclaim the Good News*. London: Hodder and Stoughton.

Myklebust, Olav Guttorm. 1955. *The Study of Missions in Theological Education*. Oslo: Egede Institute.

Myrdal, Gunnar. 1968. *Asian Drama*. Three volumes. New York: Pantheon.

Needleman, Jacob, and George Baker, eds. 1978. *Understanding the New Religions*. New York: Seabury Press.

Neill, Stephen. 1948. "The Worship of God," in *The Triumph of God*, edited by Max Warren. London: Longmans, Green and Co. 114-39.

——————. 1964. *A History of Christian Missions*. Harmondsworth: Pelican.

——————. 1968. *The Church and Christian Union*. Bampton Lectures for 1964. London: Oxford University Press.

——————. 1970. "The Church," in Neill, Anderson, and Goodwin 1970.

Neill, Stephen, Gerald H. Anderson, and John Goodwin, eds. 1970. *Concise Dictionary of the Christian World Mission*. London: Lutterworth Press.

Nevius, John L. 1958. *The Planting and Development of Missionary Churches*. Philadelphia: Presbyterian and Reformed Publishing Co. Reprinted from the 1899 edition.

——————. 1886. *Methods of Mission Work*. Shanghai: American Presbyterian Mission Press. Reprinted as *The Planting and Development of Missionary Churches*. Third edition. New York: Revell, 1899.

Newbigin, Lesslie. 1983. *The Other Side of 1984—Questions for the Churches*. Geneva: WCC Publications.

——————. 1986. *Foolishness to the Greeks*. Grand Rapids, Mich.: William B. Eerdmans Publishing Co.

——————. 1989. *The Gospel in a Pluralist Society*. Grand Rapids, Mich.: William B. Eerdmans Publishing Co.

Nicholls, Bruce, ed. 1985. *In Word and Deed—Evangelism and Social Responsibility*. Grand Rapids, Mich.: William B. Eerdmans Publishing Co.

Niebuhr, H. Richard. 1937. *The Kingdom of God in America*. New York: Harper & Row.

Oakley, Frances. 1961. "Christian Theology and the Newtonian Science: The Rise of the Concept of the Laws of Nature," *Church History* 30:4 (December): 433-57.

Oldham, J. H. 1916. *The World and the Gospel*. London: United Council for Missionary Education.

Oliver, Roland. 1952. *The Missionary Factor in East Africa.* London: Longmans.

Oosterwal, Gottfried. 1973. *Modern Messianic Movements as a Theological and Missionary Challenge.* Elkhart, Ind.: Institute of Mennonite Studies.

Orchard, Ronald K., ed. 1958. *The Ghana Assembly of the International Missionary Council.* London: Edinburgh House Press.

——————. 1959. "The Concept of Christendom and the Christian World Mission: A Question," in Hermelink and Margull 1959.

Orme, William. 1828. *Memoirs of Urquhart.* Volume 1. Boston: Crocker and Brewster.

——————. 1830. "Preface," in William Swan, 1830.

Orr, J. Edwin. 1949. *The Second Evangelical Awakening in Britain.* London: Marshall, Morgan and Scott.

——————. 1973. *The Flaming Tongue.* Chicago, Ill.: Moody Press.

——————. 1974. *The Fervent Prayer.* Chicago, Ill.: Moody Press.

——————. 1975. *The Eager Feet.* Chicago, Ill.: Moody Press.

Padilla, C. Rene. 1985. "Evangelism and Social Responsibility: From Wheaton '66 to Wheaton '83," *Transformation* 2:3:27-33.

——————, ed. 1976. *The New Face of Evangelicalism.* London: Hodder and Stoughton.

Pannikar, K. M. 1959. *Asia and Western Dominance: A Survey of the Vasco da Gama Epoch of Asian History, 1498-1945.* London: George Allen and Unwin. First published in 1953.

Parrinder, Geoffrey. 1963. *Witchcraft—European and African.* London: Faber and Faber.

Paz, Octavio. 1985. *One Earth, Four or Five Worlds.* New York: Harcourt Brace Jovanovich Publishers.

Peachey, Paul. 1965. "The New Ethical Possibility: The Task of 'Post-Christendom' Ethics," *Interpretation* 19:1. Reprinted in *New Theology No 3.*, edited by Martin E. Marty and Dean G. Peerman. New York: Macmillan and Co.

Peel, J. D. Y. 1967-68. "Syncretism and Religious Change," *Comparative Studies in Society and History* 10.

Perrin, Norman. 1963. *The Kingdom of God in the Teaching of Jesus.* Philadelphia: Westminster Press.

Pfeiffer, Edward. 1912 [1908]. *Mission Studies: Historical Survey and Outlines of Missionary Principles and Practice.* Columbus: Lutheran Book Concern.

Phillips, Clifton Jackson. 1969. *Protestant America and the Pagan World: The First Half Century of the American Board of Commissioners for Foreign Missions, 1810-1860.* Cambridge: distributed by Harvard University Press.

Phillips, Godfrey E. 1939. *The Gospel in the World.* London: Duckworth.

Phillips, James M., and Robert T. Coote, eds. 1993. *Toward the Twenty-first Century in Christian Mission.* Grand Rapids, Mich.: Wm. B. Eerdmans Publishing Co.

Pickett, J. Waskom. 1933. *Christian Mass Movements in India.* Lucknow, India: Lucknow Publishing House.

Pierard, Richard V. 1990. "Pax Americana and the Evangelical Missionary Advance," in Carpenter and Shenk 1990, 155-79.

Pierson, A. T. 1889. "Christian Missions as the Enterprise of the Church." *Missionary Review of the World.* NS 2:1.

Pope, Stephen. 1991. "Expressive Individualism and True Self-Love: A Thomistic Perspective," *Journal of Religion* 71:3:384-99.

Rahner, Karl. 1979. "Towards a Fundamental Theological Interpretation of Vatican II," *Theological Studies* 40:4 (December):716-27

Ranger, Terrence O. 1972. "Missionary Adaptation of African Religious Institutions," in *The Historical Study of African Religion*, edited by T. O. Ranger and I. N. Kimambo. Berkeley and Los Angeles: University of California Press, 221-51.

Rawlinson, F., Helen Thoburn, and D. MacGillivray, eds. 1922. *The Chinese Church As Revealed in the National Christian Conference*. Shanghai: The Oriental Press.

Records of Missionary Secretaries. 1920. Compiled by J. H. Ritson. London: Turnbull and Speers.

Rennstich, Karl. 1982. "The Understanding of Mission, Civilization, and Colonialism in the Basel Mission," in Christensen and Hutchison 1982, 94-103.

Reyburn, William D., and M. F. Reyburn. 1956. "Toba Caciqueship and the Gospel," *International Review of Missions* 45:2 (April):194-203.

Ridderbos, Herman. 1962. *The Coming of the Kingdom*. Philadelphia: Presbyterian and Reformed Publishing Company.

Rieff, Philip. 1966. *The Triumph of the Therapeutic*. New York: Harper & Row.

Ritchie, John. 1946. *Indigenous Church Principles in Theory and Practice*. New York: Fleming H. Revell Co.

Roszak, Theodore. 1968/1969. *The Making of a Counter Culture*. Garden City, N.Y.: Doubleday and Company.

Rouse, Ruth, and S. C. Neill, eds. 1967. *A History of the Ecumenical Movement 1517-1948*. London: SPCK.

Rowland, Henry Hosie. 1925. *Native Churches in Foreign Fields*. Dayton: Methodist Book Concern.

Saayman, Willem, and J. N. J. Kritzinger, eds. 1996. *Mission in Bold Humility: Responses to the Missiology of David Bosch*. Maryknoll, N.Y.: Orbis Books.

Sanneh, Lamin. 1989. *Translating the Message: The Missionary Impact on Culture*. Maryknoll, N.Y.: Orbis Books.

Scharpff, Paulus. 1964. *History of Evangelism*. Grand Rapids, Mich.: William B. Eerdmans Publishing Co.

Schmidlin, Joseph. 1931. *Catholic Mission Theory*. Techny, Ill.: Mission Press, S.V.D. Translated from 1919 German edition.

Schnackenburg, Rudolf. 1963. *God's Rule and Kingdom*. New York: Herder and Herder.

Schreiter, Robert J. 1985. *Constructing Local Theologies*. Maryknoll, N.Y.: Orbis Books.

Seeley, John Robert. 1971. *The Expansion of England*. Introduction by John Gross. Chicago: The University of Chicago Press. Originally published in 1883.

Setiloane, Gabriel M. 1975. *The Image of God among the Sotho-Tswana*. Rotterdam: A. A. Balkema.

Shank, David A. 1973. "The Shape of Mission Strategy," *Mission Focus* 1:3:1-7. Republished in W. R. Shenk, ed. *Mission Focus: Current Issues*. Scottdale, Pa.: Herald Press: 1980, 118-28.

————. 1993. "Jesus the Messiah: Messianic Foundation of Mission," (37-82) and "Consummation of Messiah's Mission" (220-41), in Shenk 1993.

Shaull, Richard. 1991. *The Reformation of Liberation Theology*. Louisville, Ky.: Westminster/John Knox.

Shenk, Wilbert R. 1983b. *Henry Venn—Missionary Statesman*. Maryknoll, N.Y.: Orbis Books.

————, 1984. "The 'Great Century' Reconsidered," in *Anabaptism and Mission*. Scottdale, Pa.: Herald Press, 158-77, and *Missiology* 12:1 (January):133-46.

————. 1990. "The Origins and Evolution of the Three-Selfs in Relation to China," *International Bulletin of Missionary Research* 14:1 (January):28-35.

—————. 1993. *The Transfiguration of Mission: Biblical, Theological, and Histori-cal Foundations*. Scottdale, Pa.: Herald Press.

—————. 1995. *Write the Vision: The Church Renewed*. Valley Forge, Pa.: Trinity Press International.

Shenk, Wilbert R., ed. 1983a. *Exploring Church Growth*. Grand Rapids, Mich.: Wm. B. Eerdmans Publishing Co.

Shorter, Aylward. 1988. *Toward a Theology of Inculturation*. Maryknoll, N.Y.: Orbis Books.

Siewert, John A., and John A. Kenyon, eds. 1993. *Mission Handbook: USA/Canada Christian Ministries Overseas*. 15th edition. Monrovia, Calif.: MARC.

Smalley, William A. 1958. "Cultural Implications of an Indigenous Church," *Practical Anthropology* 5:2.

—————. 1991. *Translation as Mission: Bible Translation in the Modern Missionary Movement*. Macon, Ga.: Mercer University Press.

Smith, A. Christopher. 1992. "A Tale of Many Models: The Missiological Significance of the Serempore Trio," *Missiology* 20:4 (October):479-500.

Smith, A. Christopher, comp. 1993. *Index 1912-1990: International Review of Mission*. Geneva: International Review of Mission.

Smith, Edwin, ed. 1961. *African Ideas of God*. London: Edinburgh House Press.

Smith, George. 1879. *The Life of Alexander Duff*. Volume 1. London: Hodder and Stoughton.

Smith, Timothy L. 1957. *Revivalism and Social Concern*. New York and Nashville, Tenn.: Abingdon Press.

Soltau, T. Stanley. 1954. *Missions at the Crossroads*. Wheaton, Ill.: Van Kampen Press.

Solzenitsyn, Alexandr I. 1972. *The Nobel Lecture on Literature*. New York: Harper & Row.

Soper, Edmund. 1943. *The Philosophy of the Christian World Mission*. New York: Abingdon-Cokesbury Press.

Speer, Robert E. 1902. *Missionary Principles and Practice*. New York: Fleming H. Revell and Co.

—————. 1910. *Christianity and the Nations*. New York: Fleming H. Revell and Co.

Stanton, Graham, ed. 1983. *The Interpretation of Matthew*. Philadelphia: Fortress Press.

Stock, Eugene. 1899. *History of the Church Missionary Society*. Four volumes. London: Church Missionary Society.

Strong, Josiah. 1891. *Our Country: Its Possible Future and Its Present Crisis*. New York: Baker and Taylor. First edition 1885.

Sundkler, Bengt. 1960. *Bantu Prophets in South Africa*. London: Oxford University Press. First published in 1948.

Swan, William. 1830. *Letters on Missions*. London: Westley and Davis.

Sweazey, George E. 1953. *Effective Evangelism*. New York: Harper and Brothers.

Taber, Charles R. 1991. *The World Is Too Much with Us: "Culture" in Modern Protes-tant Missions*. Macon, Ga.: Mercer University Press.

Taylor, John V. 1958. *The Growth of the Church in Buganda*. London: SCM Press.

Taylor, William. 1867. *Christian Adventures in South Africa*. London: Jackson, Walford, and Hodder.

Templeton, Charles B. 1957. *Evangelism For Tomorrow*. New York: Harper and Broth-ers.

Theological Education Fund. 1972. *Ministry in Context*. Report for 1972. Geneva: Theo-logical Education Fund.

Thompson, H. P. 1951. *Into All Lands.* London: SPCK.

Thrupp, Sylvia L., ed. 1970. *Millenial Dreams in Action.* New York: Schocken Books.

Troeltsch, Ernst. 1960. *The Social Teaching of the Christian Churches.* Translated by Olive Wyon. New York: Harper & Row. Reprint of 1931 edition.

Trompf, G. W. 1979. "The Future of Macro-Historical Ideas," *Soundings* 62:1:70-89.

Turner, Harold W. 1973. "Old and New Religions among North American Indians," *Missiology* 1:2.

——————. 1977. *Bibliography of New Religious Movements.* Six volumes. Boston: G. K. Hall.

——————. 1979. *Religious Innovation in Africa.* Boston: G. K. Hall.

——————. 1980. "African Independent Churches and Economic Development," *World Development* 8.

——————. 1981. "Religious Movements in Primal (or Tribal) Societies," *Mission Focus* 9:3 (September):45-55. Reprinted as a *Mission Focus* pamphlet, 1988.

——————. 1982. "The Relationship between Development and New Religious Movements in the Tribal Societies of the Third World," unpublished.

——————. 1984. "Reflections on African Movements during a Missiological Conference," *Missionalia* 12:3.

——————. 1985. "New Primal Religious Movements," editorial essay in *Missiology* 13:1 (January):5-21.

Union Missionary Convention. 1854. *Proceedings of the Union Missionary Convention held in New York, May 4-5, 1854. Together with the address of the Rev. Dr. Duff.* New York: Taylor and Hogg.

van den Berg, J. 1956. *Constrained by Jesus' Love: An Enquiry into the Motives of the Missionary Awakening in Great Britain in the Period between 1698 and 1815.* Kampen: J. H. Kok.

Van Engen, Charles E. 1990. "A Broadening Vision: Forty Years of Evangelical Theology of Mission," in Carpenter and Shenk 1990.

——————. 1992. *God's Missionary People: Rethinking the Purpose of the Local Church.* Grand Rapids, Mich.: Baker Book House.

Varg, Paul A. 1958. *Missionaries, Chinese, and Diplomats: The American Protestant Missionary Movement in China, 1890-1952.* Princeton: Princeton University Press.

Venn, Henry. 1861. "Instructions to Missionaries," *Church Missionary Intelligencer* 12:8.

——————. 1866. "Third Paper on Native Church Organisation." Combined with policy statements of 1851 and 1861 and released as *The Native Pastorate and Organisation of Native Churches.* London: Church Missionary Society.

——————. 1868. "Instructions to Missionaries," *Church Missionary Intelligencer* NS 9:10.

Verkuyl, Johannes. 1978. *Contemporary Missiology.* Grand Rapids, Mich.: William B. Eerdmans Publishing Co.

Vicedom, George F. 1965. *The Mission of God: An Introduction to a Theology of Mission.* Translated by G. A. Thiele and D. Higendorf. St. Louis, Mo.: Concordia Press.

Viviano, Benedict T. 1988. *The Kingdom of God in History.* Wilmington, Del.: Michael Glazier.

Von der Mehden, Fred R. 1986. *Religion and Modernization in Southeast Asia.* Syracuse, N.Y.: Syracuse University Press.

Wagner, C. Peter. 1971. *Frontiers in Missionary Strategy*. Chicago: Moody Press.

Walls, Andrew F. 1979. "The Anabaptists of Africa? The Challenge of the African Independent Churches," *Occasional Bulletin of Missionary Research* 3:2.

——————. 1987. "The Old Age of the Missionary Movement," *International Review of Mission* 76:301 (January):26-32.

——————. 1988. "Missionary Societies and the Fortunate Subversion of the Church," *Evangelical Quarterly* 60:2:141-55.

——————. 1990a. "The American Dimension in the History of the Missionary Movement," in Carpenter and Shenk 1990, 1-25.

——————. 1990b. "Conversion and Christian Community," *Mission Focus* 18:2 (June):17-21.

——————. 1992. "Missions: Origins," *Dictionary of Scottish History and Theology*. Edinburgh: T. and T. Clark, 567-94.

Walls, A. F., and Wilbert R. Shenk, eds. 1990. *Exploring New Religious Movements: Essays in Honor of Harold W. Turner*. Elkhart, Ind.: Mission Focus Publications.

Warneck, Gustav. 1883. *Modern Missions and Culture*. Translated by Thomas Smith. Edinburgh: James Gemmell Publisher. German edition 1879.

——————. 1897-1905. *Evangelische Missionslehre: Ein Missionstheoretischer Versuch*. 5 volumes. Gotha: n.p.

——————. 1901. *Outline of a History of Protestant Missions from the Reformation to the Present Time*. Translated from the seventh German edition. Edinburgh and London: Oliphant, Anderson, and Ferrier.

Warren, Max. 1965. *The Missionary Movement from Britain in Modern History*. London: SCM Press.

——————. 1967. *Social History and Christian Mission*. London: SCM Press.

Warren, Max, ed. 1971. *To Apply the Gospel*. Grand Rapids, Mich.: William B. Eerdmans Publishing Co.

Webster, Michael. 1959. "Simeon's Doctrine of the Church," in *Charles Simeon (1759-1836)*, edited by Michael Hennell and Arthur Pollard. London: SPCK.

Wilder, Robert P. 1936. *The Great Commission, The Missionary Response of the SVM's in North America and Europe: Some Personal Reminiscences*. London: Oliphants.

Williams, C. Peter. 1990. *The Ideal of the Self-Governing Church: A Study in Victorian Missionary Strategy*. Leiden: E. J. Brill.

Willis, Avery T. 1977. *Indonesian Revival: Why Two Million Came to Christ*. South Pasadena, Calif.: William Carey Library.

Willis, Wendell, ed. 1987. *The Kingdom of God in 20th-Century Interpretation*. Peabody, Mass.: Hendrickson.

Wilson, Monica Hunter. 1961. *Reaction to Conquest: Effects of Contact with Europeans on the Pondo of South Africa*. Second edition. London: Oxford University Press.

Wink, Walter. 1993. *Engaging the Powers*. Minneapolis, Minn.: Fortress Press.

Winter, Ralph D. 1984. "Unreached Peoples: The Development of a Concept," in *Reaching the Unreached—The Old-New Challenge*, edited by Harvie M. Conn. Phillipsburg, N.J.: Presbyterian and Reformed Publishing Company, 17-43.

——————. 1984. "Unreached Peoples: What Are They and Where Are They?" in *Reaching the Unreached—The Old-New Challenge*, edited by Harvie M. Conn, 44-60.

Woodberry, J. Dudley, Charles E. Van Engen, and Edgar J. Elliston, eds. 1996. *Missiological Education for the Twenty-first Century*. Maryknoll, N.Y.: Orbis Books.

World Council of Churches. 1982. "Mission and Evangelism—An Ecumenical Affirmation," *International Review of Mission* 71:284.

Yamauchi, Edwin M. 1972. "How the Early Church Responded to Social Problems," *Christianity Today* 17:4.

Yinger, J. Milton. 1957. *Religion, Society and the Individual*. New York: Macmillan Company.

Zwemer, Samuel M. 1943. *Into All the World*. Grand Rapids, Mich.: Zondervan.

Index

Allen, Roland, 47, 55, 111-12, 164-65
American Indians, 51-52, 60-64, 97
Anderson, Rufus, 39-41, 53-54, 109-10, 145-46, 147

Baritz, Loren, 171
Bible, 48; and church, 8-9, 120-22, 128; on mission strategy, 105-107. *See also* gospel; scriptures
Bosch, David J., 9
British, 168-69; missionaries, 44-45, 142
Busia, K.A., 79

Carey, William, 109-10, 153
Catholicism, 51-52, 77, 156
China, 88, 99-101, 163-64
Christendom: defined, 143; and development, 146-50; and role of church, 15, 16; and role of mission, 122-24, 131. *See also* Christianity
Christianity: changes in, 184-45; and Cold War, 170; cross-cultural transformation of, 124-28; conversions to, 94-95; and science, 22; statistics, 154. *See also* Christendom
Christian witness, 22-29
church, 27, 150-52; and culture, 57; future of, 188-89, 190; history, 108-109; and missionary society, 144, 178-79; and modern mission movement, 157, 162-63; relationship with mission, 7, 83-84, 107, 122-24, 131-32; relationship to world, 118-22; replication of, 51-53. *See also* indigenous church
Coe, Shoki, 56, 57, 174-75
Cold War, 169-70
colonialism, 89, 168
conferences, 110-11
contextualization, 56-57, 75-78, 174-76

conversion, 86-87; evangelicals on, 91-93; factors in, 87-91; failure of, 97-98; reactions to, 93-97
counterculture, 136
culture: American, 170-72; contextual approach to, 56-57; as evolving, 53-56; and mission strategy, 107; modern, 89-90; relationship with church, 118-20, 127-28; replication of Christian, 51-53; views of, 48-50, 51; and worldview, 87-88. *See also* indigenous culture; Western culture

development, 146-50; omission of, 63; and religion, 81-82
Diaspora, 162-63
Dida Harrists, 64-67
Duff, Alexander, 39, 110

ecclesiology, 8-9, 130-31, 150-51. *See also* church
Eliot, John, 51-52
Enlightenment, 154-55, 161
eschaton, 18-19
Europe, history, 166-69. *See also* Western culture
evangelicalism, 25-27, 91-98, 109-10, 129n.2, 180-81

Forman, Charles, 36, 46
frontier, 125-26; defined, 2, 117
fundamentalism, 22-25. *See also* evangelicalism

God, 9-11; through Jesus, 11-13; and mission strategy, 105; relationship with church, 16; relationship with humankind, 17-18; as source of mission, 106, 177

205

gospel, 15; and culture, 56, 127-28, 157-
58, 160-61; model of mission in, 132-
34; recovery of, 24-29; redefined, 20-
21. *See also* Bible; scriptures
Great Century, 143-50; defined, 142; role
of church during, 150-52
Great Commission, the, 24, 131-32

Harris, William Wadé, 64-65
Henry, Carl, F.H., 25-26
Hesselgrave, David J., 70-71
Hobhouse, Walter, 118
Holy Spirit, 13-15, 107

Idowu, Bolajui, 79
India, 40-41
indigenization model, 53-56
indigenous church, 42, 45-46, 47, 145-46,
175; in China, 99-100; criticism of, 76-
77; as goal of mission, 53-54, 62-63,
75-76; and politics, 145-46; post WWII,
172-75
indigenous culture: importance of religion
in, 80-81; through music, 65-66; need
to understand, 49-50, 54-55, 73-74, 95-
96, 126-27, 159; reactions to conversion by, 93-95; theology of, 62-64, 66-
67, 78-80. *See also* new religious
movements
individualism, 135
institutionalization, 180-81

Japan, 88n.4
Jesus, 14, 16; and eschaton, 18-19; and
God's mission, 7, 11-13, 106; and gos-
pel, 28-29

Kennedy, John F., 171
Kingdom of God, 134; as criteria for cul-
ture, 50; and Enlightenment, 161; in-
terpretations of, 28-29
Kirby, Jon, 98
Krabill, James, 65
Krabill, Jeanette, 65
Kraemer, Hendrik, 172
Krass, Alfred C., 98

language, 49-50, 77, 159
Lawrence, Edward A., 42-43

liberalism, 23
London Secretaries' Association, 38-39

Mennonite mission, 62-64
Minear, Paul, 120-21
missiology, 69-71, 74-75 (def., 71). *See
also* mission; mission theory
mission: and church, 7, 15-17, 122-24;
cross-cultural, 125-28; defined, 1; and
Enlightenment, 155-56; and eschaton,
18-19; failure of, 97-98, future of, 183-
85, 186-90; and God, 10-11, 106, 177;
and indigenous church, 62-63, 75-77,
98-101; model of, 132-34; and modernization, 156-58; and new religious
movements, 72-74; relationship to
world, 17-18; vs. state, 144-45; and
view of culture, 50-58; world, 184. *See
also* conversion; missionary society;
mission strategy; mission theory; modern mission movement
missionaries: nineteenth century, 142-43;
conferences for, 110-11; first, 85-86; on
mission theory, 41-46; reactions to conversion by, 95-96; training for, 129-30,
134-38; understanding indigenous cultures, 143-44, 178-83
missionary society, 143-44, 178-83. *See
also* missionaries
mission strategy, 145-46; criticism, 111-
12; defined, 103; history of, 108-11;
and scientific method, 112-13; shaped
by culture, 104-105; theological, 105-
107
mission theory, 39-41, 175; contributions
by missionaries, 41-46; history, 34-39,
47
modernization, 21-22, 89-91. *See also*
Western culture
modern mission movement, 131-32, 156-
58; and church, 162-63; and culture,
159-61; end of, 186-87; failure/success
of, 163-65; and institutionalization,
180-81. *See also* evangelicalism; new
religious movements
modern self, 135-36
Moffat, Robert, 92
music, 65-66
myth, 123